DOUGA...
THE PHILOS...

DOUGAL HASTON:
THE PHILOSOPHY OF RISK

JEFF CONNOR

CANONGATE

First published in Great Britain in 2002 by Canongate Books Ltd,
14 High Street, Edinburgh EH1 1TE

**This edition first published simultaneously in
Great Britain & the United States of America in 2003**

10 9 8 7 6 5 4 3 2 1

British Library Cataloguing-in-Publication Data
A catalogue record for this book is available on request from the British Library

ISBN 1 84195 340 7

**Typeset by Hewer Text Ltd, Edinburgh
Printed and bound by Creative Print and Design (Wales), Ebbw Vale**

www.canongate.net

I still feel the urge to fight with the forces of unknown walls.
It has almost become a necessary part of life for me.

– Dougal Haston, unpublished diary entry

CONTENTS

ACKNOWLEDGEMENTS

This book would not have been possible without the co-operation of Ariane Giobellina, Annie Haston, Guy Neithardt, Allan Rankin, Blyth Wright, Alec Haston, Russell Sharp, Dave Bathgate, Sir Chris Bonington, Doug Scott, Paul Braithwaite, Robin Campbell, Jimmy Marshall, James 'Eley' Moriarty, James Stenhouse, Graham Pate, John Cleare, Davie Todd, Beth Bevan, Sigi Hupfauer, Deutsche Alpen Ferien, Mike Thompson, John Fowler and the Scottish Mountaineering Club, Royal Robbins, Tom Frost, Jim Brumfitt, John McLean, Rusty Baillie, Maude Tiso, Peter Gillman, Ken Wilson, Bev Clark, Andy Wightman, Davie Agnew, Joy Kor, Chic Scott, Ian Nicholson, Allen Fyffe, Jim Cruickshank, Norman Dhyrenfurth, Clint Eastwood and Malpaso Productions, Larry Ware, Pat Littlejohn and the International School of Mountaineering, Eddy O'Hare of Currie Youth Club, West Calder High School, the Burgh of Currie, Midlothian, Jim Gilchrist of *The Scotsman*, John Gibson of the *Edinburgh Evening News* and the National Archives of Scotland.

The Dougal Haston articles originally published in the *Edinburgh University Mountaineering Club Journal* and the *Scottish Mountaineering Club Journal* are reproduced by kind permission of these two bodies, and the extract from *Calculated Risk* appears courtesy of Ken Wilson, Diadem Books and Annie Haston. The extracts from *In High Places* are also used with the permission of Annie.

As so often, Tracey Lawson was a fund of sound advice, and the finished manuscript owes much to the linguistic abilities of Tina Laukkonen and Stephanie Roetger. Duggie Middleton was a superb editor, offering his usual sage suggestions, and Frances Rendall performed wonders at short notice with some of the transcripts. Finally, a word of thanks to Jamie Byng, Mark Stanton and the staff of Canongate Books for their continued support and enthusiasm.

CALCULATED RISK

'My time has not yet come either; some are born posthumously'
– Friedrich Nietzsche, *Ecce Homo*

There are many, those who knew the time, the place and the man, who believe that the day of Dougal Haston's death was the most perfect day of his life. It was a departure replete with irony, and yet of almost mythical appropriateness. Sad and sorrowing but fulfilling and satisfying, in many ways the death mirrored the life.

Three days of Alpine storm in Leysin had finally retreated and given way to a high front that embraced most of central Europe. The sun glared out of a cloudless Swiss sky so blue as to be almost black. The clear, cold air, as it does on perfect mountain days, seemed to throb with a pulse that could belong only to nature, and there was renewed beauty even in Leysin's traditional travel-brochure view across the Rhone Valley to the Dents du Midi and beyond. Above, there was the tingling expectation of untouched fresh powder snow more than 60 centimetres deep.

The outlook was fine elsewhere. The day before, Sunday, he had completed the last of the 190 laboriously handwritten pages that made up his first novel. It would eventually be called *Calculated Risk*, although at the time he had not given thought to a title. All that remained was a final check and some minor rewriting, once Ariane had typed it into a workable proof from his scrawl, and then he could start to look for a publisher. It had taken almost a year of unfamiliar effort, but his ordered psyche had seen him through. In the end, it had been simply another challenge to be met, another discipline digested and mastered. Already, the seeds of a second novel were planted in his mind, a story in which the life of the hero would start at his death. Ariane had liked that one. She even argued that the book should go backwards; instead of growing old, the process would be reversed into growing young and dying at birth. The idea had appealed to the mystic in both.

The future held a rich promise: total, happy immersement in a relationship that amazingly seemed to climb to a different plane daily, and plans, great plans for great mountains. As contentedly optimistic people often do, a few months previously he had sketched out, in one of the school exercise books which he used to jot down his random thoughts and ideas, a hypothetical calendar of the 12 months ahead. It was a year that would include the indolent pleasures of Goa and Corsica and the Med with Ariane, mixed with the necessity of work as director at the International School of Mountaineering in the summer, and the Calvinistic delights of new climbs in Alpine winters. There was a trip to the Karakoram and K2, the second-highest mountain in the world. He had already climbed the highest. There were also hints of a return to Nepal with Chris Bonington, and advanced plans to start an offshoot of his Leysin climbing school in Canada, based mainly in British Columbia. The demons that had pursued him for most of his life, too, seemed to have receded. Many had remarked on the change over the past 12 months; the anger and contempt were gone, and even the drinking had moderated. If this was happiness, he appeared to have found it.

It would be untrue to say, as some did, that he had ignored the avalanche warnings that had closed the main *téléphérique* to La Berneuse; rather he had digested the message and, as he had done all his life, weighed the odds for and against. He judged them slightly in his favour, and that was enough to send him striding up into the powder fields.

Until that afternoon, the gods who overlooked mountains and mountaineers had always smiled on him. Above the Central Pillar on the Eiger, the fraying rope had broken with the next man on it, a few minutes after he had kicked and swung and sawed his way up the fragile line. Two years after Everest, and he still held the world record for the highest night out in the open without oxygen. He hadn't even got frostnip from that one. On Mount McKinley, they had been so sure of themselves that, on the second day, they had given the mountain a sporting chance by discarding half their bivouac gear and much of the food. And still he came through four days later.

Remember, as a gangling, bumbling 16-year-old on a misty Ben, when he and Jim Stenhouse had walked out over the North-East Buttress instead of heading for the Carn Mor Dearg Arête? Another few feet north and there would have been no Annapurna, no Eiger and no Everest. And, of course, no Leysin and no Vagabond and no Annie and Ariane, and no days like this when he owned every mountain in sight.

And those little crosses dotting his memory: Smith in the Pamirs, Harlin on the Eiger, Clough on Annapurna, Bahaguna and Burke on Everest. Even Lehne, his taciturn, hard-drinking German alter ego on the Nordwand, had been on borrowed time, as it turned out; a single stone on the Walker Spur had done for him. There was strong evidence that he was the ultimate survivor, and even if this was proved not to be, he could rationalise, like his fatalistic soul-mate Ariane, and face the future in the belief that they were simply performing to a script already written.

He had wanted her along on that Monday, but her employer had found some extra work. And anyway, six months earlier, on one of their many summer walks above the village, when he had abruptly looked up at the North-east face of La Riondaz and announced his intention to ski it – speculating on the snow cover it would require, where he'd go from the summit and the number of turns it would take – something had made her look round and tell him that this was one expedition he could do on his own. Later, she would recall that strange feeling of unease about that hill – it would be an exaggeration to call it a mountain – and that January day, in particular. The indefinable feeling of apprehension intensified as they walked together from lunch in their apartment in Leysin's Rue du Commerce up towards the Esplanade and the offices of the American School where she worked. As they parted with a kiss something, she never understood what, caused her suddenly to sprint as fast as she could up the four floors to the office balcony in order to catch a glimpse of him. But that elongated stride had already taken him out of sight towards the Solacyre and the first lift of the afternoon. Inexplicably, as the day wore on, she picked up the telephone to call him, only to put the receiver down again. She had nothing to say, just a sudden urgent need to make contact. She felt even stranger when she realised that he would not even be home yet.

He had skied down La Riondaz before, but rarely in conditions like this, and never down that face to the Col Luisset. Thanks to the extreme temperatures – around minus 20F, they reckoned – the powder lay undamaged in perfect off-piste conditions. The danger was equally obvious, but the run was short, and he probably reasoned that it would be easy – as he had caused one of the heroes in his novel to do – to find the safety of the rocks on the edge. If the worst came to the worst, he was confident that he could outrun any small slides, and he thought it unlikely the whole slope would go.

It wasn't difficult to work out the rest. At the top of the lift, Haston must have paused to take the sealskins out of his rucksack and slip them over his Miller Deep Powder skis, painted a bright orange like the avalanche warning signs, before setting off for the top. The months spent wrestling with nouns and verbs indoors had had little effect on his fitness, and 40 minutes after leaving the lift he was folding the skins back in the sack, and looking down and out over Leysin and across to the Alps from the summit, a view that was almost a panoramic picture book of his early European climbing career. The first few jump turns through the topmost rocks were tight, but the evidence of those tracks, read by friends later, showed that he had managed them perfectly. The deep carvings, like a spoon riffling through white sugar, were immaculate and told of a man completely in tune with his sport and environment. The slope must have gone when he hit the broad, main central area eleven, maybe twelve turns from the col and safety. When they found him, there was evidence that, as the avalanche and snow-structure experts recommended in the textbooks, he may have deliberately discarded the sticks and attempted to shed the skis. He may even have survived for a time, but for that trendy scarf round his neck. Ultimately, he did not have the opportunity, as do so many others buried and drowning under snow, to wonder why it should all end here. Nor where it all began.

CURRIE BOY

'Wealth I ask not, hope nor love,
Nor a friend to know me;
All I seek the heaven above
And the road below me'
– Robert Louis Stevenson, *Songs of Travel*

The beginning was a green, rounded hill far away, and as insignificant in its own context of the Pentlands, Edinburgh's indigenous range of lowly fells, as La Riondaz, amid the grander summits surrounding Leysin. If La Riondaz was an innocuous peak on which to close a climbing career, Black Hill, at a posturing 501 metres above sea level, was an equally humble opening.

The expedition had been a low-level nature trek from Curriehill Primary School, Currie being a Midlothian village six miles from Scotland's capital city planted on the northern flank of Black Hill. It took the party of schoolchildren across Lanark Road West and up the brae past Whitesides Plantation, carefully skirting the rifle range at Malleny and terminating where the track gave out into open moorland. For six-year-olds short of limb and shallow of lung, reaching what was certainly for them a dauntingly distant summit was out of the question, and when they did turn to retrace their steps, the only complaint came from one skinny boy with the long shanks and a mop of unruly, fair hair. Duncan – as he was known then – Haston had wanted to go all the way to the top.

They had called him Duncan Curdy McSporran Haston after his paternal grandfather, and he was born at 21 Dolphin Road, Currie, at ten fifty-five on the night of April 19, 1940. His father Robert, unusually for those times, attended the birth, but then his wife Margaret, like him, was almost 40, and middle-aged motherhood was an unusual and risky concept at that time. Robert was a journeyman baker, Margaret an occasional domestic, and an elder son Alexander had been born 11 years earlier. Alec was to leave home, though not the village, in his late teens for marriage and children of his own, and Duncan spent his formative years as what amounted to an only child. He was an uncle by the age of 15. Alec, who still lives on the council scheme, but round the corner in Dolphin Avenue, showed not the faintest interest in hills or climbing them: 'I get dizzy just looking out of windows,' he says.

Until the 1960s, when the village began to market itself as a viable rural habitat for Edinburgh's noveau riche, Currie was in the main a farming community, its other main industries being a tannery (still going) and two paper mills, long redundant. Dolphin Road lay a few hundred yards from the main road in the midst of a large estate built for the workers of the mills and farm labourers. Currie, with its steady supply of incomers, lost its working-class ambience long ago, but it has managed to retain the fierce independence of a rural community, perhaps represented best by a rugby team who have delighted in administering ferociously unforgettable workings-over to the toffee-nosed Edinburgh private schools a few miles down the road or the arrogantly uncouth Borders sides. 'No one likes us, and we don't care' could well have been the motto on tribal Currie's coat of arms.

The autonomy of the population, at least until recently, may have its roots in the fact that children in the village were used to finding their own amusement, and Duncan was no exception. By the age of 11, when he entered Currie Junior High, his mother and father were in their early 50s, and though there was active encouragement for a nascent sporting prowess, Robert often worked night shifts, and was not given to kickabouts with a football in the street, or on one of the local playing fields, with his younger son. But for any boy or girl with a taste for adventure, Currie was a marvellous place for growing up. Lying at a height of 600 feet on a ridge running along the Water of Leith valley, the unspoiled countryside that surrounded the village in those days was primarily mixed farmland with sheep on the higher land and arable land with some cattle elsewhere. There were long-established tree belts of cypress, willow and ash providing cover for wildlife, including badgers, fox and deer – and for michievous schoolboys. The Water of Leith, running past Currie's northern flank, offered a challenge of its own. Swimming was not an option, at least not a healthy one: the waters may once have been clear and sparkling, with brown trout beneath the surface and coots and mute swans atop, but as Edinburgh's New Town grew and villages outside the city expanded with the establishment of industries along its banks, it became too convenient as a ready-made drain and rubbish dump. Currie's tannery and mills added their effluents, but for Duncan and his friends there was adventure on the river banks, with walls to cling to and traverse spider-like, and fallen logs to dangle from above the noisesome waters, the forfeit for losing their grip a scolding or even a beating from parents when they got home stinking and bedraggled. If they got really bored, they could always pull faces at passengers or throw stones at the engines of trains that passed by occasionally on the other side of the river en route to Glasgow or Edinburgh.

And there, challenging on the near horizon, were the Pentlands. Stretching for just over 16 miles east to west, the city hills were beloved of Robert Louis Stevenson and were also the occasional inspiration for Sir Walter Scott, who wrote about 'nothing more beautiful than the ridge of Carnethy against a clear, frosty sky'. Although perhaps six miles at their widest, the turf-covered summits, encased in trackless moorland, cut by silver burns and dotted by remote farmsteads, offered peace and seclusion combined with easy access from the surrounding villages. The range's modest tops offer extensive views over the Forth Valley to the Ochil Hills in the north and, on a clear day, round to Ben Lomond in the west. The Pentlands culminate in a highest point at Scald Law (579m), but for Haston these lowly fells stirred a passion that was to guide his life. Thirty years later, in the last twelve months of his life and with the summits of the 8000m giants of Annapurna and Everest behind him, he would return to his native hills to find a new beauty there.

The young Haston was a diligent pupil at school, and at the insistence of his father and mother also attended the local Church of Scotland every Sunday without finding any convictions there. In any case, he was soon to discover other distractions and adventurous and mischievous soul-mates in two junior high school pals, James Moriarty and Jim Stenhouse. Moriarty, who grew into a 6ft 2in,

16-stone giant known universally as Big Eley, was born exactly a day later than Haston in the same street, at No. 39, with all that implies in terms of closeness and familiarity between schoolboy companions. Over the years, Moriarty was to become Haston's unofficial minder and longest-lasting friend, though several others were to fall by the wayside. His protective instincts towards Dougal survive today, way beyond the grave.

Stenhouse, who lived round the corner of Dolphin Road at 12 Stewart Avenue, was a year older and marginally more responsible, but there is little doubt that these three brought out the worst in each other. They were the type of schoolboys we can recall with horror, the noisy ones who commandeered the back seat of the bus on outings, tugged the hair of protesting girls in front, pulled faces at passing motorists and threw rolled-up paper balls at the teachers. Stenhouse says: 'Dougal and the rest of us were all fairly anti-establishment, even in those days, socially not very acceptable at all. We got up to all sorts of mischief, and even climbed the church in Currie at night and called it the Currie Eiger. We put women's pants on the various little baubles and, of course, the next morning when they were all going into church, there was this great flag flying from the top, which was just a sheet saying: "Long Live the King". They never found out who it was.' Moriarty recalls: 'We had secret gang huts up in the Pentlands, and our philosophy was: "There's Black Hill, let's attack it." I think we were all naturally fit and determined, Dougal especially so. We used to walk over the other side of Black Hill, swim one of the big reservoirs, about three-quarters of a mile of it, then walk home again, maybe with a longer diversion on the way back.'

Stenhouse recalls the three friends beating for the grouse-shooters up in the hills, and that after a long day 21 Dolphin Road was always a good place to go back to because of Robert Haston's skills as a baker. 'Always a great spot for a meal. Dougal's folks were just very ordinary people, just hard-working. I think his father worked shifts, and I don't recall him being a fanatical football supporter or keen bowler or hard drinker, or anything like that. He was just an ordinary guy. Currie was full of ordinary guys.' Currie was also full of people who lived in dread of an appearance in their street of the terrible trio: other youngsters were urged to give them a wide berth by concerned parents. They were adept at leading anyone astray – and not just each other – but fortunately for all three, instead of spending their formative years removing the hub-caps from cars or throwing stones at street lights, they were to find a different, less anti-social channel for youthful high spirits.

Currie Youth Club was formed in 1954, the brainchild of Alick Buchanan-Smith, a popular and respected landowner and later Member of Parliament, who farmed Copland Farm at Balerno. The club started life as Currie Kirk Boys' Club, and meetings were held every Friday evening from late September to April in the old railway buildings at Currie Station and in the school gym. Two years later, three timber huts were bought from the old army camp at Riccarton, and erected on the present club site in Lanark Road West. There were eighteen original members with an age range of fourteen to eighteen years, and Haston, Moriarty and Stenhouse were among the founders. Buchanan-Smith was the first club leader and chairman of the management committee and, as it turned out, the first, and unlikeliest, of the major mentors in the climbing life of Haston. From the first year, Buchanan-Smith ran annual camps, a long weekend at the April holiday and a week-long summer jaunt in July. His family owned an old, unoccupied cottage near Crianlarich, and that proved a useful base for his and his boys' forays further north to Glencoe and beyond. While initial expeditions were simply trudges over the Munros and a bit of scrambling, they did give the Currie boys a formative fitness base and an appreciation of the great outdoors, and Buchanan-Smith was no mean performer on the hill. 'Buchanan-Smith was really the guy who got us into the hills and, in fact, his mother was actually killed in a climbing accident, which had never put him off,' says Stenhouse. 'His father was Chairman, I think, of the Conservative Party in Scotland, so they were well connected and, of course, totally different from Eley, Dougal and myself, but he was very keen to get the local kids out walking, and we were very keen to follow him. I think it's fair to say he had a big influence on us all.'

Haston's first rock climb was late in 1954 when a friend of Buchanan-Smith, during an expedition to Glencoe, produced a hemp rope and took the wide-eyed schoolboys, moving one at a time, up Curved Ridge, one of the easier climbs on Buachaille Etive

Mor, but one that finished directly on the summit. It is also an excursion that passes through some of the grandest scenery in the glen, skirting the great rock-climbing face of Rannoch Wall. The athleticism of their youth made up for poor technique, and as he pushed feet down on the large holds and sent hands scrambling out to grasp and haul, something else began to stir with the hammering of Dougal's heart, a realisation that this was an environment of overt risk and yet reassuring security. There was a large drop below, and a fall would almost certainly be fatal, but there was a rope in front and careful, controlled movement of the leader to mimic. He was clinging to a ridge that seemed to lead all the way to the sky, and the surroundings, perched high above Rannoch Moor, were breathtaking. Later, he was incredulous when told that there were several climbs on Rannoch Wall, which appeared to his untutored eyes a massive, hold-less precipice. The only cliffs over 100 feet high he had seen were the pictures in the classic climbing books in Currie Library or the occasional magazine, and no one he knew in his home village had ever done mountaineering; it was a sport for lunatics, and well-off lunatics at that. No matter, he was convinced from the start that this was the reason he had been brought into the world.

'We did Curved Ridge via the Crowberry Tower, and thought: "This is it",' says Moriarty. 'This was something different altogether. Dougal could have been a useful goalkeeper – that's where he played for the school – and he was also a very good athlete, but after that there was only one way he, all of us, were going. We were inspired by it, although I quite honestly don't think we knew what we were doing at the time. After that, we decided we had better do some training.'

At first, their training was the gym at Currie Junior High, where they would climb ropes, swing from the two slings they had attached to rings in the ceiling, and traverse the wall bars. Then they remembered they had a secret 'crag' of their own, the two tiers of mossy, lichen-covered retaining walls, one above the railway line and one above the river hidden in the undergrowth on the other side of the main road. A short walk up to the tannery and across the bridge above the Water of Leith led to the 'Wa's' (pronounced Woz) and though only 15 feet in height, they were to become Haston's modest equivalent, in terms of climbing evolution, of Hermann Buhl's

Karwendel, Ricardo Cassin's Lecco limestone or Joe Brown's gritstone. On the walls at Currie and at another railway bridge at the nearby village of Balerno, the boys evolved ascents, descents and traverses, some of them, after long rehearsal and several falls, reaching freakish levels of difficulty.

'We decided these would be great training for rock-climbing,' says Moriarty. 'The idea was to go along and try not fall into the water. We could go there any time because they were right on our doorstep. We used to meet up after school, and we got so good that eventually when we came to the proper mountain stuff, there wasn't a lot to stretch us. There was another wall at Balerno, and although they were maybe only 15 feet high at their highest, there were named routes – and eventually even a guidebook for them.' Stenhouse adds: 'It was really naïve. We used to think that the mountains and the rock faces would be like the Currie Walls but 1000 ft high or something like that, so it really was ignorance about climbing that allowed us to get good very quickly. We just had no ideas about climbing and, of course, if you think like that, there's not a lot to be scared of. When we got away to mountain crags, we just couldn't believe how easy climbing was and, in turn, they couldn't believe how good we were. It was basically because we had trained ourselves to be able to hang on on these little holds, and obviously our arms and legs were strong. I remember going on the Cobbler with this guy Jim Clarkson and a pal of his from near Lochearnhead, and neither of them could get up, and after a few goes they came back down and were having this debate while I sat there like a bag of crap. So I piped up: "Do you mind if I can have a look at the thing?" and, of course, I got up no bother at all.'

Apart from the odd train and the swirling, murky waters, there were other dangers on the Currie Walls. Other kids thought it great fun to bombard them with stones as they clung on above the river, and by the time the climbers reached the top, their tormentors had vanished into the undergrowth. Confronted later, they always had big, older brothers. Haston, however, had Eley, the ultimate deterrent. Then, and for many years to come.

Stenhouse left school at fifteen to take up an apprenticeship as a draughtsman, and Haston and Moriarty were separated, during daylight hours at least, at the age of 16 when Haston, Church of Scotland, was sent to West Calder High School to study for Highers while Moriarty, Church of Rome, headed for Holy Cross in Edinburgh. But the three stayed united by climbing, or dreams about climbing. 'We still used to knock around together,' says Stenhouse. 'Dougal and I climbed together quite a lot, summer and winter, although Eley tended not to climb snow and ice. I think he just preferred rock-climbing, and he was a superb balance climber for a boy, a man, his size. But we all used to read all the mountaineering books at that time, like Buhl's *Nanga Parbat Pilgrimage* and Gaston Rebuffat's *Starlight and Storm*. They were like our Bibles, as it were. When we were not climbing, most of the time we would think and read and talk about it.'

Haston continued his formal education at West Calder High – a Haston House exists there how – which he joined in August 1955 and left in July 1958. For incomers from Currie, travelling the ten miles to West Calder could have posed problems, but Haston was almost universally popular, according to Graham Pate, one of his first school pals at West Calder. 'He was definitely different, a daredevil who would have a bash at anything,' says Pate, who was later to teach at the school. 'Everyone got on a treat with him, and I recall him strolling through the school corridors thinking quietly to himself, and rolling those shoulders of his. He was inclined to slouch, and would outwardly give the impression of a boy who was quiet and very much a loner. He had this peculiar build with broad shoulders, very long back and a concave chest. He was also incredibly pigeon-toed.'

Haston's physical peculiarities – so pronounced were his inward-turned toes that some were later to wonder how he managed to walk wearing crampons – did not prevent him from becoming the county 400m champion at Musselburgh in 1956 with a time of just over 65 seconds, and proving himself a capable all-rounder at football and cricket, sports which his parents were far happier to indulge than climbing mountains. At West Calder, he astonished his school teammates by arriving for a cricket match in a full set of whites – this at a school where playing kit tended to be whatever they turned up in – and he always had the latest spiked shoes for his track running.

But there were always the eagerly awaited treks into the hills, usually with Moriarty or Stenhouse, and occasionally Pate and other boys from West Calder, or the youth club back in Currie. All these trips started and finished with the scenarios that were to become familiar to Dougal's companions in the hills later: the long stride taking him rapidly out of sight, the others panting along in his wake. He was always first back to the transport, too, and whatever the constituency of his mountain experience, it was certainly not for sharing. Pate was struck even then by sixteen-year-old Haston's economy of effort, obvious stamina and leadership qualities.

On one of the first expeditions in fifth year at West Calder, the party were on Schiehallion at Loch Rannoch when the teacher, Pat McAndrew, took cramp, and Dougal and Pate carried the burly chap, a county pole-vaulter, two miles back to the road. Pate recalls: 'It was Pat McAndrew who got most of the fifth and sixth years to go climbing. He also had us doing acrobatics, walking on our hands, things like that. Dougal seemed good at most of these things. With the Loch Rannoch episode, the girls – I think Dougal was going out with one of them at the time – went with a female PE teacher, and just walked along the road. We went up on the hill, and had timed it to get back for the bus, but Pat McAndrew took bad cramp, and we had to take turns in carrying him. He was a hell of a weight.

'It got to the stage when Dougal and me were out every weekend, either with the school or on our own. We would leave the school on Friday evenings, and stay overnight with my mum at Breich. In the morning, we caught the milk lorry to Longridge, and from there hitched to Glencoe. There was competition all the time: we used to race back from everywhere. If you stayed at a youth hostel, you had to be back by 10 p.m., so that was another race back from the pub. I have to say Dougal always won. We did have the occasional pint at the Clachaig Inn [in Glencoe]. We didn't have a lot of money, just enough for a couple of beers, but it was all part of going away. When we went out, Dougal was the natural leader; he always seemed to have everything planned out, when I think back about it now. He would say this was what we were going to do, and we would follow. But he was considerate, too. Colin MacDonald, another of the lads keen on walking, was a wee bit heavier, and Dougal always made allowances for him.'

In his autobiography, Haston starts the early chapters by 'searching [his] memory for rock' for the benefit of his readers, but all he had to do was to look in the diaries which he kept from the age of 16 on and off until he died. The first volume, starting in the summer of 1956, graphically illustrates his remarkable progress in the first two years of serious mountaineering. They begin with a misty walk up Bidean nam Bian in Glencoe, escalate swiftly to the then hardest rock climbs in Britain, and mature on the way from wide-eyed innocence on Bidean wondering if they should have brought a rope to tackle the easy Stob Coire nan Lochain Ridge to matter-of-factly describing an early ascent of the then extremely severe Cemetery Gates in North Wales in a thunderstorm. There is also strong evidence that the artless young boy grew up rather swiftly; in 1956 Dougal was delighting in the views and brilliant sunshine of Wester Ross, but by 1958 he was taking part in stone fights in Glencoe, trundling boulders down the Chasm on Buachaille Etive Mor with 'the shower' and, after an ascent of Minus One Buttress on Ben Nevis, making off 'with an old ice-axe and a watch that must have belonged to a party that was killed while climbing Zero Gully'.

The later diaries – to so describe them may be a misnomer as most were undated, and often simply extended notes written in school exercise books – were used as the basis for his books *Eiger Direct* and *In High Places*, and all are addressed to a third party. They are full of chatty asides like 'you may think this' or 'as you know' and initially are simply the naïve and earnest outpourings of a boy in love with the novelty of mountains and the climbing of them (unknown to him, Stenhouse was also keeping a contemporaneous record of their experiences). It is only the later writings that reveal Haston's deeper searchings and longings. The change is startling.

The first volume begins in July 1956, and is in what became the standard format: name of the place and climb, members of party and description of ascent. There are postcards and cuttings of photographs of mountains from magazines and newspapers and occasional photographs taken by one of the party. Some of the photographs, to the certain astonishment of later climbing partners and their recollection of the technologically illiterate Haston, must have been taken by Dougal himself. The first recorded expedition begins at Glencoe

Youth Hostel, and includes ascents of Bidean nam Bian (1150m), Aonach Dubh and Buachaille Etive Mor, walking seven miles down the valley on the road to reach Glencoe's easternmost peak during school holidays. Examples of a nascent, dry sense of humour shine through: 'From the top of the Buachaille we saw the summit of Bidean. You may not think anything unusual about this, but considering we had climbed it on two successive days and had not seen the summit [it] seemed rather unique to us.' There are also some failures in bad weather, the hint of the occasional epic, and one hair-raising near miss.

From Glencoe, Dougal and Stenhouse moved on to Glen Nevis Youth Hostel just above Fort William, and from there on July 12, 1956, they set off for Ben Nevis (1344m), and their first ascent of Britain's highest mountain. Again they had diabolical luck with the weather, starting off in good conditions up the north-west shoulder in shorts and boots, but then finding the summit was encased in mist, and spending 'a miserable ten minutes' trying to get a bearing on Carn Mor Dearg. It could all have ended there and then for both, as they made the classic Ben Nevis mistake, walking out over the North-East Buttress, spotting their error just in time as the precipices loomed out of low cloud. 'One look was enough to take us back to the summit,' Dougal records. 'Eventually, we found the Carn Mor Dearg Arête, which was narrow and exposed, and some excellent scrambles gave us the best ridge climb of our climbing days.' Not satisfied with the classic Ben Nevis/Carn Mor Dearg round, a good day's work for many, the adventurous pair, clad in the standard Lillywhites' nailed boots, struck off for Aonach Mor in a straight line, where 'I met my first defeat' . . . Dougal, as schoolboys will do, wrote up every expedition, however minor, in terms of a major ascent, in the manner of his hero Hermann Buhl, and he recorded: 'I led off, but was forced off a slab by lack of holds, but a route up a wet gully on the right was forced by JS. After this pitch, we both failed to make a wet chimney go, being turned back by a loose chockstone and brittle rock. A way was finally forced up a steep scree slope to the left of this gully. An easy walk then brought us to the summit.'

The next day was spent climbing Mullach nan Coirean (939m) Stob Ban, Sgurr a Mhaim – with a short nap to recover on the summit – and Am Bodach, on the opposite side of Glen Nevis, before the holiday for the two sixteen-year-olds came to an end, Dougal not surprisingly admitting to 'feeling the week's climbing in my leg muscles' as they headed home to Currie.

By the start of 1957, Haston was a short way down the concentric path familiar to climbers everywhere: Black Hill and the Pentlands had undoubtedly awakened something inside the boy from Currie. There were the hill walks, a bit of scrambling and the gradual realisation of the primitive joy to be had in hauling oneself up unknown rock. There was the inspiration, too, of climbing literature, and while most of his schoolfriends worshipped the Famous Five at Hibs, Marilyn Monroe or Elvis Presley, Dougal's mind was elsewhere. *Nanga Parbat Pilgrimage*, the great Austrian climber Buhl's classic work on his progress from an Innsbruck rookie bumbling round the limestone faces that overlooked his home to his solo ascent of the Himalayan peak, 'was like a Bible to Dougal', Moriarty confirms. 'I think he used to take it into his room at home and read it over and over for hours, when he should have been concentrating on his school books. But most of the time we had no idea what we were about on the hill. We hadn't even learned ropework.'

It was plain to all three that Haston, Moriarty and Stenhouse were swiftly outgrowing the comparatively modest aspirations of Alick Buchanan-Smith – the friend with the rope on Curved Ridge had moved on to other good works – and Currie Youth Club. However, it was ABS, as Haston called him, who introduced them to the dubious delights of Scottish winters. The expedition, in April 1957, was to the Cairngorms, the rounded, featureless – but often extremely hostile – range of hills on the 4000-ft contour above Aviemore, and ABS, in typical style, ran it with all the precision of one of Chris Bonington's later Himalayan expeditions. Base Camp was close by Glenmore with ABS and six other boys, including Haston, Moriarty and Stenhouse, in three tents, followed by a four-mile hike up into Coire Cas, carrying packs of around 50lbs, where Camp 1 was pitched on the 3000-ft contour. 'It was incredible,' says Moriarty. 'We had never camped in winter before, and it was a major expedition in a way. But we loved it.'

It was here that the boys from Currie caught their first sight of skiers, Coire Cas and its single tow being part of the fast-developing Cairngorms winter sports complex, and Stenhouse recalls Haston's sneering attitude to this strange breed. 'There was a stage when he was younger, he used to hate the skiers. I think he thought they were all toffs. When we were in the Cairngorms, Dougal and I were sharing a tent. It was before the lifts were there and before the road [up to the Coire Ciste car park at the foot of Cairn Gorm] was in, and the skis were all left at the bottom. We were actually camping in the snow above that, and we just couldn't understand the mentality of people who went skiing. They were going down the hill to a hot dinner, and we were staying in a tent and taking half an hour to get our boots defrosted, and trying to crack a frozen egg in a pan. We thought we were so superior: so much harder, I suppose.'

After the relatively straightforward ascent of Cairn Gorm (1244m) on the first day, the party set off for their second 4000-footer, Ben Macdhui, at 1309m Scotland's second-highest peak. It was typical Cairngorm plateau visibility of around ten yards and, as so many have done before and since, the party progressed carefully by map and compass along the five-mile walk, eventually missing the summit by just five yards. This was a valuable lesson in the importance of navigation, and an ABS feat that prompted Dougal to spend some of his pocket money on a compass the next week. There was a glissade on old snow down to Loch Avon, an exploration of the Shelter Stone, the traditional boulder doss beneath Shelter Stone Crag, followed by the 1000-ft climb back to the plateau via Coire Domhain.

On the Sunday, the young team – Haston and Moriarty were still ten days away from their seventeenth birthdays – began with a descent into the Lairig Ghru, the gloomy pass that links Aviemore with Braemar, and an ascent of Braeriach (1296m) during a day that eventually took in fifteen miles and 4000 feet of climbing in just eight hours. Haston recalled the stupendous views from Braeriach, 'breaking through the clouds into the sunlight, like being in an aeroplane. Everywhere to the north and west was a sea of cloud, with the occasional dark peak pushing through like a rocky island.'

It turned out to be Haston's last weekend on the hill with Buchanan-Smith; his ambitions were already beginning to outstrip mere hillwalking, and ABS had never formally climbed rock. Haston had met Ronnie Marshall, a shipwright from Edinburgh and the brother of the legendary Jimmy, one of the most important figures in post-war Scottish climbing, late in 1956 on a trip to Glencoe. Ronnie was an experienced climber and, what is more, a member of the Junior Mountaineering Club of Scotland. He was also without real ambition, and was happy to show Haston, Moriarty and Stenhouse the ropes, patiently shepherding them up Staircase Buttress, a low-lying crag on the path up to Coire an Tulaich, the walker's normal route up Buachaille Etive Mor. Marshall taught them how to move one at a time, how to belay, and 'the use of the karabiner', as Dougal wrote it in his diary. There was also an ascent of Agag's Groove, the Glencoe classic on the same Rannoch Wall at which Dougal had gazed up in wonderment a mere twelve months previously. He found the crux move 'exhilarating,' adding breathlessly: 'One must look for holds, and on looking downwards can see the foot of Rannoch Wall between your legs, truly an enjoyable climb'.

Haston's first lead, with Stenhouse as second, followed two days later – Crowberry Ridge via Greig's Ledge, a classic Buachaille 'Difficult' – and he soon began the classic climber's ticking-off process through the guidebook current at the time, mixing appreciation of his surroundings with earnest analysis of his performances. On North-East Zigzag on the lower tier of Buachaille Etive Mor's North Buttress, 'I had to take a high step with no handholds to support me, and I just made it. Incidentally, I thought this move was more than V Diff, but I think I wandered off the route and did a harder pitch that was not on Zigzag.'

A week later, there was an ascent of Observatory Ridge on Ben Nevis in two hours (Dougal, by then, was a keen timer of routes) in foul weather followed by a descent of Tower Ridge, and then a trip to the Cobbler above Loch Long, where Dougal and a JMCS friend, Randall Coe, groped their way up a slime-covered Recess Route. An attempt on the severe and unprotected Chimney Arête forced them into Right Angled Gully, where 'we only reached the top because it was easier to climb up than fall out of. As we were using rubbers, this climb was certainly more than diff because of the slimy rock.'

The Cobbler was a rare excursion away from Glencoe because, in common with many Glasgow and Edinburgh climbers whose cash resources did not run to a car, a motorcycle or even public transport, most of Dougal's climbing had perforce taken place on Buachaille Etive Mor and its neighbours. Scotland's most accessible mountain rock-climbing area to its two major cities could be reached in three hours' hitch-hiking. Nowhere else, either, could match the charm or convenience of the 'Coe' with its two pubs situated at either end of its ten-mile length, and the whole glen lined with crags and peaks sweeping down from the Buachaille at its entry past the Three Sisters of Gearr Aonach, Beinn Fhada, Aonach Dubh and Bidean nam Bian. Ben Nevis involved a long weekend with a journey across the Ballachullish ferry at the western end of Glencoe, and then that long, gloomy walk into the jaws of the Allt na Mhuillin with the misty precipices of Carn Dearg glowering a warning.

But the rest of Scotland and its unexplored hills suddenly became more accessible once Ronnie Marshall persuaded all three Currie Boys to join the JMCS, who ran a bus north from Edinburgh every Friday night. With the JMCS, there were to be trips further afield to Creag Meagaidh, near Loch Laggan, the Cairngorms north and south and the far north.

Dougal and Stenhouse, in the company of the JMCS, visited Skye and Wester Ross for the first time, with horrible weather chasing them off Skye and Haston, to his disgust, being severely jilted by four of the Five Sisters of Kintail, though he did manage Sgurr Fhuaran, the highest at 1067m.

Stenhouse says: 'Ronnie mentioned that there was a Junior Mountaineering Club in existence, and although we weren't all that keen on joining clubs, we found out that they had bus meets, and you could pick up the bus in Edinburgh, which saved a lot of hassle. Edinburgh University ran a bus as well, and although I was never at university, it was useful to know by meeting people exactly what was happening and what transport was available, because we were always fairly keen on getting away. Originally, we used to go away with a guy called Jim Clarkson from Dunfermline – he was killed on Ben Nevis [Carn Mor Dearg] years ago. He wasn't a Scottish lad, but he was a keen climber and he had a car, and he used to come up to Currie and pick Dougal and I up and take us off and pick up another guy, and then used to take us away a few weekends. I was an apprentice and had money, and Dougal was broke, but it didn't really matter: it was share and share alike. In the summer, we got motorbikes, and that used to be the big thing then with climbers, because they were cheap to run and good fun. I bought myself a bike; both Ronnie and Jimmy Marshall had one each, and eventually Dougal and Eley got one between them, which wasn't really a good idea as it turned out.'

The JMCS was considered a less-stilted, more-dynamic version of the Scottish Mountaineering Club, and a natural progression into the senior club once youthful high spirits had worn off, if one was prepared to submit to the rules, etiquette and regimentation for which the SMC was famous. Although closely linked and with a lot of toing and froing between the two, they were separate bodies with their own committees, members and activities. The idea was that young climbers joined the JMCS, and they could climb with the more experienced SMC men, but it was soon apparent that the JMCS individuals were climbing at a far higher standard than their more ponderous and restrained elder brothers. With the arrival of Dougal and his anti-social pals into the JMCS and later the SMC, problems were inevitable.

* * *

Jimmy Marshall, later to play a pivotal role in Haston's development as a climber in summer and winter, along with a small army of young Scottish climbing aspirants, first met the Currie Boys at Caerketton, a conglomerate rock outcrop on the western side of the Pentlands, close to where the Hillend ski slope is now. Caerketton is loose and undefined, and the boys preferred the Wa's for training, but it did have several boulder and low-level problems in a minor mountain environment. Marshall was pottering around there on a Sunday morning in May 1957 when the three appeared after walking over from Pentlands via Capelaw Hill.

'They were wandering around without much sense of purpose, so I took it upon myself to show them around. They never had any problems with any of the routes,' says Marshall, who was eight years older than Haston and a qualified architect. 'My brother Ronnie had met them first, and he liked them, but then Ronnie was a great individualist who, believe it or not, was actually sacked from Granton shipyard for using foul language. At the time, they were just wee hooligans trying to be mountaineers. They climbed on the Railway Wa's at Currie, which they had invented. They were fantastic the climbs there, and technically very, very difficult. You would be pulling up on a fingerhold, and you would have to have someone at the top to catch you if you couldn't make it. Sometimes they didn't, and went whang, bang into the river. Stenhouse has always been in the shadow of Dougal, but he was always a fantastic climber and a hard man. I later researched a book on the Ben with him, and we used to do thousands of feet of rock-climbing a day. Eley, surprisingly, was an excellent balance climber. At the start, they were closer to my brother, and he took them along in their cautious development, which must have lasted all of six months. Dougal wanted to be a climber more than any of them. Eley and Jimmy were as keen as normal climbers are, but Dougal had that particular, aggressive thrust. Looking back, I don't think there was any difference in their ability, but the other two, if they thought they couldn't do it, they would turn back. Dougal would just go on. I think, too, there was a hierarchy there. Dougal and Eley were like twins, and made most of the decisions; Jimmy took the back-seat role, but was a kind of intellectual climber; he had more understanding of lines up mountains.'

Marshall was also impressed with the youngsters' precocity in other fields.

'They were prodigous drinkers, even at 15, Eley and Haston in particular. Stenhouse was more responsible. Eley's sister was courting an American soldier at Kirknewton base, and they had all the drink out there, like Philadelphia rye and dubious stuff like that. The girls used to get them bottles of this hooch, and they would take it away and drink it. They were all three totally mental, and different from any youngsters I have ever met before or since, really way out, but with this incredible zest for life. Eley was a beautiful, tall young man in those days, and a lot lighter than he is now, of course. As climbers, I think they contributed to each other's development, but boozing and fighting were the other big things. There was a New Year's party when they were sixteen or seventeen, in a pub at Corstorphine, and we had a wee monster called Ronnie Anderson and his van to get us round to the first-footing. They had taken their Philly rye into the pub with them for their halves and their beers. We were all smashed by the time we came out and climbed into a car, a lovely car outside, and the monster was going to drive us away, but the owner came out at the same time. It's incredible thinking about it now, just coming out and getting ready to drive off with a vehicle belonging to a total stranger, but we never thought anything of it at the time.

'Later on that night my sister was having a party, and she was a soldier's wife, very much into army etiquete. The major was there, and a lobster buffet all set up. We went in the back door and reduced the place to a shambles. Dougal was dead keen on jiving, and so was my wife, and they are thrashing around while on the settee the major was saying to Eley: "You're the sort we need in the army!" Trying to talk him into becoming a soldier. Dougal eventually threw up, but had the decency to open the front window while we held on to his legs. He was a little, black bastard, with absolutely no feeling for others – it was just the way he was.

'His brother was a well-known bruiser in Currie, so maybe that's part of the family genes, but it certainly helped Dougal to have Eley around because, while there was boozing, there were always punch-ups. Eley's timing was immaculate: he could punch anyone out. A total natural. And if a boxing trainer had seen him, they would have signed him up at once. In pub brawls he would stand upright and just clock people around, and there were always people willing to have a go at him. Dougal was a scrapper without skills. He would just fight and bite and tear. On Friday nights, he would take a karabiner out with him to use as a knuckleduster. That's how his mind worked. I think all three of them were born to be frivolous and irreverent. But Dougal was a lovely lad as a schoolboy. I could show you pictures of him digging the foundations of my house in Currie at the age of 16, and playing ring-a-ring-a-roses with my bairns. No sign of a dark side then. He was just great fun, always larking about, always liked. I recognised him as an evil bastard at the time, but I was very fond of him.'

Stenhouse recalls: 'If we were climbing away, there was always a dance somewhere. People would have one too many, and there would be a bit of trouble, particularly in Glencoe, where we used to get into a few scraps. They used to have a dance down in the village hall, and invariably you attracted the bother. You went in there with your climbing clobber on, and tried to start pulling some of the local lads' girls and, of course, they objected.' Moriarty, the modest enforcer, simply smiles: 'There was the odd bit of bother, but we always seemed to get out of it.'

Marshall, though a respected committee member of the SMC and a successful architect with a large house and car, 'was also a roughneck at heart, weltering for years in a morass of Scottish climbing politics', according to Haston. They called him the Old Man, but it was a title replete with respect. For his part, Marshall, who despised the SMC at the time as 'a bloody moribund shower, run by mediocre guys, who were just trumped-up arses,' believed he had seen the way of changing Scottish mountaineering in the unlikely, rebellious shape of Haston and his friends. And in the next few years, in their company and the company of others, he was to climb far harder things than he had in the past. 'At first, I stayed out of the SMC because, basically, it was a bunch of old women,' Marshall reflects. 'But I thought: "Bugger it! I'll move in and bring in all these youngsters, and change it." And it did change, into an energetic club, although I don't think Dougal ever became their favourite member. I suppose I was like an old man to them, a father, although they never showed the slightest respect for their seniors, and that included me.'

Stenhouse insists, however: 'You couldn't have a better teacher than Jim Marshall. He was just incredible, and he was like a sort of Godfather – I suppose he still is. I think Jimmy brought out Dougal's competitive nature. I mean, he was very competitive at anything. He thought it was failure if you came second; you had failed, and when we got into climbing, we found through Jimmy and some of the other Edinburgh guys that there was quite an intense sort of rivalry between the Aberdonian crew and the Creagh Dhu and Jimmy Marshall. Robin Smith and us became the Edinburgh team. There would be a group of about ten of us who tended to climb together, and we used to go to the Cairngorms in the winter hoping to try and put a new route up, maybe something that the Aberdeen lot had tried for.'

To understand the rivalry and competition that was to be the catalyst for escalating standards in Scottish climbing, and the strange feudal world in which the boys from Currie suddenly found themselves, it is worth considering its history after the Second World War into the late 1950s, when it was dominated almost exclusively by groups from Glasgow and Aberdeen. Each had heterogeneous factions, too, with Edinburgh poorly represented until Marshall, Smith and later Haston got into their stride. Glasgow was represented, in the main, by a few members of the SMC or JMCS and the university, but was best known for its working-class climbing clubs from Clydeside, such as the Lomond, the Ptarmigan and Creagh Dhu. These were confined by work circumstances to weekends in Glencoe, and occasionally Ben Nevis. The Aberdeen group dominated the southern Cairngorms, particularly Lochnagar, above Braemar, and were headed by a doughty bunch drawn mostly from Aberdeen University, but including the Cairngorm and Etchacan clubs. The acknowledged leading Aberdonian lights were Tom Patey, Graeme Nicol, Kenny Grassick, Mac Smith and Bill Brooker.

These Scottish entities mirrored similar, informal climbing groups which had grown up in the north of England's industrial cities after the war, particularly in Manchester, Sheffield and Liverpool, and apart from climbing, all had one thing in common to a greater or lesser degree: an anti-establishment view of virtually everything. Clubs like the Creagh Dhu, the Wallasey Gang, the Alpha and the Rock and Ice became almost as famous for their mafia-like entrenchment and intolerance of anyone outside their immediate circle, as for their innovative pioneering work in the hills. There was, allegedly, a fatal stabbing one night when the paths of the Wallasey and the Creagh Dhu happened to cross in a pub – a story, possibly apochryphal, that is still doing the rounds.

In a climbing sense, forays into 'alien' territory were barely tolerated, though Patey and Nicol, in the company of Scotland's best-known renegade, Hamish MacInnes, snatched the Ben Nevis plum of Zero Gully in 1957. The balance was redressed to some degree when Marshall raided Lochnagar in winter the same year for Parallel Gully B, a grievous blow to local pride. As for climbers from England, they were with few exceptions persona non grata, the bolder ones invariably heading back down south after fruitless weekends with tales of 'nice wee routes' in pouring rain that they had been recommended by the natives. An article by the noted Yorkshire climber Allan Austin, in the book *Classic Rock*, tells of a hilarious misadventure from the early 1960s when he and a friend had been pointed at Clachaig Gully in a typical Glencoe downpour by an unnamed, but recognisable, group of local experts that included 'one called the Old Man, who seemed to be in charge [Marshall]; a dark, black-visaged giant [Moriarty]; one with shifty eyes, who seemed incapable of telling the truth [Haston]; and another with strange, round eyes who giggled a lot [Robin Smith]'. The adventure ended predictably: the Scots were first to the top of the climb, but last to the bar at the Clachaig Inn, where the bedraggled and bloodied English had to buy the drinks.

The Creagh Dhu did not recognise demarcation lines, real or imagined. Founded in 1930 by Andy Sanders, a shipwright from Clydebank, they cultivated an image as aggressive, anti-social hardmen for whom a smack in the mouth was as satisfying as a pint. Many of their fringe members early on were not even climbers, but dubious characters who would take a fishing pole or rifle on to the club bus for poaching trips up north. Stories, like the famous Battle of Zermatt, in which a small group of the Dhus allegedly tamed an army of Swiss guides in a drunken brawl, were exaggerated, but there is no doubt that members like Davie Agnew, Pat Walsh and John McLean were not men to meet at arm's length in a dark alley. Membership of the Creagh Dhu was almost impossible to attain, and depended as much on mountaineering ability as what one member described as 'a touch of evil'.

But between the brawls, boozing and all-night card schools, they were no mean climbers. And while the SMC had Lagangarbh, a distinctive, posh cottage 300 yards from the Buachaille car park at the eastern entrance of Glencoe for weekend visits, they found they had the ultimate neighbours from hell when the Creagh Dhu built their own 'club hut', a notoriously dank, unlit hovel called Jacksonville – without the formality of planning permission. The 'Ville', unlike Lagangarbh, was never locked, the Creagh Dhu's reputation ensuring the unlikelihood of unwanted visitors. Invitation was strictly limited, but Haston, Moriarty and Stenhouse found the door open to them, the Dhus recognising that in the three Currie schoolboys, doggedly and independently camping and climbing and exploring in Glencoe virtually every weekend, they perhaps had kindred spirits, even if they did come from posh Edinburgh. Agnew and McLean became firm friends with Haston, and climbed with him a lot down the years, Agnew later teaching Dougal, Mick Burke – and amazingly Don Whillans – how to ski in Leysin.

Agnew, like many of the Creagh Dhu, had been through a sickly, elemental upbringing on Clydeside, but had found freedom and good health in the hills with his companions in the club. 'I always remember my first day out when I was on top of the Campsie Fells looking over the smog in the shipyards at Clydebank, and I had never seen a blue sky. I didn't realise there was such a thing as a blue sky.' He had begun climbing with Haston mainly because of a shortage of partners, many of the Creagh Dhu following a fashion in the late 1950s and early 1960s of spending a year or more with the British Antarctic Survey 'down south'. Agnew, a wrestler of inordinate strength and no mean performer on rock, says of Haston: 'I always got on fine with him, although there were differences. The Glasgow guys were mostly apprentices; they had to go back to work on a Monday, which was the main difference between those and Edinburgh lads who had university. But I have always simply thought of Dougal as a guy who loved to climb and, in fact, thought of very little else.'

McLean, too, found Haston easy company: 'All the boys climbed with each other, and this east-west rivalry thing is a load of nonsense. It was Jimmy Marshall who brought them on, but a lot of the Creagh Dhu were down in Antarctic, so I gravitated to the Edinburgh lot. They used to camp on Gunpowder Green, near the "Ville", and before long I started climbing with Dougal, Eley and Jimmy.'

Friends or not, the rivalry was fierce, and laced with that ghoulish humour beloved of all climbers. McLean says: 'One season the weather was terrible, and we were all in Ravens Gully – Dougal, me, Ronnie Marshall and Robin – and all of us, the supposed cream of Scottish climbing, went creaming off the chockstone. Eley managed to fight his way up, and then we all abseiled off and left him there!' On another occasion, on Aonach Dubh, Haston beat Agnew and McLean to the foot of a longed-for first ascent, much to the Glaswegians' disgust. 'A terrible beating of the English language ensued. At last, McLean calmed down enough: "We'll eat your chocolate instead." We rolled rocks down on them, and they scattered cursing and swearing great revenge. They had our chocolate, and we had our first ascent.'

In between the climbing and desperate exploits and the under-age drinking, came the necessities of an education and the Higher exams looming in late 1957. Dougal and his parents were keen for him to proceed to higher education, and there was the opportunity of a state scholarship to university or teacher training college, if he could get the right grades. At West Calder High, Dougal proved an able linguist with an ear for French and German, in particular, and in those days at least devoted time to studies and homework. He was popular with the staff, and was eventually elevated to the heady heights of a school prefecture. Some teachers, however, dismissed him as 'a bloody tearaway', possibly after one master, out for a meal with his wife in Edinburgh one night, saw Haston staggering out of a pub in Rose Street. School staff seemed evenly divided between those who believed that the teenager who would turn into their most famous old boy – and have a school house named after him – would finish up as a ne'er-do-well, and others, like art teacher Arlo Santini, who believed Haston was destined for greatness, though in which field he knew not. Santini proved himself a remarkably good judge of character when he recalled: 'He was the type of boy you looked at after teaching for three years, and said: "From little acorns grow great trees." He had the type of eyes which looked at you, and said: "You are mere mortals you people. Just get out of here to get on with life. I have greater things to do." There was once a young PE teacher proud of his fitness [Pat McAndrew] and he would get burned off by young Haston. Most boys are just faces, but with Haston you recall his restless spirit and the will he had for winning. He was, when you look back, one of those boys who said: "I am something special. I am one of the minority who will go on to greater things."'

Santini must have been psychic. It took a long time for those greater things to arrive; the learning curve proved to be extremely steep and occasionally traumatic, and as Dougal was to write in 1970 of his teenage days in Scotland: 'Years later, in the mellowness of many mountain experiences, some of our behaviour at the time seems strange. But when you are unaware of your capabilities, have grandiose plans, don't know if you can fulfil them, are moving in new social directions, fighting constant criticism and going through at the same time all the normal formative teenage problems, then it is no surprise that what exists is a strange form of human animal. In all, a wild, crazy, sometimes disastrous period that was still a very essential part of shaping the mountaineer that I am now.'

If those experiences shaped the boy, then so, usually graciously acknowledged, did many of the people around him. Alick Buchanan-Smith (later Baron Balerno of Currie), the Currie Boys and the Marshalls were all to play lesser or greater roles in that development. But it was a young Edinburgh University student, a climber who in a few short years was to leave an indelible mark on British mountaineering, who was to have the most marked influence on Haston.

On a lousy, wet Sunday morning in July 1957, as Dougal and Stenhouse sat in their one-skin tent on Glencoe's Gunpowder Green watching the rain infiltrate the faded canvas and wondering if they would have to move as the River Coupall rose higher and higher, there was a commotion outside, and a head pushed through the tent opening to ask: 'I'm Robin Smith, do you want to do a climb?'

REVELATIONS

Two things fill my mind with ever-increasing wonder and awe, the more often and the more intensely the reflection dwells on them: the starry heavens above me and the moral law within me.
– Immanuel Kant, *Critique of Pure Reason*

Haston and Stenhouse looked out of their tent to discover that the voice belonged to a short, stocky figure clad in oilskin jacket and Wellington boots and with the customary Glencoe monsoon bouncing off a bright yellow sou-wester. A suspiciously worn climbing rope was draped round his shoulders. Their visitor, they noted, was given to giggling a lot, and much of the time wore a mischievously endearing grin that split most of his lower face.

They had certainly heard of Robin Smith. He was already a legend in Scottish climbing circles, if that is possible before the age of 19, and Haston's initial reaction was one of surprise that someone of his climbing pedigree should want to consort with two ill-equipped, naïve rookies. It was only later that they realised that most of Smith's climbing contemporaries tended to give him a wide berth. There were rumours of a relentless search for extreme difficulty without the formality of prior consultation with companions, and he trailed tales of all-day ascents, a disregard for the prevailing conditions, and the occasional benightment. He was always looking for new partners, or at least seconds, and would climb with anyone prepared to hold his rope for an inordinate length of time. He had done a lot of soloing.

Stenhouse takes up the story: 'Jim Clarkson and the other guys were away walking, it was such a bad weekend, and the rest were in their tents when Robin showed up. He wanted to go up Slime Wall, which took us aback a bit, but in the end we just strung along. We had really inferior gear, but then so had Robin. I don't think anyone else would climb with him because he was so good, to be honest.' Moriarty adds: 'Robin was slightly older, and had more aspirations than Dougal at the time. On most of the JMCS bus meets, no one would climb with him because he was so obviously in a different league. Everyone was astonished when we started climbing with him, although I have to say, if you climbed with Robin, you had to be prepared for a long day and usually finishing in darkness, because he didn't believe in early starts, and wouldn't quit on anything.'

Smith was born on August 30, 1938, in Calcutta, India, where his father was based as a naval architect. The family came to Britain in 1946, establishing themselves in Edinburgh's Morningside district, from whence Robin was dispatched to George Watson's College, a notable Edinburgh private school half a mile down the hill in the city's most genteel suburb. Haston was later to make great play of Smith's 'public school' background, but Smith's biographer Jim Cruickshank, who also attended Watson's, is at pains to point out that many of the pupils there, Smith included, were helped by state funding, and that he was not a boarder. After Robin's father died, he was almost as impecunious as 'working-class' Haston, whose parents and older brother indulged his every whim, and he certainly had fewer readies than the Marshalls (architect and shipwright) and Moriarty and Stenhouse, who were also working by then.

At the time of his meeting with Haston, Robin was a student of Philosophy at Edinburgh University, his academic brilliance – unlike Dougal later – allowing him the leeway to ignore the occasional tutorial, disappear for midweek climbing trips, and still sail through exams. When he and Haston met, Smith had been climbing for only three years, beginning in 1954 on Edinburgh's Salisbury Crags, where the objective dangers included irate Holyrood Park constabulary charged with keeping climbers off one of the city's favourite tourist attractions. But in that short time he had fast-tracked into the top echelon of British climbing. He had had no formal instruction, apart from a one-week winter course at Glenmore Lodge, the National Mountaineering Centre in the Cairngorms, and like Haston was helped with the technicalities and safety procedures by the ubiquitous Jim Clarkson, to whom Scottish, and world climbing, owe an obvious, unacknowledged debt.

Smith had appeared at the campsite beneath the Buachaille on a foul day unfit for even the easiest climbs, but typically wanted to go out and confront the hardest thing he could find. According to Haston, this was because he had to make things hard for himself, to even up the odds, as he found most climbing, whether on rock or ice, intolerably easy. 'This was his challenge, the way he played the game,' Haston confirmed. But Smith was also the ultimate amateur recreational climber, totally in tune with the mountain environment and conscious of his place in it, but without a single thought about making a living from the sport, or a name for himself.

'If Robin and Dougal were on the Currie Walls, to take an example,' says Andrew Wightman, who was also at Edinburgh University, and climbed with both, 'it was plain that Robin was there because it was fun, a good laugh. Dougal was there because it was serious training.'

Smith's choice of climb that July day in 1957 was Revelation, on the Buachaille's most forbidding precipice, the West Face of North Buttress, known popularly as Slime Wall because of its continuous weeps. The route, which aims for a large undercut flake at midheight, was first ascended in June 1956 by the Creagh Dhu duo of Patsy Walsh and Charlie Vigano, and its reputation for difficulty had not diminished a year later. Today, it is graded Hard Very Severe with the crux 5A, but is still definitely not considered a suitable outing for a wet day. As virtual novices, however, Haston and Stenhouse harboured no preconceived notions about climbing difficulty, though they certainly knew of Slime Wall, had heard of Revelation, and may have had a vague notion that venturing on to a climb like that on a day like that was not quite the norm . . . 'But then we were just so naïve,' Stenhouse reflects.

Marshall, who was to forge a notable winter climbing partnership with Smith within two years, says: 'It was Wheechie [Smith was named thus because of the high-pitched cry with which he would heartlessly taunt fellow climbers *in extremis*] who picked them up, and gave them a real shot in the arm by showing them a real climb. They were apprentices, and Wheechie took them up, and everyone else was tut-tutting and saying how irresponsible it all was. That so enthralled them, Revelation, and from that day forward they were climbers.' In Haston's diary, the neat schoolboy script reads: 'Glencoe 21st July, Revelation (Very Severe). R. Smith, J. Stenhouse, D. Haston. (This climb is reputed to be one of the hardest and most exposed in Glencoe)'.

It is interesting to compare his record of the ascent, written in his bedroom at Dolphin Road the following week, with the account that appears in his autobiography *In High Places* fifteen years later. In 1957, with little hindsight and the benefit of immediacy, he wrote: 'On Sunday morning, Robin Smith popped into our tent and asked us to accompany him on a climb called Revelation. Our acceptance seemed to have a profound effect on the rest of our companions. They thought us a little crazy. One o'clock saw us at the foot of the climb, which starts halfway up North Buttress. The first pitch is a traverse on to an extremely exposed face which overlooks Ravens Gully. The only trouble about the pitch was the thought of the third man coming off. If this had happened he (I) would have pendulumed into space and landed on unclimbable rock. However, everyone managed this, and arrived on a belay stance of about a foot square. This was where Jim and I were destined to wait for an hour and a half. As Robin had only an eighty-foot rope, he had to split the pitch into two. He then brought Jim up to underneath the crux. There he had to untie and pass my rope up to Robin, so that he could belay me as I made the traverse. I was then suspended from a running belay about twenty feet above, and I had to remain there for an hour. Eventually, Robin managed to reach the top of the pitch. Then Jim successfully tackled the crux, and led through to the top of the climb.

'When my turn came, I found the climbing tremendous. One must do a layback to get over round the overhang, and then climb another crack for about twenty-five feet. At the top of this crack, I had to untie the runner and then traverse under two more overhangs to the top of the pitch. I also led through, and climbed a slimy crack to the top of the climb. The climb took us five hours, but this was mainly because of trouble with rope and belays, and also slimy rock.'

The *In High Places* version presents Haston as more dramatic in his descriptive powers, but marginally less accurate. He gets the month wrong for a start: 'Again 1957, in August, Stenhouse and I lying in our tent on Gunpowder Green beneath the Buachaille. It was a normal Glencoe day; the rain was skidding along horizontally, and we were idly watching the rising river wondering if we'd have to move our tents. Frustration was the mood. We'd spent precious money taking a JMCS bus instead of hitch-hiking, as usual. It looked like a wasted weekend. A head appeared in the door to interrupt our mutterings.

' "I'm Robin Smith. Would you like to go climbing?"

' "Sure." We never stopped to think why he would want to climb with us. We got out of the tent to find a thick-set, medium-height figure with incredible, bowed legs. He was dressed in the then fashionable oilskin jacket, sou-wester and Wellington boots.

' "Where do you want to go?" say we. He looks distant for a moment. "There's a wee route on Slime Wall called Revelation, which should be interesting in the wet." '

And on the climb: 'The memories are still clear today of Robin taking hours over the second pitch, yet I was not feeling unhappy as we stood belaying on a small foothold each. Conditions and his decaying boots were terrible; his climbing was great. We were amazed at the quality of his equipment. It was as bad as ours. Four old beaten-up slings with ex-War Department karabiners and an old nicked and scarred nylon rope.

'We found it strange that Robin Smith had such bad equipment. But on getting to know him better – and when my powers of character analysis had perhaps had some of the rough edges taken off – I realised this was the way he played the game. This was his challenge. He had to increase the challenge by climbing at night, in the wet or sometimes solo, often in bad conditions, and always with the worst equipment.'

Haston's ascent of the Slime Wall route, as might be gathered from his original, matter-of-fact, description, was not quite the quantum leap into the sixth grade that it was later portrayed. No blinding revelation here. His climbing progress, in fact, was far more structured and deliberate than that of Smith, whose thirst for extreme adventure and madcap spontaneity was almost obsessive.

Historians seeking clues to the workings of Haston's mind have searched long and hard into the relationship between two widely differing personalities still regarded as seminal figures in Scottish mountaineering history. Some saw them as rivals, but they climbed together, though not always amicably, over a period of three years from 1958 to 1961, their most notable collaboration producing an epic first ascent of The Bat, at the time one of the hardest routes in Britain, on Carn Dearg Buttress, Ben Nevis, in September 1959. Contemporaries, however, leave no one in doubt that Smith remained the senior partner, and not just in climbing, until his death in the Pamirs in 1962, when Haston began the gradual ascent to the global status that many still believe would have belonged to Smith one day.

John McLean of the Creagh Dhu, a friend and climbing partner of both, insists: 'We always felt Dougal took the role that Robin would have had.' Wightman says: 'Dougal was definitely in Robin's shadow, and it's interesting to speculate on what might have happened if Robin had lived.' He recalls catching an embarrassed Haston in what he, and Haston, obviously believed was secret training: press-ups and sit-ups in an effort to improve, and 'catch Robin up', adding: 'Would there, for example, have been room for two major climbing talents, both coming from Edinburgh? There is little doubt that Dougal blossomed after Smith died.'

According to Stenhouse, who also got a close-up view of both in action: 'They were rivals in a certain sense, and I think it was a little bit of a put-off on Dougal's side that Robin was probably a better climber. I'm sure he wanted to become better than Robin, but he – all of us, for that matter – were slightly behind him at the time.'

Jimmy Marshall, however, is unequivocal in his view that 'Robin had far more natural ability as a climber than Dougal'.

Their manner of tackling steep rock could not have been more different. Smith, sturdily built at 5ft 9in, was physically in the Joe Brown/Don Whillans mould, and tended to cling like a limpet and move slowly, and with great certainty. Haston, an inch and a half taller, but weighing less than eleven stones, had more delicacy about him, and liked to get close to the rock, using his long arms and the strong fingers developed on the Currie Railway Walls. Sessions at the sports hall with Pat McAndrew at West Calder High, and in the school acrobatics team, had also given him a gymnastic ability useful for high steps, bridging and mantleshelf movements.

Haston later had no hesitation in naming Smith as 'the greatest influence on my early climbing career', but while both were to be remembered as reckless, almost crazy, and willing to take any risk to complete a climb, Haston's diaries make it plain that from the period 1956–8, he was far more prudent and conservative in his approach, content to ascend almost anything without the qualification of great difficulty. In terms of quality new-route output, too, Haston trailed conclusively behind, and while there are numerous climbs still looked on with respect as 'Smith routes' – Shibboleth on Slime Wall, the Needle on Shelter Stone Crag, Marshall's Wall on the North-East Face of Gearr Aonach and even The Bat come to mind – Scotland lacks the definitive 'Haston Route', perhaps the nearest being the classic Hee Haw on the West Face of Aonach Dubh, and even on that most of the credit belongs to Eley Moriarty. Much of Haston's most notable pioneering work was done on Creag Dubh at Newtonmore, which, though containing a number of bold, high-grade routes, is little more than a roadside training crag. Most of the twenty or so first ascents Haston put up in the current Glencoe guide are eminently forgettable.

On snow and ice, the gap was even more marked. While Smith, usually in the company of Marshall, literally plastered Scotland, in particular Ben Nevis, with first winter ascents, Haston's contribution was minimal. On Ben Nevis, his contributions number just three – and two were made as a second to Marshall. Haston can be likened to a world-class decathlete: way above average in several disciplines, but not really excelling in any. It was only later that the combination found a true arena on higher hills.

In the pub or at a party, Haston, Moriarty and Stenhouse may have 'left Robin in the corner while we chased after girls', (though there is evidence that this, too, was a fallacy) but on the mountain, Smith proved to be the catalyst for most of their more outlandish adventures. Where he led, Haston followed.

The evidence is there in Haston's first diary. After Revelation, while Robin set out immediately on a first trip to the Alps and an early British ascent of the South Ridge of the Aiguille Noire de Peuterey with Clarkson, Haston and Stenhouse departed for a scrambling holiday in Skye in weather so vile that they cut it short to return to the mainland and a few middle-grade routes on Ben Nevis. Even there came failures, and a circumspect willingness to turn back rather than push things too far. On Raeburn's Arête (Severe) the pair were driven off by rain, 'because we were wearing plimsolls', and the next day they turned back from Clachaig Gully. In September of 1957, Haston failed on Sunset Groove, an innocuous Very Difficult on Buachaille Etive Mor's Great Gully Buttress, and also retreated from the overhang of the Very Severe Shattered Crack, the only consolation being an ascent of the old favourite, North-East Zigzag, a task described resignedly by Haston as 'a climb that needs no description. This was my fourth ascent'.

On a trip to the Lake District a month later, there came more evidence of his variable performances and, perhaps, a hint that he was outgrowing his climbing partners of the time. He badly needed the renewal of impetus so demonstrably offered by Smith on Revelation. In the Lakes, however, Smith stuck with Gordon Burns, a science lecturer at Edinburgh University, and Haston climbed with Clarkson, which at least gave him more experience on the sharp end of the rope.

Clarkson, however, failed to follow up Amen Corner on Gimmer Crag's Severe B Route and on Asterisk, a Very Severe, and Haston recorded somewhat sarcastically that 'old man Clarkson declared it impossible, but this time he managed to second it'. On the way down, Haston spotted Smith and a partner in the act of doing the same climb, but 'in pitch darkness'. The next day, Haston and Clarkson blitzed Raven Crag, by the road in Langdale, climbing Original Route, Revelation, Bilberry Buttress (Clarkson again failing to follow), Centipede, Evening Wall and Oak Tree Wall where, 'though he didn't know it, JC climbed this pitch without protection, as my belay kept slipping off its spike'. But back at the campsite, by the Old Dungeon Ghyll Hotel, they found Smith had climbed three Very Severes on Gimmer Crag, one after the other. Smith, unconsciously and without really trying, seemed consistently and effortlessly able to one-up everyone else. And he always appeared to be the overriding driving force, with Haston happy to tag along or loath to lose face by saying no. Occasionally, their ambitions outstripped their abilities or form, as one would expect from young climbers, and led to incidents of almost farcical proportions.

The weekend of October 26–27 found Haston, Moriarty, Smith and Stenhouse in Cameron's Barn, a famously popular farm doss at the eastern end of Glencoe, where initially there were plans for a midnight ascent of Ravens Gully on Buachaille Etive Mor, a route graded Very Severe, and as black and forbidding as its name implies. Torrential rain managed to put even Smith off that idea, and the weekend went downhill from there. Haston was stopped by Fracture Route and Grooved Arête and then, persuaded by Smith to attempt Satan's Slit, a Very Severe on Rannoch Wall, they were forced to retreat in the darkness, sacrificing one of Smith's precious nylon slings for the abseil. On the way down, Moriarty took a tumble to be held on the rope by Stenhouse, and 'we eventually fumbled down Curved Ridge with our tails between our legs'.

In early November, they were back in Glencoe with a plan to climb all 4000-ft peaks in Scotland within twelve hours, another grandiose notion that lasted as far as Kinlochleven where, on a bright, moonlight night, Smith decided conditions were ideal for a nice walk. Haston agreed without hesitation, and while Stenhouse and Burns took their sacks round to Glen Nevis, the pair set out. By one-thirty in the morning, they were making pace along the crusted snow on the summit ridge of Binnein Mor, where 'the view from the summit was wonderful. Buachaille thrust its dark bulk skywards to the left of the spiky Aonach Eagach ridge. Straight in front was Ben Nevis with the Carn Mor Dearg Arête shining in the bright moonlight. The snow was rather soft in places, and the going became heavy as we ascended Na Gruagaichean. It was a long way from this summit to Am Bodach and we were now rather weary, but we reached it soon after six a.m. The next part entailed going along the famous Devil's Ridge, which joins Am Bodach to Sgurr a'Mhaim. The going was tremendous, and we had to use our hands in places. Just before we reached the summit, the sun rose abruptly in the east and we were soon picking our way laboriously down towards Polldubh. At nine-thirty, we met Gordon [Burns] and Jim [Stenhouse] and we eventually decided to go down to Glencoe.'

The madcap behaviour was becoming contagious. As all four lay recovering in the back of his van Burns, who perhaps should have known better, suddenly announced his intention of climbing

Clachaig Gully solo, and set off up the hill towards the 1000-ft long Glencoe classic. The other three turned over and went back to sleep, but half an hour later, Haston thought they had better follow him, 'and it was just as well we did, because we found him stuck on some slabs above the Great Cave Pitch'. After effecting a rescue, all four continued to the top solo, finishing in total darkness, as tradition by then demanded. To complete a hectic weekend, Haston and Stenhouse, while Smith and Burns went for a hill walk, this time out-Smithed Smith by climbing Agag's Groove on the Buachaille, collecting the discarded abseil sling on the way, but neglecting, naturally, to return it to its owner. Finally, they ascended Shackle Route in bitterly cold conditions before heading, happily exhausted, for home.

* * *

With the advent of winter 1957–8, Haston and Stenhouse decided it was time to graduate from mere winter hillwalking and to learn the rudiments of snow and ice climbing, though they did not even own a pair of crampons. Before the advent of curved picks, 12-point crampons and front-pointing, winter climbing was far more laborious, difficult and technical in many ways. Winter ascents required a dogged ability to hang on to steep ice for hours at a time, while hacking a ladder of steps. But far from requiring the arms and skills of a lumberjack, there was an undoubted subtlety in reading the varying qualities and types of ice and an art to crampon placement, resting and placing of protection. For many it was a long learning process, but fortunately Dougal found in Marshall not only a master of all the winter arts, but a teacher prepared to devote time to his education. On December 15, the night after the JMCS dinner at the Kingshouse Hotel in Glencoe, a hungover Haston and Stenhouse had battled their way up an out-of-condition North Buttress of the Buachaille – where crampons would have been superfluous anyway – finishing in a howling blizzard, and then narrowly missed being avalanched out of NC Gully on Stob Coire nan Lochan on the way back down to Lagangarbh. Then it was over to Fort William and the long plod up the Allt a'Mhuilinn where, after the round of Ben Nevis and Carn Mor Dearg on New Year's Day with Moriarty, Stenhouse and Ronnie Marshall, 'we enjoyed a glissade on the slopes above the CIC Hut, and on reaching it, found that Jimmy Marshall and his party had arrived'.

Marshall has always consistently underplayed his role in Scottish mountaineering, and in the education of Smith and Haston in particular. He insists vehemently that they would have found their rightful place in mountain history without his help, but there is little doubt that in this unlikely duo he saw a chance to drag Scottish climbing up by its bootlaces. His encouragement and occasional prodding of the two youngsters was, he admits now, a quite deliberate campaign to make Scottish climbing a force to be reckoned with. 'I climbed with the boys in winter, and I suppose you could say it was part of their education. But I taught them only by example. I told them not to catch their troosers and how to run down slopes, basically how not to kill yourself. They had these ex-army axes, and I told them what had or hadn't been climbed, and away they went to do it. But they were always going to be good with or without me. Basically, I just pointed them at things. They were dead keen on what is now Neanderthal at the head of the Lost Valley in Glencoe, but it was never in condition – it needed this overhang to ice over – so they always did things round it. But then I said: "Gully A has not been climbed, go and do it." They were apprentices, but went away and did it. They also climbed on the Ben with me, which gave them a good start, I suppose. I took Dougal and Jim Stenhouse up Minus 2, and as a prelude to that, we were over on Creag Meagaidh, and I sent them up to straighten out Centre Post. They didn't quite manage that, so as consolation I took them up 1959 Face Route, the first ascent.'

On January 2, 1958, Haston and Stenhouse, while Marshall and his party put up the Italian Climb on the Western Flank of Tower Ridge, spent almost six hours fighting their way up Staircase Climb on Carn Dearg, a first winter ascent, and an epic involving verglas-covered rock, cracks choked with ice, combined tactics and the occasional piton for aid. It was Marshall again who had recommended this, discounting their naïvety in snow and ice, and telling them: 'That's a nice wee route; go and have a go at that.' Later, Haston had little hesitation informing his diary that 'the crux, a crack filled with tough ice followed by a verglas-covered slab I had to wriggle up on my stomach was the hardest pitch that I had ever led'. Stenhouse did not disagree.

Above the first crux, Dougal reported that 'we then proceeded up some snow pitches to the second obstacle – The Tower. Our summer direct route seemed out of the question, so we tried to climb a bulging wall at the col between The Tower and the face. Eventually, we had to resort to combined tactics, and after a grim struggle, we reached The Tower. We then scaled the chimney behind, and landed at the top of the climb. It had taken us five and a half hours, and in our estimation was about Hard Severe to VS [Dougal forgetting that winter routes had their own one to five grading]. We then proceeded to the top of Carn Dearg before glissading, whooping and shouting our heads off, down No 3. Gully to the [CIC] Hut.'

As Marshall puts it: 'I think they had a great time on that. I think I just took away the barriers and, although I think Dougal was probably still not 18 at the time, he began to realise then exactly what he could and couldn't do.'

Haston's mentor must certainly have been impressed by the schoolboy's accelerating prowess on snow and ice, for at the end of the month he was back with his protégé climbing as a rope of two, and it says much for Marshall's opinion of the abilities of his teenage partner – or perhaps his disdain for normal climbing protocol – that their first goal was Point Five Gully, unclimbed at the time.

'On arriving at the foot, we found water dripping from the ice,' said Dougal. 'So we decided to seek a higher climb, namely Gardyloo Gully.'

While Marshall worked with Smith as an equal, sharing leads in arguably one of the most powerful combinations seen in Scottish winters, Haston was still the novitiate. Nonetheless, Marshall pushed Haston into the lead up the Grade Three Gardyloo Gully high up above Observatory Gully – 'Jimmy had been up the gully before, so I led a lot of it' – and then they decided that, as the day was still young, they would descend Tower Ridge, still considered in those days a major ascent, and one on which several notables had been benighted. Haston recalled: 'Three hundred feet of easy climbing brought us to the Tower Gap (normally the upwards crux) and we climbed this by hitching the rope around a spike and sliding down, and then we stepped across and up the other side. We rappelled from the top of the Great Tower, and after this the only obstacle was the rock pitch on the Little Tower. We were soon over this, and then ran the rest of the way to the CIC Hut.' An ascent of Comb Gully, high up in Coire na Ciste, followed on the Saturday, and the pair rounded off a memorable weekend by racing up the classic Observatory Ridge, Haston noting happily that 'we took four hours from hut back to hut'.

If Dougal thought he had graduated as a snow and ice climber, however, there was an advanced class to come from Marshall. Twelve months later, after warming up on the unclimbed Smith's Route on Creag Meagaidh – an ironic nudge at Robin, who had failed on it – the 'Old Man' led Haston and Stenhouse first on the six-mile plod across the frozen wastes of the Allt a'Mhuilinn to the CIC Hut and then up Minus Two, the finest of the big Ben Nevis gullies. On this, a 'stunner and a mind-awakener', Haston recalled that it 'was taking us as long to second as Jimmy to lead. His experience and ability were still beyond ours. He seemed able to cut steps like a simple and economical machine.' Dougal still had much to learn.

* * *

The 1958 rock-climbing season began on April 1 with a ten-day holiday in North Wales, at that time the acknowledged home, even by parochial Scots, of extreme British climbing. With Haston in the main on the end of Smith's rope, the pair ran through what were then the hardest routes in the area. Smith, by this time maturing into one of the finest rock-climbers in the country in his own right, and with a canniness far beyond that of his partner, invariably managed to plan matters so that he led the harder pitches, with Haston never objecting. They warmed up with Belle Vue Bastion on Tryfan, and followed that with the hardest route at the time in Cwm Idwal, Rowan Tree Slabs, before moving round to Llanberis Pass, where an aura of immense difficulty still surrounded many of the routes on the so-named Three Cliffs. Although 'rather apprehensive at the start', the pair made short work of Ivy Sepulchre on Dinas Cromlech, their first Extremely Severe (climbs in Wales still had two gradings above the normal Scottish Very Severe, though there was quite often little to choose between them in terms of difficulty). Both, however, exhausted themselves trying to extract the famous twelve-inch ice piton below the crux bulge. Some Glencoe habits were hard to break.

Jericho Wall and an abseil down the famous open book of Cenotaph Corner followed, and they slowly ticked their way through Peter Harding's 'bumper fun book' guide of Llanberis Pass classics before they stood at the foot of Clogwyn y Grochan. They had their eyes on the Joe Brown route, Hangover, and a chance to test themselves for the first time on a route created by the most notable rock-climber in the land.

Haston's writing, like his climbing, still had not lost its ingenuousness, and his powers of description had not yet broadened (he was, after all, still two weeks away from his eighteenth birthday) but are endearing for all that: 'This is a Joe Brown XS, and it makes the Harding routes look like V Diffs. The route starts up a strenuous crack, which is very fine. The next pitch provided another very good lead from Robin. The wall is tremendously steep, and you have to hang on all the time. This leads to the traverse on Kaisergebirge Wall which, in turn, leads to the sensational last pitch of Hangover. If you look through your legs as you bridge the chimney, the only thing visible is a dark bulge which curves over, then thin air and finally, 150 feet below, terra firma. On following up, I found this groove the best that I had yet had the fortune to climb.'

The climax of the holiday for the young Scots came with the Pass's Big Two, Cemetery Gates and Cenotaph Corner on Dinas Cromlech, again Brown/Whillans routes, and graded Extremely Severe. The Gates, which follows a crack line in the vertical right wall of Cenotaph Corner, went without great difficulty, but then came a typical Smith piece of impetuosity when he took the extraordinary decision, having polished off one of the famous pitches in Britain, to head across to the other side of the pass and try The Grooves, another Brown classic, on Cyrn Las, a good hour's walk from the road. 'We were benighted on the second pitch, and had to abseil off in the darkness,' Dougal noted resignedly. That setback did not stop them from trudging next day up the steep, unstable scree slopes to the foot of Cenotaph Corner, the climb on the top of every aspirant's wish-list of those days. Although any Brown/Whillans route was regarded as a coming-of-age in climbing terms, the Corner, because of its dramatically photogenic appearance, history and demanding technicalities, was the absolute yardstick at the time. Theirs was only the route's seventh ascent in six years, and the second by a Scottish party. Smith, as so often, was in Wheechie mode once he had got up after a lengthy struggle, laughing at Haston's efforts to get his two pitons out – in 1958, the climb still required two pegs for aid – and then burning himself on the abseil back down the Corner. Dougal found much laughter in the company of Smith.

* * *

If his education was continuing apace on the hill, by early 1958 Haston had to give some consideration to his learning off it, and the necessity of a career. By now he was totally addicted to climbing, and his thoughts were fixed on a vocation that would allow him to indulge his sport totally. With his Highers at West Calder High School out of the way – he passed German and French in his sixth year, having passed English in his fifth – he applied to Jordanhill College of Physical Education in Glasgow, an establishment that put great store in the value of outdoor pursuits as part of education, with rock-climbing, sailing and canoeing courses on its agenda. Dougal's paper qualifications were acceptable, but first he had to pass a few physical tests. After that, he would be able to look ahead to a career of excellent pay, long holidays and a future of full-time climbing punctuated by the occasional need to demonstrate the use of map and compass, or the tying of a bowline knot, to a classroom of students.

It was not to be.

Moriarty had spent £20 of his wages as an apprentice engineer on a 350cc Royal Enfield motorcycle and, as was the norm, a half-share in the machine went to his best pal, despite the fact that the impecunious Haston could not afford a cash contribution. Dougal certainly upped his street cred by roaring into school at West Calder on his machine, but while travelling at top speed – just over 60 mph – through Juniper Green early in May 1958, on the way from Currie, the front forks collapsed, and he skidded sixty feet down the road. He woke to find his right arm dangling at a strange angle, and a shoulder so badly dislocated that even ten years later it was wont to pop out occasionally, much to the alarm of his wife, Annie. The lengthy convalescence and the damage ended his chances of becoming a PE teacher, but more worryingly took three desperate months out of his developing climbing career. He was back on Buachaille Etive Mor by the weekend of July 26–27, but his haste to return to the world of Very Severe nearly proved his undoing. He followed Moriarty up Mainbrace, but then almost fell off leading the layback section of the far-easier Hangman's Crack – both on the East Face of North Buttress – arriving 'pretty chastened' on the finishing ledge. A week later, he had his revenge on Shattered Crack, and by September, with a return to Wales, he was back to something close to his old form, and with the fears about long-term damage to his shoulder allayed.

The keyword was still caution, however, and though he had determined beforehand that he would lead, in Llanberis Pass he simply headed off up most of the routes that he had seconded with Smith four months earlier. However, as Marshall insists: 'That's what makes a good mountaineer, building up a good vocabulary.' Haston took great delight in his anointed role of climbing mentor to Stenhouse, introducing his friend to Brant Direct, Spectre, Hangover and Cemetery Gates, the latter proving an eventful lead. He wrote: 'We were gradually working up the scale, and we were going to try the awe-inspiring Gates as a prelude to an attempt on the Corner, but things didn't quite work out as planned. I was about halfway up the climb when the thunderstorm broke. But I was determined to climb the Gates, and to the accompaniment of peals of thunder and flashes of lightning, I eventually pulled myself on to the sloping ledge at the top of the crack. The rock here was very greasy, and I tied myself to some loose flakes to avoid slipping off. The whole climb was streaming wet, so it was decided that Jimmy should not try it. I then fixed a sling and karabiner round a dubious flake and abseiled down to the piton, which is about fifty feet up, [and] he abseiled down the rest of the way on the second rope.'

The weather had broken, and it was the end of their holiday. When their tent, on the small unofficial campsite opposite the Cromlech Boulders, was flooded, they simply duplicated another time-honoured Glencoe habit, and broke into the Climbers' Club Hut down the road at Nant Peris to sleep there.

* * *

With his prospects of becoming a teacher of Physical Education ruined by his road accident, Dougal turned his mind elsewhere and came up with an alternative – a Philosophy honours course at Edinburgh University. To many it seemed a long stride from a life as a sweaty jock studying the teachings of Percy Cerruty and the mechanics of anaerobic and aerobic exercise to becoming a cerebral undergraduate pondering the works of Hume, Kant or Hobbes, but both courses offered opportunities for climbing, and Haston reasoned that between listening to discourses on logic, metaphysics and psychology, he could always slip out of Edinburgh midweek and head for the hills. Smith, midway through his four-year honours course in Philosophy, had already demonstrated the viability of this approach, 'The idea of going to university had nothing to do with a compulsion to study philosophy,' Jimmy Marshall explains. 'It was simply the easiest course he could find. He didn't have to attend much, and the fact is that a lot of it involved reading, rather than written work. I think that's what Smith sold him on: they could bone up on philosophy late at night and discuss it between them, because the fact is Dougal was going to become a mountaineer – there was no other course in life.'

Andrew Wightman, who started his science course at Edinburgh University at the same time as Haston, came from a similar background with a state scholarship from Broughton High School being his means of entry. He had been introduced to climbing while in the Boy Scouts when Jimmy Marshall turned up as a sort of freelance instructor, and he proved no mean performer. He says: 'I think he took the course because Smith did it, and he was always following Smith. But the problem for Dougal and others was that people like Dick Holt [a Smith climbing partner] and Robin would seem to simply swan around all day doing absolutely nothing, and we thought this was the norm. I, for one, can't recall ever seeing Smith do any work, but he was a brilliant academic and had the tutors eating out of his hand. Once one of them wrote to him: "Dear Robin, *please* do try and hand in an essay sometime this term."'

Dougal was not due to go up until late 1959, however, and he had time to kill. He worked for a time at Scottish Equitable, in St Andrew Square, Edinburgh, mulling over insurance proposal forms, day-dreaming about weekend climbing plans, and getting sniffy about the rows of faceless suits there. 'He was just a clerk, and he hated it,' says Wightman. 'He just hated the environment, he hated the job. Whatever he should have been in life, it was not a clerk.' Unsurprisingly, Dougal failed to last the course as a white-collar worker, and signed on the dole, virtually living in Glencoe and hitching down to the city once a week to collect his benefit, a trick that he had learned from a generation of the Creagh Dhu. But he, or rather Jimmy Marshall, was by now looking further afield than gloomy Glencoe, with its small peaks lashed by constant rain and walls of greasy rock.

* * *

The classic convergent progress of British mountaineers of ambition invariably runs: native hills, native rock, Scottish snow and ice, Dolomite rock, mixed routes in the Western Alps and finally, if they have survived so far, the Himalaya or similar lofty ranges. In the summer of 1959, Marshall, who already had seasons in the Alps, decided that the Currie Boys were ready for stage four, and announced that they would be heading for Europe in the summer, and the limestone towers and vertical faces of northern Italy. The party was to consist of de facto leader Marshall, brother Ronnie, Haston, Moriarty – Stenhouse had retired by this time – and John McLean, the 'Great White Hope' of the Creagh Dhu, who had been invited to make up a famous five at the last minute. As always, Marshall did the planning, the organising and delegating, with the rest happy to tag along. 'Jim was in charge, without a doubt,' says Moriarty. 'I wouldn't say he was the schoolmaster, but he was ancient, about 30 by then, and we tended to do what he said.'

Marshall, always extremely well prepared, had spent twelve months working in Geneva, where he had got to know some of the local climbers. They had passed on topos and route descriptions of many of the major routes in the Alps and Dolomites, and Marshall had them translated and written out on a sheet of paper. He was extremely well armed when it came to climbing. If the 'Old Man' was his usual, methodical self, the same did not apply to the younger members of the party. McLean, who had saved £29 for the seven weeks away – £10 of which had been donated by Creagh Dhu colleague Bill Smith to buy a duvet – was arriving late, and Moriarty had told the big Glaswegian that they would meet him in London, without specifying where. After a night in a jazz club, the advance party emerged bleary-eyed into The Strand, to find the familiar figure of McLean shambling down the street towards them. So far, so good.

It turned into a reasonable first season. Though not without occasional setbacks. Their base was close to the foot of the Vajolet Towers in the Catinaccio region, where certain members of the party slipped into the traditional habits of British climbers abroad, drinking themselves senseless on local red wine, and shopping in supermarkets without bothering to pay. 'They were always nicking things,' says Marshall. 'I remember walking through Cortina one afternoon with McLean, when we saw Dougal and Eley approaching at high speed from the other direction with a bunch of people in hot pursuit, shouting at them.'

McLean notes mordantly: 'Dougal got us into more trouble than anyone else. He would start something, and Eley and me had to get him out of it.'

At Marshall's insistence, they had carried out tins of bully beef, important for iron rations, and 'I also made them drink milk for the calcium, but it wasn't much of a diet. Later on, on the way up to the Civetta, we were going up the foresters' track to the usual campsite, and we were really sweltering and struggling – McLean had been put out of the army because of his bad feet – and when we got to this clearing, there was a big dropping of sacks. That's when I noticed a nice pair of trousers hanging over a boulder, so I took them and passed my old ones over to Dougal. They were carrying up a huge tin of pressed chicken they had stolen from somewhere, and we were all looking forward to getting into that. We went up for the climb next morning, and when we got back someone had nicked the chicken. Disgraceful!'

The party had warmed up with a traverse of the airy Vajolet Towers en masse before Jimmy Marshall announced that they would go up to the Ombretta Pass next day, and try the South Pillar of the

Marmolada. Haston recalled *Nanga Parbat Pilgrimage* and Buhl's epic on one of the toughest climbs in the Dolomites, but faithfully followed the leader. Conditions were appalling, and after eleven hours of climbing, Marshall and Haston were in the notorious Exit Couloirs, soaked to the skin and looking up at the ice glistening on the rock, then down at their rubber-soled PAs. They were eventually repulsed by the noted Waterfall Pitch, sheathed in a layer of verglas, as so often. 'If we had had ice axes, we would have got up it,' claims Marshall, but a 1500-ft abseil retreat and a discarded rope followed. Dolomites 1, Haston 0.

Unabashed, Dougal, Ronnie Marshall and Eley were handed by Jim the description of the Comici Route on the Cima Grande de Lavaredo, a famous pre-war Grade Six, and the pair muscled their way up that, learning the rudiments of artificial climbing on the way. While Marshall and McLean headed for first the North Face of the Cima Ouest then the North-West Face of the Civetta and a night out in a lightning storm in the final chimneys, Haston and Moriarty were pointed at the North-West face of the Valgrande. Initially, they climbed the wrong side of the approach gorge, bypassed a supercilious bunch of Germans halfway up, and after being driven back by a fierce crack, spent a night in the open in the rain. When they came to in the morning, they spotted the roof of a hut a few metres below. They retreated valleywards to their chosen lodgings, in a graveyard, where they discovered that their passports had been stolen. It was turning into a painful learning process, but the various epics were filling up the logbook of experience, and even the failures and seemingly continuous setbacks could not keep them down for long. Leafing through the tattered pages of Marshall's makeshift guide, Haston came across the description of the Cima Su Alto – 'one of the hardest climbs in the Dolomites' – and off they went.

At the start, as they bivouaced under a clear, starlit sky, Haston began to experience, for the first time, a state of mind that he would call upon during many mountain days in future. He looked forward to the total commitment of a difficult climb; he felt a sort of controlled excitement and, above all, a burgeoning belief in his ability. The Su Alto, however, turned into an epic which even Robin Smith could not have contrived, though the actual ascent went without a hitch. On the summit, they tucked into their meal of two pre-boiled eggs, and prepared for another night out and a descent the next day. It began to rain heavily, then to snow. 'We were absolutely knackered,' says Moriarty. 'How we survived, I just don't know because we had left the sleeping bags behind to save on weight, and all we had on were shirts, jeans and PAs. We didn't even have socks. At one time during the night I woke up, and Dougal was buried under the snow: it was bloody freezing.' On the way down, the rope jammed, and Haston had to reduce it to two 40-ft lengths with his piton hammer. Eventually, Moriarty could hear the sound of running water – a sure sign of the approaching valley – but the cloud had closed in again.

'We set up one last abseil, and Dougal disappeared. I never heard anything, then a voice came floating up: "I'm stuck, I'm jumping it. I canna go any further." I never heard anything, but then, lucky for me, the cloud cleared. Dougal had jumped the last twenty feet, but he didn't know that in the mist. It could have been 200 feet for all he knew. We got down to the meadow, and were both violently sick, the bile. But all through it there was no moaning and groaning from Dougal, just a determination to get out of there.'

On the walk down to the valley, Marshall's former trousers, now in the care of Haston, fell to pieces in protest at all the abseiling. The guardian at the Allhege Hut took pity, and handed over his spare pair.

Marshall's original plan had been to spend three weeks in the Dolomites, then head for 'the big stuff' in Chamonix, where they hoped to meet up with Robin Smith, who was there with a group of other Scots. The Dolomites party eventually caught up with Smith on his way down from the Grandes Jorasses, where he had made the first British ascent of the Walker Spur with Gunn Clark, a feat alongside which their Dolomites ramblings noticeably paled. The season was ended by a series of massive storms, and when Smith and his party were caught out by several feet of new snow in the Vallee Blanche, between Chamonix and Courmayeur, following a set of ski tracks that terminated in a large hole big enough to put a bus in, all prudently decided to call it a day. They headed for home.

*   *   *

Back in Scotland, the climbing relationship with Smith continued its erratic course later in 1959, with their ascent of The Bat on Carn Dearg Buttress, Ben Nevis, an elongated epic typical of the chaotic, impromptu and occasionally confrontational partnership. The line of The Bat had long been coveted by both men. After the English raiding party of Brown and Whillans had stolen the Ben Nevis plums, leaving a festering sore on the Scottish climbing psyche with Sassenach (1954) and Centurion (1956), nationalistic eyes turned to the huge tracts of unclimbed rock in between, and the chance to regain some Caledonian pride. Between Centurion's boiler-plate slabs and obvious corner and the massive overhung chimney of Sassenach further right, a large, bottomless diedre had winked invitingly at a number of climbers on their way up to the CIC Hut down the years.

Smith had first tried to get into the big corner with Dick Holt from the Edinburgh University Mountaineering Club, but had been stopped by the first crux section, named imaginatively by Smith the Hoodie Groove, 'because it looked as happy as a hoodie crow', and his usual scenario of loss of daylight. He returned with Haston in September 1959, though the pair were hardly talking after Haston had failed to meet Smith in Switzerland after the Dolomites/Chamonix excursions for an attempt on the North Face of the Eiger, a concept that again illustrates Haston's willingness to be towed along by Smith's irrepressibility, and his own ambition. It would have been his first route in the Western Alps. Smith was also severely disenchanted when he heard that Haston and McLean had been up to attempt 'his' route while he swotted for university exams, the justification of McLean being that 'Robin has had his time on it. Now it's our turn'. Rain intervened to save Smith on this occasion, and McLean had to make do with the second ascent, with Bill Smith, a year later.

The first attempt by Robin and Dougal in September got off to a typically shambolic start. Haston's climbing was going through a perennial erratic phase. He was either useless or brilliant, but in Smith's company somehow always managed to find something extra. He failed to get off the ground on Carnivore, the famous John Cunningham test piece on Creag a'Bhancair in Glencoe, but returned with Smith the following weekend to climb it in style. This was their warm-up.

They arrived in Fort William on the Monday ready for the tramp up to Ben Nevis too late to buy food, and after a night out in the local hostelries finished up sleeping in an SMC member's garden shed. Haston had to leave on the Wednesday to collect his benefit in Edinburgh, and though Haston cracked the groove, both failed on the big corner, despite Smith borrowing a reluctant Haston's PAs. Dougal had made steady progress, but took a long fall, swooping into the gathering gloaming like the eponymous Bat, and pulling Smith off his stance and into space. The attempt fizzled out in the darkness, and the climbers were forced to make a hairy retreat down Sassenach.

Next weekend, they were back again with money enough for a week-long siege after a raid on the Creagh Dhu pontoon school in Jacksonville, Smith clad in a new pair of specialist PA climbing shoes: his earlier pair had been stolen while climbing at Harrison's Rocks, near Tunbridge Wells. This time, after another comfortable night in the same accommodating garden shed in Fort William, the route went almost without incident, though they were forced to finish in familiar moonlight again, and up the final pitches of Sassenach. It remained only to work out an independent finish for The Bat, and a week later Haston, by now a keen advocate of the philosophy of Stephen Potter, returned with Jim Marshall and one-upped the exams-tied Smith by traversing across from the top of the Sassenach chimney to the top of The Bat's big corner, and following a new line of none-too-difficult grooves to the top. The route was complete.

The first ascent of The Bat became a classic incident in British climbing, mainly because of Smith's brilliantly evocative telling of the climb in the *SMC Journal* of 1960, an account that not only hinted at the extreme nature of the climb, but at the background rivalry between two men pushing each other past the limit.

Smith's writing style was unique, and with perhaps Jimmy Marshall as his only equal, he had discovered a gift of capturing the essence of the chaotic, anarchic yet essentially disciplined business of climbing, first with his articles in the *EUMC*, and later *SMC Journals*, the latter long distinguished by the quality of mountaineering writing under a series of enlightened editors. Using innovative phraseology that employed ands, sos and thens to elongate rambling sentences followed, invariably, by a short, cryptic one of just six or seven words, Smith's writing became much imitated, particularly in university climbing journals. Whether by design or coincidence, Smith's *The Bat and the Wicked* could also be considered the template for Haston's later contributions to the *EUMC Journal*. It was only much later, when he came to write *In High Places*, that Haston managed to find a laconic style of his own.

Robin Campbell, later to become the erudite editor of the *SMC Journal*, but then simply a fellow Philosophy student at Edinburgh University, believes that Haston had to work on his writing, like his climbing. 'I don't think he was a natural writer. There were a lot of people at the time who fancied a go at writing under the influence of Smith. But he had a gift with words, a gift for getting down on paper the flavour of difficult climbing. He could also be funny. There is not a lot of humour in Dougal's writing. If he had a goal in that direction, it was a sort of existential goal.'

For even more evidence of this, it is useful to compare Smith, in the *EUMC Journal* of 1961, describing his and Marshall's ascent of Orion Face Direct on Ben Nevis in February 1960, with Haston's *Night Shift In Zero* in the same journal a year later. Smith: 'Then I went by iced slabs and he went by iced slabs, and I went over a snowfield and we found ourselves into the night with the moon hidden in clouds below the final towers of North-East Buttress with 1400 ft of climbing behind us, and the perishing Old Man in the lead again. First he wandered leftish, but 100 feet without any runners he came back right and sent all the rubbish thundering down on my head while I froze from cold and terror, and thought about the twenty-four points of his crampons.' And Haston (climbing with Smith and Wightman) in Zero Gully: 'Andy got stuck in a corner moaning the blues while I pecked miserably at the first pitch and had done ten feet in half an hour when he told me to get a grip and move, and I threatened to drop on him and put twenty-four holes in his head, which shut him up, and the slanging warmed me up, so I charged up seventy feet within the hour.'

And again: 'We had a ten-minute session and I got the urge to lead, and started up the next pitch. This got me gripped, and eventually I stopped under an ice bulge leaving a line of buckets to salute the evening sun, which was charging down with so much haste that it forgot to tell the moon to come up, so that it was getting dark rather quickly. Andy was brought up to Wheech, and Wheech was brought up to me, and proceeded on to the bulge.'

Haston, in fact, seems to have lost his innocence, in his view of climbing at least, not long after joining university, when his writing changed abruptly from the artless romantic of his early diaries to cold-blooded pragmatist. The disbelieving naïvety turned into almost world-weary matter-of-factness, interspersed with the normal, laddish carping at partners forever reluctant to get their fingers out.

In the *EUMC Journal* of 1960, Haston wrote marvellingly of his 1959 ascent with Moriarty of the Su Alto: 'The passage of this roof provides the crux of the climb, and hard on its heels there follows another long, artificial pitch. The climbing here was tremendous – there can be no thrill like that of swinging from etrier to etrier with 2000 ft of space beneath one's heels. There were signs of desperate battles in the vicinity, pegs which were in about half an inch, an occasional sling, at one point even an abandoned etrier – the latter was hastily added to our collection. Eventually, we were both left gasping on a small ledge with the glad thoughts in our mind that there was only one pitch of VI to be climbed.'

Three years later, describing his ascent of the Aste Diedre on the Crozzon di Brenta, Haston wrote: 'Now there's a climber in Italy called Aste, and on the Crozzon di Brenta he has a diedre named after him. This guy is reputed to say his prayers before going climbing, so he's honest, and we read his description of 108 pegs used and harder than the Gabrial Livanos on the Su Alto, which is hard enough after we had an epic on the face using only 30 pegs, due to a cock-eyed description by a bum Belgian, Claudio. He did the third ascent, and finds climbs easy once he is back at the hut. So here's the story for a grip. Ian Clough was my partner, and porridge the breakfast.

And later: 'The top soon I said – not on your life said the rain and poured. The real berries of a storm ensued. Great farting thunder-claps and whining ironmongery. The diedre oozed slime. Clough wanted to bivvy and I didn't, but in the end we had to as darkness overtook us. The night was cold – there was no supper and two barley sugars for breakfast. Muttering nasty remarks about Aste, Cloughy set the morning ball rolling, cunningly halting under a bulge with a peg in it. Nothing but bulges, and the next pitch was the bees knees of a bastard. I eventually collapsed retching with effort on a small stance. Cloughy's tight rein confirmed the hardness; later we found that 13 pegs were used on it.'

* * *

In September 1959, Haston, with Marshall pushing hard from behind, took the plunge and decided to apply for membership of the Scottish Mountaineering Club, a joining together of disparate parts that began as a marriage of convenience, but declined swiftly into a union made in hell. Bickering, strife, separation and divorce were to arrive within half a dozen years.

The SMC had been founded in March 1889, the brainchild of William Wilson Naismith, of Naismith's Rules for hillwalkers fame, who strongly believed that Scotland should have its own 'Scottish Alpine Club' independent from the London-based big brother. Like the Alpine Club, the original membership of 94 were drawn mainly from the Scottish gentry or white-collar classes, and like the Alpine Club also came to harbour an exaggerated view of their own importance. Membership of both was hard to come by, with climbing ability low on the list of qualifying priorities – the great English mountaineer Albert Mummery, an inspiration to climbers even today, was blackballed by the Alpine Club because of his humble origins – and the advancement of British mountaineering post-war owes less to the figurehead associations and more to the rise of the working-class clubs that sprang up in the 1940s and 1950s, mainly in the industrial north of England and on Clydeside.

Although the SMC was to produce some hardy mountaineers and first ascentionists in the likes of Harold Raeburn, W.H. Murray and J.H.B. Bell, and provided a succession of definitive climbing guide-books, it was not until Marshall managed to get Smith, Haston and others on board that they began to catch up in terms of domestic climbing output with English counterparts, notably the Fell and Rock, Climbers' and Rucksack Clubs. While vast tracts of Scottish rock remained unexplored – many of the SMC membership considered native hills suitable only for Alpine training – Welsh and English climbing had vibrant, self-contained lives of their own. For a long period before Marshall began his recruitment drive, the SMC had all the stately stolidity of an exclusive gentlemen's club. It took 100 years, for example, before women were allowed to become members, the number of committees and sub-committees would not have disgraced a municipal council, and the rules and regulations attached to membership and use of club huts were similar to those of an officers' mess.

Hardly surprising, then, that Haston, like many others of his generation, regarded the club as an archaic figure of authority and with disdainful resentment, even after he was admitted to membership. His desire to join had less to do with a wish to find new climbing or drinking partners – the usual justification for joining a club – and more with the fact that the SMC owned two of the best mountain huts in Britain, and members had preferential use.

In particular, the Charles Inglis Clark Hut, the one at the foot of Ben Nevis, was opportunistically situated for climbing on Britain's highest peak, but had space for only eight, SMC members having priority. Usually it was booked up 12 months in advance. Although he had used the SMC's Lagangarbh Hut – small house is a better description – in Glencoe for some time, Haston was probably getting weary of having to break in through the skylight to gain entry.

Marshall, who had his own agenda, had also proved persuasive. 'At the time, I thought the SMC was moribund, particularly in the Edinburgh section,' he says. 'They were basically socialites, very nice people, but typical New Town Edinburgh, lawyers or clerks without a clue about enjoying the wilderness. I was actually a barrier for a number of years for people going from the JMCS to the SMC, until I thought we'd better get on with it, and introduce all the hoodlums. Believe me, it was a positive, controlled effort to make the SMC the best climbing group in the country. We had the best climbing grounds; we just had to go and develop them. The Creagh Dhu used to go down to Wales for education that gave them an insight into what they could climb. The efforts of Brown and Whillans were extraordinary for the time, and that's why I always admired them as climbers. I wanted Scotland to catch up.' Robin Campbell adds:

'Dougal was to have a short and troubled relationship with the SMC, joining in 1959 and being defaulted eventually for not paying his subs. He didn't get expelled for that and, in fact, I can't recall a case of expulsion in the SMC. Like many others, Dougal felt the SMC didn't give due recognition to the climbing efforts of himself, Robin Smith and Jimmy Marshall. I think he thought they discounted his efforts in a way, and he may have had a point. There were other differences. The president in the early 1960s was Ian Charleson, head of the George Street branch of the Bank of Scotland, and the membership included similar people with status in Scottish life. It was difficult for people like that to feel comfortable with breaking and entering, fighting, petty theft and drunkenness. But there was a tension of that kind in the 1960s. It was the battle between generations everywhere. In those days, you had to get keys to the huts from the Hon Hut Custodian, which could be inconvenient if you wanted to go to Ben Nevis on a Friday night. But you could still get in one hut in one way or another. It was difficult at the CIC, because the club defended it with iron bars. At Lagangarbh, it was always possible to jemmy open a window, which Dougal did frequently.'

Dougal's formal written application to the SMC, which gave his address as 48 Dolphin Road – his parents had moved into a larger, semi-detached house opposite No. 21 – was proposed by Ronnie Marshall and seconded by his brother, Jimmy, and is dated September 16, 1959. It consisted of the standard club form, which demanded a list of snow and ice climbs in Scotland, a list of rock climbs in Scotland, a list of hillwalking expeditions in Scotland and a list of expeditions elsewhere, Dougal painstakingly filling all four pages to the last line with an impressive collection of achievements that included several first ascents. The space left for 'statement of contributions to science, art or literature in connection with Scottish mountains, or any other relevant note' was left blank. With the Marshalls on the committee, he was inducted almost immediately, setting off an astonishingly fraught relationship that was terminated two years later, when he neglected to renew his subscription. Indeed, Haston's association with Scotland's mountaineering father club turned into a microcosm of the 1960s struggle between the generations in society: protesting, high-spirited youth versus middle-aged, disapproving conservativism. While Smith managed to become, almost, the acceptable face of young Scottish climbing, Haston most definitely did not, and with his total inability to conform, he must have occasioned more disapproving committee minutes than all other members put together.

'Robin was definitely more tolerated by the SMC than Dougal,' Marshall confirms. 'I don't think it was anything to do with his educational background, more the fact that Robin was brought up to be more respectful to his elders. He enjoyed being bloody awkward and all the rest of it, and could be unpleasant, but he wasn't a master at it, like Dougal. He had old-fashioned values, like being nice to his girlfriends, which Dougal definitely did not have.'

Haston's confrontational relationship with the SMC culminated in the notorious Lagangarbh Painting Incident, which has gone down in the annals of Scottish climbing.

'He did get into trouble for that,' says Campbell. 'He and Ronnie Marshall spent a wet, frustrating weekend in Lagangarbh, and decided to amuse themselves by painting the walls in the manner of Kandinsky, and there is a famous photo of Dougal in a funny hat admiring his handiwork. It earned him some approbation, but it wouldn't get him expelled, because there was a long history of this sort of behaviour. Malcolm Slesser got so upset about the rule forbidding dogs that he borrowed a horse off someone, and took that into Lagangarbh. There was no rule against horses.'

Marshall recalls: 'I think Eley, Stenhouse and my brother were involved. Of course, the only reason Dougal wanted into the SMC was to use the huts without having to break in, and at Lagangarbh one weekend a working party had just painted the whole of the interior green, when Ronnie and Dougal arrived. They were pissed off with the weather because it had rained for a week, and they just got hold of the paint the working party had left behind and mixed it with boot polish, and painted this mural on the wall in the style of Kandinsky. It was green and yellow, black and red, with all these mysterious symbols, and Dougal and Ronnie were pictured standing by with candles lit on top of their heads. But then, I think a lot of people had problems with the rules and regulations of the SMC.'

The Lagangarbh incident did have an odd denouement when a

party from Corriemulzie Mountaineering Club arrived the following weekend to find the interior freshly decorated. One of the party was so impressed by the art on display that he signed the painting 'J. Gibson, CMS'. The SMC at first assumed the painting was Gibson's handiwork . . . and he and his club were promptly banned from all SMC huts for a year.

Dougal's unsteady association with the Scottish Mountaineering Club, however, is best captured not by his attempt at abstract exhibitionism at Lagangarbh, but by an extraordinary, extended, three-sided correspondence involving the club's Hon Librarian Robin Inglis, the Hon Secretary Stanley Stewart and Dougal (though Haston's contribution consisted of one cryptic letter). This uproarious affair was to last almost two years from April 19, 1965, when Inglis, who took his job most seriously, first attempted to get Dougal to return the books *The Conquest of Fitzroy* by the French mountaineer Marc Azema (out since December 1963) and the *Alpine Journal of 1960–61* (out since January 1964). Also on the Inglis overdue list were the *Oxford University Mountaineering Club Journal* (out since June 1964) and the *Climbers' Club Journal* (May 1964).

Addressed to 'Dear Haston', the Inglis letter, after reminding Dougal of his obligations as an SMC member and that he had been attempting to have the books returned for almost 12 months, turned threatening and concluded: 'I ask you to return all these four books to the library without fail by 29th April, 1965, otherwise I shall be forced to bring the matter the the attention of the Club Committee, and ask them to take whatever action they deem necessary.' To which Haston, with undisguised sarcasm, replied: 'I shall make some effort to return them within the next few days in order to avoid summary court-martial by the committee – of which I am a member. I hope your patience can hold out.'

This roused Inglis to even more apoplexy, with letters flowing backwards and forwards between him and Stanley Stewart until events – Dougal was in jail – took the likelihood of the return of any book from this borrower out of the realms of possibility. Inglis, incidentally, as faithful club servants usually do, found his reward when he was appointed Vice-President of the club in October 1971, writing to the new Club Secretary Donald Bennett: 'I would count it as a real honour, not only for myself, but also of following in the footsteps of my dear father, who was "Vice" 32 years ago.'

In an effort to improve security – the library rooms at 369 High Street, Edinburgh, were open to just about anyone – Inglis gave the SMC use of an office in Newington rent free. Unfortunately, when he departed to the great library in the sky in late 1975, the executors of the Inglis estate immediately asked the SMC to vacate. The saga of the SMC library failed to arrive at a happy ending.

* * *

In 1959 Haston began what were to be his three and a half years at Edinburgh University. As was customary, on the second Tuesday of October he joined an institution renowned for innovative tradition in the arts, medicine and sciences, and which had attracted an impressive roll-call of intellect. Eminent staff and students included the philosopher David Hume – who failed to graduate, a comforting thought for Dougal when he dropped out early in 1963 – Charles Darwin, the physicists Edward Appleton and James Clerk Maxwell, and Joseph Lister, who introduced antiseptics into surgical practice. The university's esteemed literary figures included Walter Scott, Robert Louis Stevenson, and Arthur Conan Doyle, whose Sherlock Holmes is said to have been modelled on one of his medical lecturers.

At the time that Dougal matriculated, the Swinging Sixties were just around the corner, but in many ways Scotland's capital had got there first; Edinburgh already had a deserved reputation as one of the most sybaritic, free-spirited suburbs of Europe. Drugs, soft or hard, were easy to obtain if you knew where to look, and the city had its own music, drink and vice culture. The era coincided with Haight-Ashbury, flower power, the birth of the Beatles and the Rolling Stones, protest and promiscuity. It was the age of that new phenomenon, the coffee bar, all lit by bright, fresh and optimistic faces, and with Elvis crooning on the jukebox in the background. At night, the young of Edinburgh would pack into subterranean clubs, like the catacombs of The Place, a darkened, multi-storey venue in Victoria Street. Intimate, mystical, smoky cellars with strange, long-haired pop groups playing in the gloom became the 'in' places, but for anyone under the age of 20, there was also a sense of coming out of the darkness of the post-war era, a burgeoning spirit of identity, and a feeling that the future really did belong to them. They had never had it so good.

Scottish culture became more and more influenced by Continental and American trends in music and fashion. The antidote to this conformity was to look as weird as possible, but it was a time of rebellion, the age of CND marches, student sit-ins and missile crises. Dougal preferred climbing and drinking, both to excess. At university, like many others at the beginning of the 1960s – Andrew Wightman blanches even now at the memory of his wearing a cravat from time to time – Dougal took great pride in his appearance, and cultivated the foppish elegance of the conventional image of a philosophy-studying aesthete. The fashion was a sharp suit or the tightest possible drainpipe trousers, finished off with a pair of winkle-pickers or, in summer, open-toed sandals. He got his skin-tight moleskin breeks from a shop in Victoria Street, not far from the main university campus, and would spend up to half an hour trying to lever them past his feet. He also grew his hair long, and neglected to comb it. He was, insists Wightman, a 'bit of a poser', but so was virtually everyone else. Dougal was a child of his times.

Even in that age of affection and free love, however, he found friendships difficult, particularly with the opposite sex. A majority of the Edinburgh University students in Haston's day were definitively middle class and, hardly surprisingly, the baker's son from rural Currie had few acquaintances outside climbing. He was soon to discover that he had virtually nothing in common with anyone unfamiliar with the language of crag and icefall.

'He was happiest in the hills,' Wightman affirms. 'There was one holiday up at Carnmore which, of course, is very remote, and he revelled in the privacy and solitude and the companionship of people he liked and trusted. He was always on edge with others. Apart from the climbing, we were also very keen hillwalkers, and Dougal was just incredibly keen to get out, whether it was climbing or not. If the weather was bad, that wouldn't stop us when we went away, and we would often all meet and go out walking on the Pentlands, just trudging for miles. I did a fantastic walk with Dougal once when things were covered in snow, and we got the bus out to

West Linton and walked back over the Pentlands in the snow, and then got a Corporation bus back to Edinburgh.' Haston was to define true friendship in his diaries thus: 'For me, it is hard to have a friend who is not a climber. He needs to have shared the many close-to-death experiences, and not have panicked; backs one up through trouble, and is not jealous of success. On this basis, I have few friends.'

The unworldly 19-year-old, fresh from West Calder High School, also saw Edinburgh as a sniffy, cold-hearted place, with a reputation as a refuge for bourgeois snobbery, despite its pockets of rank poverty in the 'outer darkness' that still exist today. A place where the opening question of a first introduction was likely to be: 'And which school did you go to?' but whose contrasts have often been likened to Stevenson's famous creation of Dr Jekyll and Mr Hyde, a dichotomy of the one face presented to the world, and the other struggling to suppress an inner darkness. The metaphor could equally well have been applied to the life of Haston.

While at university, he still clung to known acquaintances, such as the Marshalls and Moriarty, though Eley, like Stenhouse, was soon to fade from the climbing, but not the boozing, picture almost entirely. There was Robin Smith, too, the pair now discovering that in Hume and Hobbes they had a discussion forum almost as stimulating as the works of Buhl, Bonatti and Terray. Wightman recalls lengthy student discourses, in common room, pub, climbing hut or occasional bivouac, on Friedrich Nietzsche and Immanuel Kant, with Dougal 'quite taken with their views'. It was fashionable in the 1960s and 1970s to turn to the traditional philosophers in an effort to discover why one climbed – the fact that it was enjoyable was considered too simplistic – and Kant's view that 'individual actions should be regarded as self-contained necessities within themselves, without reference to any other purpose' struck a chord with Haston. He was to apply it to himself, and extreme climbing, writing in his notebook later: '[Climbing] tests are not stepping-stones to one big test. They exist as separate wholes, the tackling of which is one complete function within my terms of existence.' He also became a keen disciple of Nietzsche and his concept of an *Übermensch*, who can create and impose his own law. Haston later developed the habit of signing off every diary entry: 'Thus spake DH.' Smith, too, was still an inspiration, if a daunting one.

Wightman recalls: 'I think in the first year Dougal became quite close to one of the tutors, but probably the tutors found anyone who climbed interesting, particularly a wild man from Currie, who drank like a fish. He had no friends in the Philosophy Department, and never went to any of their parties, whereas Robin revelled in it all. Robin had the social graces which Dougal didn't have, but certainly aspired to have. University was a good opportunity for kids from our background to develop intellectually, and Dougal definitely had aspirations in that direction, although it would be true to say that there were not many others there from West Calder High School on campus. But whereas Robin could hold his own in any company, Dougal would be stood silent in a corner on his own. I remember it was an education going to Robin's house – a bungalow, for heaven's sake. There was a Hieronymous Bosch print on the wall in the hallway, which made a mighty impression on us all, particularly Dougal.'

To Davie Agnew, 'Dougal had a bad time trying to express himself. Some people are very good at it, and Robin was one of them. Dougal struggled.'

* * *

The courses in Philosophy and Old English, his second subject, were based in the Old Quad of the main university buildings close to Edinburgh's Royal Mile, and Wightman remembers Dougal's habit of 'swaggering down the central corridor into the common room', where hot chocolate could be bought from a machine, and students lolled around trying to look as cerebral as possible. 'I think we fancied ourselves a bit: we were into Bertolt Brecht, things like that.' For Haston, Wightman and friends, it became fashionable to visit jazz clubs, where some aped the fashionable Parisian trad scene by wearing berets. Smith even took up the clarinet with some élan. The 'Steamboat' in Rose Street Lane was a favourite haunt where, according to Wightman, 'we used to eat hamburgers and chips, and think we had made it in the world'. Pop concerts, though Haston adopted the appearance and carefully cultivated rebellious image of

Mick Jagger, were considered passé, and CND and other protest marches were for the middle classes. 'We were too busy climbing for that, and when we were not climbing, we were too busy drinking. And while I would never describe Dougal as a drunk, he certainly loved to drink,' says Wightman.

In Edinburgh he could not have chosen a better place, as the city was, is, a paradise for dissipation, with a bewildering choice of pubs, ranging from the Saturday-night punch-up joints in Leith to the bourgeois charm of the Café Royal, just off Princes Street. There were pubs for poets, pubs for artists, pubs for postal workers, pubs for journalists. In the city centre Paddy's Bar or Milne's, Hugh McDiarmid and Norman MacCaig held court, and at the Abbotsford, if he felt so inclined, the jazz clarinettist Sandy Brown would give impromptu performances. There were also pubs for climbers, and their numbers were growing now, as Marshall's dream of a thriving Edinburgh scene was coming to fruition. The university club encompassed Smith, Dougal, Wightman, Neil McNiven, Robin Campbell and Dick Holt – all extremely capable – and most of the group had been railroaded into the SMC by Marshall, to add fresh legs to the tottering institution. Edinburgh was also the birthplace of another major Scottish climbing force, the Squirrels.

Like Scotland's other loosely formed groups of kindred spirits – the Rannoch, the Etive, the Lomonds, the Creagh Dhu, the Ptarmigan and the Etchacan – the Squirrels had no constitution, few rules, but a number of recognised leaders. Named somewhat pretentiously after their continental counterparts in Lecco and the Grigna in Italy, the Squirrels had leading lights in Brian Robertson, Dave Bathgate, Jim Brumfitt, Bill Sproul, Fred Harper and Alistair McKeith. Haston became closely associated with them at a later stage, around 1964, though he was never an official member. Their anarchic nature and abilities definitely appealed. Bathgate, who was later to go to Everest with Dougal in 1972, and eventually reach Camp Six says: 'Dougal was one of the guys I was trying to catch up with. At the time, he was several steps ahead of everybody, up there on a bit of a pedestal, was a year older than me, but he had been climbing a lot longer.' Russell Sharp, later to become managing director of the independent Caledonian Brewery in Edinburgh, and at the time a fringe member of the Squirrels, says: 'We were in awe of guys like Smith and Haston. There wasn't a big age gap; it just seemed it. They seemed so far ahead of us.'

The Squirrels had a two-star doss in Glencoe, an old ARP shelter above the Clachaig Inn known as The Dray, and Brumfitt also had access to a Land Rover owned by the climbing club at Ferranti, where he worked, which added to the travel options for Haston and the university group. The most reliable mode of transport for Dougal and selected friends, however, was a famous Ford Popular owned by an Englishman, Graham Tiso. Tiso was originally from Birmingham, and was working as a salesman with Cadbury – he always had a good supply of their products for climbs and bivouacs – when they posted him to Scotland. He began climbing with the Edinburgh branch of the JMCS, and married a local girl, Maude, in the spring of 1962, the same year that he opened Scotland's first specialist climbing shop in Rodney Street, Canonmills. The shop became pivotal for Edinburgh climbers, proving to be a useful meeting point, a place to exchange information, and even offering occasional, short-term employment.

Although totally realistic about his abilities on rock and ice, Tiso shared in first ascents of routes such as Smith's Route on Creag Meagaidh (1959, with Marshall), Parallel Gully B on Lochnagar (Marshall again) and Vanishing Gully on Ben Nevis (1961, with Ronnie Marshall). In 1965, he also made the second winter traverse of the Cuillin Ridge, and on Everest in 1971, though nominally there as the man in charge of equipment, showed considerable stamina and lung power by reaching Camp Four on the South-West Face. Tiso, who was to build up his business into one of the biggest retail climbing chains in the country, was killed in an accident on June 8, 2000, while working on his boat in St Lucia, West Indies, but Maude retains many memories of that era. Like many other women, she found Dougal an enigmatic character, whose personality was to prove elusive.

'Graham became, I would say, very friendly with Dougal, although I probably tolerated him rather than being a friend, because he was a very angry young man. Graham had such an great regard for him, undoubtedly for his climbing, but he puzzled me. He always drank really fast and furious. A lot of people ended up having had a lot to drink, but there was usually quite a bit of chat and banter early in the evening, but Dougal almost seemed to have demons in him. He had this kind of anger, both sober and when he was drinking. Usually, people mellow when they're drunk, or they are mellow until they drink, but he did seem to hit the bottle very quickly, and I can't see somebody doing that unless there were other things in his life concerning him.'

Climbing and drinking go together; high risk invariably translates into heavy thirst, and even at a lower level – think of all those earnest climbing magazine articles that end: 'We made it to the Clachaig/Padarn/Dungeon Ghyll just in time for a well-earned pint' – it was almost de rigueur to drink oneself insensible after a good day on the hill. Wightman, Moriarty, Smith and the Marshalls certainly enjoyed a drink, but Dougal always seemed to take it a step further. The noted American climber Royal Robbins remarked of him: 'We all drank, but Dougal just seemed a little bit more overly enthusiastic about it than anyone else.'

In Edinburgh, the favoured haunts for the climbers were the Hall Bar, close to Surgeons' Hall – where one of Dougal's more enlightened tutors would hold his weekly tutorials – Deacon Brodies, Lawnmarket, or the White Cockade in Rose Street, where conversation would invariably revolve around a climbing venue for the weekend. Another favourite haunt was the Denmark Rooms, where very strong lager, the new 'in' drink, could be purchased. Pubs at the time closed at ten p.m., but the city's gasping climbing population, with friends happy to tag along, could deal with their thirst simply by purchasing a carry-out and retiring to the SMC club-rooms at 369 High Street, where the rented first floor housed the club's collection of priceless books and a room where they held their frequent committee meetings. It also doubled as what Moriarty gleefully describes as 'our town flat'.

There were girls, massive drinking sessions and music so loud that passers-by would walk in off the street to join in. The address became like the legendary brothel housed above a branch of Mothercare, and in between discussions about the cost of repairs to Lagangarbh, the progress of the Arrochar guidebook and apologies for absences, 369 High Street rocked to some of the wildest, loudest, most debauched parties in the city. 'Members or not, we had a free run of the SMC clubrooms,' says Dave Bathgate. 'It was almost like a party venue, and someone would always have a key. I think the SMC knew it was used for parties; they could hardly fail to, but not specifically what went on there, which was just as well.'

The club-rooms also became a popular accommodation address for various climbers, and an occasional lodging house. Inglis, the club's Hon Librarian, was continually being roused to put more pen to more paper to his committee to complain about official SMC letters to the High Street address being opened, read and then replaced in their envelopes. Some of his precious books vanished forever. For Dougal, who usually travelled into the city from Currie by bus, 369 High Street became almost a second home, and he often missed the last transport home. 'I can remember sleeping all night in the library with Dougal after some binge somewhere,' says Wightman. 'We used to sit in there pissed, and read these fantastic books and journals. If he couldn't be bothered going home, he just used to put his head down there.'

While often overstepping the moral line into outright hedonism, Dougal's Edinburgh scene was a dynamic era for climbing and socialising, according to Jimmy Marshall. 'The guys in the Squirrels, the university club and the Edinburgh SMC were all independent, tremendous groups, but the club-rooms were the centre for it. It was party night almost every night, somewhere. There was one I remember in posh Buckingham Terrace, where Eley and Dougal finished rolled up in a big Chinese rug together. I would have fights with them, boxing or wrestling. I could put on a few holds, and when he was half-pissed Dougal would come at you, always to hurt you, and I would put on a headlock, pushing his face into the floorboards. But he wouldn't give up, and I would start putting him into unconsciousness and that, of course, was when Eley would step in and grab me, and tell me: "Leave him alone." '

If Moriarty was prepared to take sides in Dougal's favour against one of their best friends, it is plain that he would give short shrift to outsiders. While Dougal loved to drink, he was seldom a cheerful drunk, and there were numerous confrontations, usually settled by Moriarty. Marshall says: 'Dougal always drank himself out of sense, and in many ways he always welcomed violence. Eley was not a violent person, but he was very efficient. In the Forrest Bar, Eley took one guy outside, hit him once, and I thought he'd killed him. He just bounced off the pavement.'

Bathgate recalls an incident in the Denmark Rooms, where the formidable Moriarty came to the rescue again. 'I was there once with Eley, Dougal and some of the boys, demonstrating pinch grips on the bar, when it tilted over, and all this expensive booze smashed on the floor. I thought I was in for it, but that was the great thing about having Dougal and Eley around, especially Eley. He just stood up and looked at everyone, and that was me off the hook. He was a handy guy to have around, often too handy, too quick. He was very protective of Dougal, but he would lead Dougal astray, if that were at all possible. To be honest, I thought Dougal was an odd guy at the time, who took some getting to know. I think he even had trouble getting to know himself. It was only in the last two or three years that he became really good company. He was always a bit on edge before that, possibly because he was not satisfied with himself, or his achievements.'

Wightman, too, has his favourite Eley story: 'I always enjoyed Dougal's company, and I was relaxed with him, but when he was drinking, things could turn a bit unpredictable. We were walking one night past a pub, and I was walking at the back, and there was Brian Wakefield and somebody else at the front. Suddenly, the door opened and these two nerds came out, and there was a bit of a tussle, and it was like something out a cowboy film. Eley's punch just came up from his knees, and this guy literally was poleaxed. It was very impressive.'

For all the boozy, brawling lifestyle, Marshall is at pains to point out: 'After a party we would quite often go up Arthur's Seat in the morning to sober up.' And Wightman stresses: 'We talk about drink, but there was no way at all Dougal was a drunk. We drank a lot, and we sometimes got drunk, but there was no way we were drunks or anything like that. It didn't matter anyway, because we were always in good shape.'

And if Dougal didn't allow drink to interfere with his fitness or his climbing – his constitution was to prove extraordinary in both respects in the years that followed – nor did that other notorious hazard to the ambitions of young mountaineers. Haston was attractive to women. As Robin Campbell points out: 'He was good-looking in a particular way. I think girls found him physically attractive with the blue eyes and the squashed nose, a result of getting in a fight without Moriarty to help him out. He had the same looks as Depardieu or Belmondo, a primitive-looking face.'

In his university days, however, Dougal had a singular lack of success. His brooding reticence at the time did not have the appeal of later in the 1970s when that demeanour, allied to his fame, proved a devastating combination. Maude Tiso believes that 'he wasn't a very easy person in company, and particularly among women's company. Women, girls, fell for him. Don't misunderstand me, but I was a young, married lady, and really unless you were a potential girlfriend you really weren't within his sphere. I'm just being very honest about that.'

The acknowledged Lothario of the Lothians at the time was Fred Harper, later to become the principal of Glenmore Lodge, and a renowned and innovative outdoor educationist. Harper had done his National Service in the navy after leaving school in his home town of Stranraer, and was already a wordly, chain-smoking ladykiller by the time he went to Edinburgh – which may surprise many who remember him as the formal, somewhat stern, figure in charge at Glenmore. Fred's best climbing contributions were with the Squirrels on Creag Dubh, Newtonmore, where routes which he named Strapadicktaemi and Gang Bang, as well as giving a clue to a more frivolous side to his nature, were periodically to come back and haunt him.

Harper was two years older than Haston, and a student of sociology. A darkly handsome figure, invariably dressed in newly fashionable denim, and with the mellifluous voice of an Alan Rickman, he charmed a mighty swathe through the university's female population. Casual sex and one-night stands pre-Aids were as much a habit for climbers as heavy drinking, and Dave Bathgate recalls 'people passing around all sorts of diseases, like NSU or gingivitis. One case of crab lice, whose source shall be nameless, came from California to Europe, on to Peru, and back to California.' The overwhelming fear was 'having to get married', which would spell a certain end to any climbing career. In those days, contraceptives were purchased furtively in the barber's shop ('Something for the weekend, sir?') or at the quaintly titled medical supplies stores, where French letters were handed over, like a football bung, in a brown-paper bag. If all else failed – as it did for at least two members of Dougal's climbing circle – abortion was the option, up a back street or, for £100, from renegade GPs like the notorious Dr Roddy Ross, who was jailed for his troubles.

But the statutory, libidinous campus lifestyle appears to have passed Dougal by and Wightman noted his reserve in the company of women, Haston invariably preferring the company of girls who climbed. Joy Heron, who was to have a lengthy relationship with Haston, points out that there were not many of those around. Maude Tiso often wondered if the drinking was related to a need for non-involvement. 'I think he just was terribly single-minded about the climbing, and he liked women but, particularly in the early years, he really didn't want any encumbrance with them. That was the evening, that was it, and so it was quite a ruthless approach. I think, to be fair, you've got to put it in the context of that time. There wasn't in any sense these young men all prepared and going out with condoms in their pockets, as I understand my sons would today, and certainly there was a huge fear among the female population that you would become pregnant; you either had to have the will of whatever, or else. I think for someone like Dougal, who didn't want to have any sort of encumbrances, probably the sort of drinking and all the rest of it was to keep everything at arm's length.'

'I can only remember one girl before Joy,' says Wightman. 'I think she was a local lass from Currie, and he brought her to Lagangarbh once, and slept in a separate room with her. The next day, he was struggling up the hill behind the rest of us, and you can imagine the remarks that were being passed. There were harsh words between them, and I got the impression that relationship was coming to an end. To be honest, I never thought of him as a womaniser – I don't think he had the confidence. He lacked the self-confidence to meet and speak to women. We also had very little money, which I suppose is a bit of a factor. But you couldn't fail if you were prepared to make some sort of effort. We used to go to the Hall Bar and then to the Men's Union, which was like a cattle market, and I can't remember Dougal ever chatting up a girl. He stuck with girls who climbed, like Joy. Drinking was a macho thing for him, but when we had parties with girls available, Dougal would stand in the corner trying his best to look like a philosopher.'

His longest-lasting relationship before he met his wife Annie in 1966 was with Joy, who had been born and raised in England, and had met Dougal after she went to Edinburgh University in 1961, to study nursing. A keen and highly proficient climber, she at once joined the college climbing club. 'I climbed with Dougal a lot, and was his girlfriend for two and a half years, a relationship which ended in 1966 when he went to do Eiger Direct,' says Joy, who emigrated to the United States and married and divorced Layton Kor, the American climber who was with Dougal on the Eiger in 1966. 'The start of the relationship was the day of Kennedy's assassination in 1963 which, of course, I now remember for a different reason. We were having a meeting in a pub to elect a new president after Neil McNiven was killed, and that's when news of Kennedy came over on TV. I'd say we had a very close relationship. He was fairly quiet, although not shy, and definitely was not a bragger or publicity-seeker. Marriage? I never thought of Dougal as the marrying kind.'

Joy Heron shared a flat with Sheena Bannerman, Mary Paine and Polly Pardie in Valleyfield Street, Tollcross, and their house became a popular trysting spot for competing male climbers. While Joy became Haston's steady girlfriend, Sheena was to marry Jim Brumfitt of the Squirrels, and Mary was to become Mrs Andrew Wightman. Joy says: 'They were marvellous, sociable times, and Edinburgh was a marvellous place to be at that time. I think he enjoyed climbing with me, and we were to climb together a lot, both home and abroad. For my part, I was very much in love with him.'

* * *

In between the occasional studies – by his second year of 1960–61, Dougal had decided that he would never graduate, and he consistently struggled to pass exams – there were long holidays, and the chance to extend his Alpine experience. This required money, even for climbers prepared to rough out seasons in the most basic circumstances, and Smith, Haston and Wightman developed a routine of spending the first two or three weeks of the summer semester on pea farms in Kent, before heading to Europe. It was hard work in elemental conditions, cutting the vines in the field, loading them on to trailers, and taking the trucks into the yard for unloading, and Wightman recalls finishing work on most days unable even to close his fingers. 'We used to go down to Maidstone every year. Dougal actually worked for Birds Eye, and Robin and I worked for another company, but we used to go and see Dougal after work. It wasn't the nicest of jobs, but it did give us that chance to get to the Alps. My biggest-ever earnings at the peas was about £40 for a six-day week, and that was astronomical in those days.'

Haston still favoured the Dolomites for Alpine summers, while by 1961 Smith had extended his experience to the Western Alps, and was now considered one of Britain's leading alpinists, with a CV that included the West Face of the Blatière and the Walker Spur on the Grandes Jorasses. Though he hated artificial climbing, he agreed to set a target for that summer of the Swiss/Italian Route on the Cima Ouest of Lavaredo, Haston again returning to familiar ground – he had already done the Cassin route on the same face. The attractions of another pegging route were hard to fathom. Smith had no interest at all, while Dougal often found the technicalities of this type of climbing – this was a man who struggled to change a domestic plug – totally beyond him. But it was a famous route.

As always in terms of disorganisation, the two seemed to bring out the worst in each other. They didn't have a description, and intended simply to follow the anticipated line of pitons. They wore jeans, and had no food or bivouac gear, but their brainwave was to have two girls from the university climbing club who had come out with them attach sleeping bags and a piping hot meal to a 300m Perlon rope lowered by the climbers, who would then haul it back up, and spend the night in well-fed luxury. Unfortunately, the girls carried the offerings all the way to the wrong mountain, and though Haston and Smith dealt competently with the difficulties of the climb, it turned into another epic with tangled ropes, a bivouac dangling in étriers, cut hands and Smith finally hurling their rucksacks, and food, into space in a rage.

Haston wrote in *In High Places*: 'We began to wonder if we could ever plan an organised climb. Or, more worryingly, if we did so, perhaps it would seem so mundane that we wouldn't enjoy it so much. To many people, our innocence and lack of organisation may seem almost criminal. But one can have a certain philosophy about it. We were getting out of difficult situations successfully, by the strength of our own ability. These wearing experiences were giving us an incredible store for the future. I still had a lot to learn, but we were learning.'

As it happened, Haston demonstrated that organisation and competence were not alien concepts by returning to the Dolomites the following year, 1962, in the company of Yorkshire climber Ian Clough who, within ten days the previous year, had managed the North Faces of the Matterhorn and the Eiger, and was maturing into one of Britain's most able alpinists. They made a good team, and everything went smoothly with fast ascents of the Buhlweg on the Roda di Vael, the Aste Diedre on the Crozzon di Brenta and the Oggioni Diedre on the Brenta Alta.

By then, however, Dougal's partner in so much innocent youthful disarray was dead.

*   *   *

In the summer of 1960, as mountaineering's contribution to the thawing of the Cold War, a party of Russian climbers had visited Britain and ascended most of the classic rock routes, where they had climbed with Smith and Moriarty among others. The Russians had impressed with their strength and determination, but not their equipment, and a reciprocal trip by a British group was arranged to the Pamirs in 1962. The expedition was to be led by Sir John Hunt, who led the first ascent of Everest, and Malcolm Slesser of the SMC was asked to sound out leading Scottish climbers about their availability. Among names to crop up were Smith, Haston and Jim Stenhouse, though he had virtually retired from climbing. Stenhouse says: 'I got the opportunity to go in that direction, but I got married when I was 20 and I had a couple of lads, and the employer that I worked with wouldn't give me the time off. You also had to put something like £200 up front, and get about three months off work. Dougal could have gone on that, but I don't know if he would have been able to raise the cash. I remember before that happened, in 1961, the big thing at that time was to do the first winter traverse of the Cuillin Ridge, so we all went up to Skye and broke into this bothy, and we were in that about a week waiting on the weather improving. Robin was getting all this freebie equipment, so we were borrowing all his old stuff and he was saying: "Right, if I don't come back, you can keep it." And, of course, he never came back: I still don't know who got his clarinet.'

Smith and his partner Wilfred Noyce, the poet-mountaineer who had been on the successful Everest expedition of 1953, were killed on an easy descent on Peak Garmo. Haston had been due to meet him for an attempt on the Eiger that summer of 1962, but staggered off the night shift at Birds Eye in Maidstone to read the newspaper headlines: 'Disaster in Pamirs: British climbers fall to their deaths'. Wightman, who was preparing for his shift, says: 'It's engraved in my memory. We used to start at six a.m., and it was in the heart of the Kent countryside. Someone had heard it on the radio, and told me, and I walked over to the warehouse where Dougal was working, and he was in a state of shock. I got a postcard from the Pamirs a couple of days later saying: "See you in Chamonix" on such-and-such a date.'

Smith's death, the first of anyone close to him, was a shattering blow to Haston, and ended lingering thoughts about finishing his university course. With Smith gone, he was elevated, unwillingly or not, to the position of undisputed king of Scottish, or at least Edinburgh, climbing, and immediately set about consolidating that position. 'I think Dougal always wanted the North Wall of the Eiger on his climbing CV,' Wightman observes.

* * *

It had long fascinated him. As a schoolboy he had read and re-read *The White Spider*, Heinrich Harrer's classic account of the first ascent of the North Face by an Austro-German team in 1938, one of the sport's great epics. Its subsequent history had produced similar dramas, and a string of fatalities, and the face's extreme length, gloomy history and fickle nature had made it the yardstick for every extreme climber. Such was the pivotal role the face played in Dougal's life, he was to make several attempts on it, climb it twice by different routes, and make two films and write two books about it. By 1962, when Haston and Wightman made their attempt, it awaited a first British success, a fact that had attracted a number of other Britons: Chris Bonington, Tom Patey, Don Whillans and others had spent time on the face.

Haston had first tried it in 1960, with Moriarty, on the way back from the Dolomites, and their ascent of the Cassin route on the Cima Ouest. Moriarty had minimal experience on snow and ice, even after many years spent in Scotland, and their half-hearted attempt petered out just over 1000ft up in vile weather. It had, said Haston realistically, 'stopped us making fools of ourselves'.

Two years later, and with the face still awaiting the metaphorical raising of a Union Flag or Saltire on the summit, Dougal was back with Wightman. It is debatable whether the concept of a first British ascent, and the glories that went with it, crossed Dougal's mind, for like every other climber, he simply saw the Eiger as a logical test for his abilities, mental and physical. There were harder routes around, but none with the combination of technical dificulty, seriousness and objective danger. The Eiger and Dougal were made for each other.

When he and Wightman arrived in the Alps in August 1962, the omens were mixed. They failed on an attempt on the North Face of the Matterhorn, their warm-up, in late July. The US Army parkas they had bought from an army surplus store in Leith Walk proved a straitening burden when the fur froze solid, so Haston had spent a chunk of his university grant and the pea money on new boots, down duvet and bivouac sack. Back on the Eiger, a doomed attempt by two other inexperienced Britons, Barry Brewster and Brian Nally, ended in Brewster's death and a hairy rescue of Nally by the Chris Bonington/Don Whillans team, which effectively ended their attempt. Haston had good reason to think that this could be his year, but after disposing of the lower pitches, the Difficult Crack, Hinterstoisser Traverse and first and second icefields, the Scots were slowed by an eight-strong party of babbling Italians, and then by the usual Eiger scenario, a storm. It was Haston who counselled retreat after a sleepless bivouac, wisely as it turned out, for the descent turned into a prolonged battle with water and stonefall: wet, rotten rock and fatigue which culminated in Wightman, with all the difficulties over, taking a lengthy tumble and breaking his ankle. The accident ended Wightman's climbing career – he spent a year on crutches, then left to work in Liverpool after graduating – and Dougal's misery was complete when Bonington and Ian Clough snatched a well-publicised first British ascent three weeks after his attempt. Haston's gallant, piggy-back rescue of Wightman did earn him a nomination for Man of the Year 1962 from the British Council for Rehabilitation of the Disabled at a luncheon in the Savoy, London, but this was scant consolation, and he did not attend the ceremony. His disgust is summed up by a brief description in his diary: 'Eiger, North Face to third icefield with A Wightman'. His next entry, the description of an ascent of the Fiachill Ridge, a short and easy scramble in the Northern Corries of the Cairngorms, was written up in twice as many words.

But in 1963, Haston was back in even more determined mood, this time in the company of the 22-year-old Rhodesian climber Rusty Baillie. He had found instant fame as the flat-capped leading figure of John Cleare's cult photographic essay *Rock Climbers in Action in Snowdonia*, shot through the European climbing scene like a meteor in the 1960s, and when he met Haston was working as a climbing instructor at Benmore Centre, near Dunoon. Haston had climbed with him in Scotland and, like everyone else, found Baillie an enthusiastic and uncomplaining colleague on the hill. They arranged to make Dougal's now annual Nordwand attempt, after a tortured ascent of the North Face of the Plan above Chamonix at the end of July 1963.

The Eiger's ability to present a different face to a climber's every attempt had ceased to surprise Haston. The first day dawned cold and frosty, and what appeared to be dry rock was coated in verglas, the second icefield was black, water ice and the waterfall pitch a huge boss of green vertical ice. There was, for once, a comfortable night at Death Bivouac, and another above the Traverse of the Gods. Just past the Hinterstoisser, there had been another surprise when the pair ran into Haston's hero Walter Bonatti, in the process of retreating from his solo attempt after a battering by prolonged stonefall. For Dougal, there was to be no going back this time, though he did produce a shock of his own for Baillie, the normally withdrawn Scot bursting into song – Freddie and the Dreamers' 'I Like It' – as the summit icefield came into sight. Indeed, he did like it.

There was still media interest in the Face – these days, no one bats an eyelid over an ascent, unless there's a fatality – and Baillie and Haston were treated to a bath and a bed in the Scheidegg Hotel by the *Daily Mail* (Bonington had been sponsored by the *Daily Express*). The admittedly esoteric Scottish press had a field day, and the announcement of the successful derring-do by their famous old boy was made at morning assembly at West Calder High School, the first of many, as it turned out. Dougal was ambivalent about the exposure. More than any other climber, he eschewed publicity, but it was clear that having a famous name would help future plans, and the way ahead for him was major ascents, summer and winter, on as many unknown walls as he could find.

The long campaign on the Eiger, his ability to remain in control in the most dire of circumstances, and tolerance of cold, hunger and fatigue, had produced something close to euphoria, but eventual success had merely whetted his appetite. Climbing had to be something more than a pastime – it had to be his way of life – and in late 1963, he dropped out of university. He had hardly opened a book that year, and it was simply a confirmation of what his tutors had long suspected; Dougal's interest in the study of Philosophy and Old English was marginal.

Dougal warmed up for the 1964 Alpine season with some of the Chamonix classics in the company of Joy Heron, followed by the North Face of the Pointe Migot with London climber Grant Jarvis, following a route climbed for the first time a few days previously by Joe Brown and Bonington. Back in Chamonix, Jarvis introduced Haston to a London friend Bev Clark, who was looking for a partner. Clark was a climbing anomaly – he was rich. He had inherited money from his father, and as well as a home in Berkeley Mews, near Marble Arch, owned a series of classic motor cars. He and Dougal hit it off immediately, but Clark discounts the inevitable theory that Haston, and later Moriarty, used him simply for his money. Now living and working in Lausanne as a TV producer, he says: 'My personal relationship with Dougal revolved round who I was at that time, rather than who he was, I guess. I was sort of in awe of him, along with everyone else, but I believe he simply accepted my money because it was there. There was no conscious attempt to go looking for it. I was still, at the time, finding out who my friends were, and Dougal did become a firm friend.'

They had met at the Biolay, a Chamonix campsite traditionally commandeered by British climbers. Clark's climbing partner had had to return home to complete his medical studies, and Dougal's plans to go up to the remote Brouillard Face on Mont Blanc with Bonington and Baillie had fallen through.

As his initiation Clark, with Dougal, Joy and Jarvis, went to tackle the South Ridge of the Pelerins, and impressed sufficiently for Dougal to suggest the West Face of the Dru, this being a big ambition for both of them.

'That was where Dougal discovered I knew nothing about aid climbing, but it didn't put him off,' says Clark. 'I remember thinking at the time that Dougal had a rather peculiar physique, with extremely long thigh-bones disproportionate to his legs, which would have disqualified him for most sports. He was, in fact, very unco-ordinated, except for climbing. But out on the hill, he just burnt me off on every hut walk we ever undertook. He was potent on the hill, that's for sure, and capable of 48 hours at a hit. He probably didn't have the vision of, say, Messner to initiate, but there is no doubt he was in that league. On expeditions, you would just keep Dougal in your back pocket.'

The next target was the Walker Spur of the Jorasses, where Clark found himself the victim in what was to become an almost standard Dougal scenario: he was discarded for someone else.

'After the West Face of the Dru, he decided to go for the Walker, which was another great ambition of mine, and on the way up there we met John Harlin, who was just making a name for himself at the time. He didn't know Dougal, but said, I think to both of us: "How about going up to do the Shroud?" I was extremely pissed off with this because my dream was to do the Walker, and I wasn't an experienced ice climber at all. Harlin's dreams were getting in my way.

'So we all went off to do the Shroud. We got up to the Leschaux Hut, and there was Michel Vaucher and Walter Bonatti going for a new route on the Pte Whymper – Dougal was in the big league now – and I sort of chickened out. Dougal and Harlin went off to the Shroud, and I remember Bonatti waking up in the middle of the night and saying: "*Michel, c'est l'heure*", for all the world as if he was calling him down for breakfast. Then a huge storm broke, Dougal and John backed off, and Bonatti and Vaucher had a major epic. But as a result of that, we came back in autumn of that year, very ambitiously going for the North Face of Les Droites. We came out on a Matchless 650 [motorcycle], with Dougal on the back and all the gear. He drove for a while, but then I realised that while I was quite happy to let him lead, I was better in the driving seat. He had very bad mechanical co-ordination and eye-muscle co-ordination, and was really lousy with anything off the mountain. Ask him to change a fuse in a plug, and he would struggle. He was a terrible driver.'

* * *

Dougal had to start learning, though. Having decided that his future lay in full-time mountaineering, there were basically three options. He could emulate the likes of Frank Smythe 30 years earlier and use journalism, broadcasting, photography and lecturing as the means to explore and climb; he could open a shop and use his name for brand marketing, as Joe Brown was later to do (many still visit Brown's shop in Llanberis expecting to be served by the great man) or he could become an instructor. The first avenue seemed already closed; Bonington was already giving every indication that he would soon corner that market, and Tiso had snapped up the second. Haston, in any case, was hardly the type to spend his days helping customers to try on climbing boots or wrestling with VAT forms.

In the end, Bev Clark helped him to make up his mind.

'At the time, I was also keen to make a living out of climbing, and when Dougal mentioned becoming a full-time climber, I agreed to bankroll him and Eley and a climbing school, printing the brochures and finding the accommodation and basically paying the bills.' It was to be called the Scottish School of Climbing, and the address was given as 48 Victoria Street, Edinburgh 1, which turned out to be the address of Haston's supplier of trousers. The directors were Messrs D. Haston and J. Moriarty, but that was as far as the business formalities went.

'It was a hoot,' Jimmy Marshall contends. 'They may have created one or two good climbers, but probably frightened the others off. The introductory course was climbing up the middle of the Etive Slabs. Of course, they had no insurance and no base, but they used Lagangarbh a few times, I think. I remember I did the heading for the notepaper. At first, they were going to start a climbing shop in Edinburgh, and the alternative was a climbing school. In the end they didn't like the idea of running a shop and Tiso, a good businessman and very clever chap, picked up on the idea. Dougal dropped out of college, and Eley gave up his job to make a go of it'.

The Scottish Climbing School failed to provide Clark with his anticipated living, and his relationship with Dougal and Moriarty was to prove prohibitively costly. 'Eley managed to write off several cars, something like 33, the first being an army armoured car when he was a kid in Currie. His bike went underneath it, and it went off the road. He also did a magnificent job on a Lotus Elan I was very fond of.'

It says much about Clark's nature that he tolerated this, and even put them up in London for a time, in between some impromptu climbing courses, when they would race up and down Glencoe with white-faced clients in a transit van paid for by their benefactor. They even managed a trip to the Alps in 1964, but most of Dougal's friends could not see it lasting. He simply wasn't a teacher.

When the summer courses ended, the pair settled in Clark's home in London W1, filling in time between gargantuan drinking bouts by running a new company, Oddjob Enterprises, which was nominally a decorating business, but in which they, or rather Eley, would put hands to anything. 'They used to paint people's posh flats in London, and would ring me up and ask me what colour they would paint the walls. These obscenely wealthy people used to pay them a fortune, and they loved these outrageous characters, who could drink like fish and acted like hoodlums. They had never seen anything like them,' recalls Marshall.

In Edinburgh, meanwhile, the minutes of the meeting of the Scottish Mountaineering Club held at 369 High Street, on Saturday October 29, 1965, noted that the club had purchased £100 of stock in ICI, that Jimmy Marshall was to be elected Vice-President, and that the membership of D. Haston had lapsed under Rule 11 – non-payment of club subscription. But, by then, Haston had more serious matters to concern him.

IN LOW PLACES

I want to know how does it feel
Behind those eyes of blue
You've made your mistakes
And now your heart aches
Behind those eyes of blue
– Paul Carrack, *Eyes of Blue*

On the night of Easter Saturday, April 17, 1965, Haston, who had been drinking, was driving the transit van on the road between the Clachaig Inn and Glencoe Youth Hostel at the western end of Glencoe, when he ploughed into three young walkers in the darkness. One, 18-year-old James Orr, a student from Glasgow, died of his injuries seven days later, and Haston, who had been arrested on the day following the accident, was charged with careless driving, driving while unfit through drink and with leaving the scene of an accident. He was found guilty on the first two charges at Oban Sheriff Court, and in June was sentenced to two concurrent terms of 60 days in prison.

The accident and its aftermath produced as many theories and myths as anything else in the life of Haston, and the facts have been buried or distorted down the years. Even now, more than 35 years after the event, it is difficult to find witnesses willing, or able, to give a definitive account of that terrible night. The site of the accident, in the sinister, rain-swept glen of massacres, merely added to the incident's dark mystery, and given the lack of a true version of events, people – and climbers are as bad as anyone for gossip and invention – have embellished the incident to an even murkier degree. Such were the exaggerations that one popular tale suggested that Haston had struck the hikers deliberately after an argument in the pub, ignoring the fact that there was no intent implicit in the charges.

This fallacy was born of an extraordinary error by the Procurator Fiscal, the public prosecutor in Scotland.

Unwisely, perhaps, there is no mention of the accident in Haston's autobiography, and he spoke little of it later, even to his wife and closest friends. Some of these believed that it should have been left out of any history of Haston because 'it would open old wounds', but even supporters of this theory admitted that the accident would have had some effect on him, and deserved at least a mention. Others, Jimmy Marshall included, insisted that it did not alter Dougal's course through life in the slightest; that his fatalism and realism allowed him to put it to the back of his mind, and to get on with dedicating everything he had to the business of climbing higher and higher mountains, by harder and harder means. Marshall says: 'People have taken the whole situation and distorted its importance. It was obviously very unfortunate, but a lot of people have made a signal mistake in a moment of weakness. The theory that it coloured the rest of his life, however, is nonsense. Basically, Dougal didn't care for anyone except himself at the time.'

During the course of research for this book, for every one person who claimed that the accident changed Dougal's personality, taking him into an even more withdrawn world in which redemption would come only from extreme feats in the mountains, there was another who said it did not. Some claimed that he fled Scotland in its wake, but he was doing new routes in Glen Etive, on the Triallachearn Slabs, in October 1965 within weeks of being released from prison, and while it is popularly supposed that he did not drive again, there is at least one witness who insists he did – and under the influence of drink. All in all, the Glencoe accident and its aftermath became a classic, almost undefinable, part of the Haston legend.

April 17 had begun on Creag Dubh, close to Newtonmore, a favourite Squirrels outcrop about 15 miles from Aviemore, and one on which they had pioneered many of the harder routes of the time. The group consisted of Haston, Eley Moriarty, Fred Harper and a number of others. The arrangement had been to pick up Dave Bathgate at Glenmore Lodge, where he had been working on a course, which they duly did, before heading for the crag. The weather was vile, too bad to climb even the easiest of routes on Creag Dubh, which is an abominable place in the wet anyway, and in time-honoured climbers' fashion, they repaired to a pub, the Laggan Inn at Loch Laggan, now sadly closed. No one can recall who suggested heading for Glencoe, but there were vague recollections of a possible party at Ian Clough's house in Glencoe Village and a dance at nearby Ballachullish, as well as the familiar, cosily rustic charms of the climbers' bars at the Kingshouse at one end of the glen, or the Clachaig Inn at the other. After a few more drinks, the idea gathered impetus, as it does in these circumstances, and around six p.m. the fateful decision was made, and they climbed into the VW van that Haston and Moriarty employed to take students of their Scottish Mountaineering School from crag to crag, and set out for the 35-mile drive through Fort William via the Ballachullish Ferry – no bridge existed in those days – to Glencoe. Moriarty was at the wheel.

In Glencoe, they dropped Bathgate and his girlfriend at the road end by The Dray, promising to collect the couple on the way back from the Kingshouse. Bathgate says: 'We wanted to get a bite to eat. We were supposed to go down to the Clachaig, but the girl I was with said: "I am not going in that van." I'm glad she was there, as it turned out, particularly when Fred turned up later and told us what had happened.'

After a few drinks in the Kingshouse, the party drove ten miles back down the glen, and dallied at the Clachaig Inn until closing time, before setting out for Glencoe Village. Haston, who was still a learner, wanted to drive, and though Moriarty and Harper tried to dissuade him, after a half-hearted struggle for the ignition keys he got his way and climbed in behind the wheel.

The back route that leads from the Clachaig Inn to Glencoe Village is bad enough to drive in the daylight, in fine weather and sober, being an unlit single-track road made even more treacherous by blind humps and sharp bends. On a dark, wet night with a learner driver who had spent most of the day drinking, it was to prove lethal.

The van hit the three young hikers just before the youth hostel, Orr bearing the brunt of the impact. Some of Haston's passengers panicked and ran into the night, as did the driver, and it was left to Moriarty, Harper and one of the women in the van, who happened to be a nurse, to give first aid. The injured, all students, were Orr, of

Thane Road, Glasgow; David Hutcheon, 17, of Merchiston Place, Edinburgh; and Robin Taylor, 14, of Jordan Lane, Edinburgh. They were eventually taken to Belford Hospital in Fort William, where Orr, who had suffered severe head and chest injuries, died on April 24. It was Moriarty who later persuaded Haston that he should return to the scene and give himself up, which he eventually did, on the Sunday, having spent the night in a friend's cottage nearby. He was arrested by Police Sergeant Sandy Whillans, who was a well-known member of the local mountain rescue team, and spent the night in jail in Oban, appearing at the Sheriff Court before Sheriff John Stevenson on the Monday.

Case 267 saw Duncan McSporran Haston, a 25-year-old climbing instructor, of 48 Dolphin Road, Currie, charged with three offences under the Road Traffic Act 1960. Section 3 (1) was driving without due care and attention, Section 6 (1) driving while unfit through drink or drugs, and Section 77 leaving the scene of an accident. Dougal pleaded guilty to the first two charges, not guilty to the last, this plea being accepted on the grounds that he was in a state of shock at the time, and did report within 24 hours. Sentence was deferred to June 2, and he was released until that date. Graham Tiso, who had just finished work, drove up from Edinburgh at seven-thirty that night to take him home. 'He phoned Graham, and Graham went up and brought him back to Edinburgh,' says Maude Tiso. 'It was very late at night, and Graham mentioned a phone call from Dougal to ask if he would come, just to say he was in trouble. We were building up our business at the time, and Graham had come home, had a bite to eat and then more or less turned around and went back out to make the long, hard drive up to Glencoe.'

Haston was back in Oban in June, and was sentenced to 60 days' jail, concurrent, for the first two charges, a licence endorsement and £15 fine. He was also banned for two years. The affair, however, was to drag on a little longer. Haston was released on the day of sentence after his agent asked for a stated case, announcing the intention to appeal. But by July 5, when the time limit for lodging that appeal expired, Dougal had had second thoughts, gave himself up, and was taken in handcuffs to Barlinnie Prison in Glasgow to serve his sentence.

Two weeks into his term, on July 20, the Procurator Fiscal at Oban issued this statement: 'At the court, I stated that Hutcheon and Taylor were of Haston's party, and the impression was given that they were drinking with Haston. This was incorrect. They did not know Haston, and they had not been drinking.' Undoubtedly, this mistake gave birth to the rumour that Haston had acted with intent, that he had driven down the students deliberately after a pub fracas, with even his friend Andrew Wightman believing this was the case for more than 35 years, until he was interviewed for this book. Inevitably, the fatal accident – and there is no doubt that it was an accident – was to have lasting repercussions. Within two years, Haston was to become a major public figure, with a huge cult following in climbing circles, but he was certainly conscious ever after that when he appeared on television or in newspapers, relatives and friends of the dead and injured students would be looking on with less than admiration for the hero of the Eiger, the Old Man of Hoy and Everest, to name three of Haston's major climbs played out under the public gaze. It was always hard, for example, to persuade him to smile for the camera.

Doug Scott, who climbed to the summit of Everest in 1975 with Haston, revealed that occasionally one or more members of his audience would approach him after a lecture and tell him that they were friends of Orr, and that perhaps Dougal wasn't quite the hero he was portrayed. Sixty days in prison, to them, did not seem much for the life of their friend, and Orr's family were angered that a more serious charge had not been brought. Apologists for Haston point out that at that time, pre-breathalyser, virtually everyone, not just in climbing circles, would drink and drive. After closing time on any given weekend in Glencoe, the road would be crawling with drivers under the influence. Habituees of the pub in that era can clearly recall Whillans, the arresting officer, driving after drinking sessions, while for other locals it was a fact of life. Whillans, who claims Moriarty 'gave us all a hard time after the accident whenever we went back', was later to be dismissed from the police force, losing his pension and house in the process, for misappropriating funds belonging to the Glencoe Mountain Rescue Team. He died in 2000.

The back road from the Clachaig Inn was notorious for its

treachery, too, with several accidents and near misses littering its history. As for Dougal, he did his 60 days in Barlinnie, one of Scotland's toughest jails, where one of the prison officers at the time remembered him 'as quiet as a mouse, just kept himself out of the way, and out of trouble. I think some of the other prisoners saw him as some sort of intellectual, and anyway, a couple of months for a driving offence didn't make him worth bothering about.'

He had told Tiso that he didn't want visitors, but was seen by his brother and by Moriarty, to whom he spoke of the paedophile in the same block, 'who got done in' by some inmates. Various tasks could earn some extra pennies, and Dougal, desperate for a Sunday newspaper, traipsed round the landings with a trolley every morning selling mugs of cocoa. Ironically, in view of his long-running dispute with Robin Inglis of the SMC, he was also put to work in the prison library, history failing to record how he set about obtaining the return of overdue books from various villains comprising the Barlinnie clientele.

When he got out at the beginning of August, Dougal arrived back in Edinburgh in chastened mode and, if anything, even more taciturn and inward-looking than before. Many of his friends saw this at once as evidence of a willingness to serve some sort of atonement, to cast himself as a figure of Shakespearean tragedy. But if there was remorse, he did not express it openly, and Joy Heron, still his girlfriend at the time, recalls: 'Dougal seemed more concerned after the accident with what was to happen to him, rather than what had happened to those hikers.' His climbing friends, as climbing friends are wont to do, jestingly called him a 'murdering bastard' from time to time to which, according to Marshall, he would respond with a sheepish grin. John McLean insists that within three weeks of release Dougal was driving again, 'turning up at Jimmy Marshall's house pissed, which really annoyed Jimmy'.

'He did drive again,' Marshall confirms. 'He wrote off my partner's [in Marshall's architecture business] Ferrari. He used to go over there to Fife, and drink huge volumes of booze, and my partner gave the boys a Ferrari Dino to come home, and Dougal was driving and doing 150mph, and went through a central reservation at Inverkeithing. He hit the opposite concrete retaining wall on the far side and,

Currie schoolboys James Moriarty and Duncan (later Dougal) Haston relax on Gunpowder Green, Glencoe in 1955

Dougal hits the big-time with his own slot in the *Hornet* comic

West Calder High School chums Haston, left, and Graham Pate

Jimmy Marshall below Buachaille Etive Mor
Inset: Glencoe adventures with Jim Stenhouse, left,
Graham Pate, centre, and Colin MacDonald with Buachaille Etive Beag in the background

Dougal gets ready for a day's work at ISM in the apartment in the Rue du Commerce, Leysin

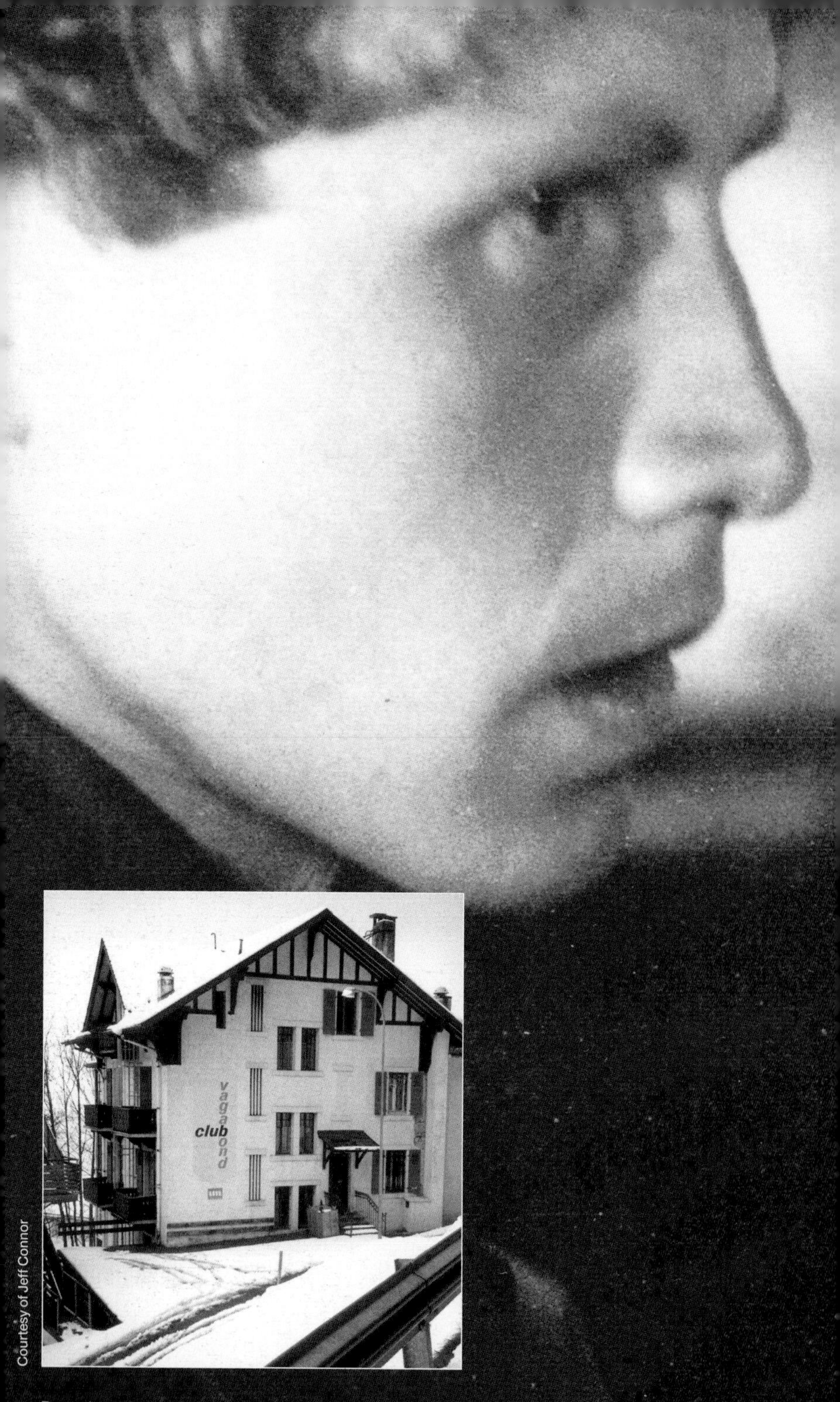

Courtesy of Jeff Connor

Dougal and Annie on a night out in the Vagabond. Inset, the Vagabond today.

Annie and VW van in the Calanques

Courtesy of John Cleare

Courtesy of UPI

John Harlin strikes a pose in the Leysin snow

Background: The retreat from the Eiger in March 1966 left to right: Jorg Lehne, Dougal, Gunther Stroebel

Dougal Haston tackles the Hinterstoisser Traverse
on the North Face of the Eiger,
August, 1963

Main picture: Dougal muscles up the Old Man of Hoy for the BBC cameras, 1967

Top inset: The cast of the Hoy TV epic: *front row*, left to right:
Pete Crew, Ian McNaught-Davis, Joe Brown; *middle*, Peter Biven, Barry Biven,
Chris Bonington, Tom Patey, Dougal, Ian Clough, unknown, the Rev Wilkinson,
Eric Beard; *Rear*, John Cleare, Chris Brasher,
Hamish MacInnes, Peter Gillman

Bottom inset: Mick Burke and Dougal after the winter ascent of the north face of the Matterhorn, 1967
All pictures; courtesy of John Cleare

for two years afterwards, there was an imprint of wheel in this concrete.'

As for the salutary effect of the incident, Marshall believes that 'the accident simply displayed to himself a weakness in character, in that he tried to run away, and it was only his pal that made him return. That must have been a personal offence to himself, that he had this craven streak. The time in the jug would affect him, but he was a fatalist. He realised there would have been nothing he could do about it, even if he had been sober. Anyway, he would have welcomed the chance to drink as much as he liked without having ever to drive again. It suited his laziness. I would love not to drive again. If you are driving others around, you're the one sat in the background sipping orange juice, and that was definitely not Dougal.'

As for fleeing the country and never returning to the scene of the crime, the SMC's Glencoe guidebook records five Haston first ascents in the area in October: Aryan with Graham Tiso and Attila with Jim Brumfitt on the Etive Slabs and, within sight of the Glencoe road end, Dick (North-East Face of Gearr Aonach), Greez (Beinn Fhada) and Smersh (Mome Rath Face of Gearr Aonach). He told Annie later that 'he rather resented the implication that he had run away from Scotland, although I believe he did have a deep remorse about it. On a lighter note, I still believe that the accident is one reason why Chris [Bonington] had to wait so long for his CBE, until after Everest in 1975, in fact. There was a thought that after Annapurna [in 1970] they would reward the successful summit team and the leader. But they couldn't very well give Chris one without Dougal, and seeing Dougal had seen the inside of HM prisons, it was a joke that Chris had to wait.'

* * *

Whatever the supposed effects of the death of young James Orr, and Haston's time in prison, Dougal's search for, and tolerance of, pain and discomfort certainly intensified at the end of 1965, and within 12 months of release from Barlinnie, he was to step into a higher grade of mountain extremism. But it would be a mistake to look upon this as his method of penance, a sort of self-flagellation. As his writings were to make clear, climbing had become a catharsis for something else. Sometime between leaving school and the accident he realised that the only happiness he could find lay in severe tests in a mountain environment. And even that would be temporary; after one test, he would have to find another, and another. To achieve this would take a degree of selfishness and self-absorption and, like his favourite philosopher Kant, he sought the freedom to live as freely as possible within laws of his own making, and nothing would deflect him from the path he had chosen. But he needed others to help him along that path.

John Harlin, his companion from the aborted attempt on the Shroud, had suggested that Dougal could spend Christmas with him and his family in Leysin, a small Swiss mountain village an hour and a half's drive from Geneva, where the American had made his home, and Haston took up the offer. Harlin was a keen advocate of winter climbing, and Dougal, too, was gradually realising that this was the future of alpinism, his alpinism at any rate, and a way of finding first ascents in surroundings where the short days, extreme temperatures, verglas and powder snow-covered rock produced an environment that suited his nature: primitive, elemental, dangerous and, above all, lonely.

He found all of these conditions in the accommodation he was offered by Harlin, who was building a chalet above the village, and allowed Dougal to use his half-finished, concrete basement. On the surface, Dougal grinned and bore it, but Bev Clark, who was working at Harlin's International School of Mountaineering at the time, believes there was 'a certain amount of resentment on Dougal's part, that he was living like a dog in this damp basement in the freezing cold, while Harlin and his family were upstairs in pine-clad luxury. But he was a hard Scotsman, so he put up with it.'

For Dougal, it was undoubtedly excellent training, as good as the refrigerators of meat-packing factories used by Arctic explorers. His heating was a Primus stove he had stolen from an empty chalet nearby, but it smoked so badly that it was a liability. His sustenance was the leftovers from the American School, where Harlin had been sports director. In Leysin in the winter of 1965, he also learned the fundamentals of skiing, though he was unable to afford lift tickets, and simply walked to the top of each run, and skied down.

He also managed a couple of winter ascents, one the North Face of the Tour d'Ai, the highest of Leysin's distinctive limestone towers, which Haston was to come to know well in the next decade. He found the alpine cold mind-blowing, though the Tour was just over 2500m high, and the contrast between winter climbing in Scotland alarming. Instead of gullies containing climable ice, there was powder snow on rock, verglas under the powder: 'All in all, a very hard business, but that made me want to get more involved in it.' Harlin, however, had had something bigger than a 1000-ft rock face in mind when he invited Dougal to Switzerland.

By 1965, John Harlin had already burned out several glamorous careers, with every indication that ISM was simply one more. Born in Kansas City in 1935, his father's career as an airline executive gave the young Harlin a cosmopolitan upbringing, with homes at various times in Ireland and France. At Stanford University, though a strapping quarterback and better-than-average track athlete, he had majored in fine arts, and even worked for a time as a designer with the house of Balmain in Paris. He found his métier, however, when he joined the college mountaineering club whereupon, with five years as an USAF fighter pilot in between, he set about making himself the most famous American name in European alpinism, climbing the Eiger North Face in 1962, and between 1963 and 1965 adding the first ascents of the South Face of the Fou, the Hidden Pillar of Freney on Mont Blanc, and the American Direct on the West Face of the Dru, to form an impressive CV. He was also a member of the All-American services football team, allegedly came twenty-fifth in the world langlauf championship six months after first stepping into a ski, and was a Californian wrestling champion, though Bev Clark recalls the smaller, and lighter, Davie Agnew making mincemeat of the American in a catchweight match at the Club Vagabond in Leysin. Not surprisingly for someone who seemed able to excel in anything to which he put his mind, Harlin was not universally popular.

Royal Robbins, his countryman and climbing partner on the Dru's American Direct, had first come across Harlin at an American Alpine Club meet in 1964, and admits that, at first, he had been taken in by Harlin's charm and hard sell, particularly when he was persuaded to come to Europe and work at a climbing school in Leysin that would have the likes of Walter Bonatti and Rene Demaison on its teaching staff, and even advertised two of the world's great mountaineers in its glossy brochure. This, says Robbins, 'turned out to be not quite the case'.

Robbins also later came to believe that Harlin was far too adept at garnering credit for achievements that rightly belonged to others; as a climber, he was certainly not in the class of Robbins or Gary Hemming and Tom Frost – his partners on the South Face of the Fou and the Hidden Pillar of Freney. Clark climbed with Harlin in North Wales in the summer of 1965, and did all the leading on routes such as Spectre and Brant Direct because 'John was unfamiliar with the rock, and not technically brilliant. I also believe he was a bit of a bully, in just choosing things that suited him.' (Later on, in the Ogwen Valley, Clark did note Harlin's skill and strength at the new American sport, bouldering.)

The relationship between the dour, cautious Scot and the extrovert, relentlessly optimistic Californian intrigued Robbins, still one of the biggest names in American climbing sport with a thriving outdoor clothing business based in Modesto, California. 'I just opened Dougal's book [*In High Places*] a while back for some reason, and I happened to open it at the part where he was at loggerheads with John because I guess John was being a little pushy, and Dougal wasn't one to be pushed. But on balance, Dougal had rather a personal liking and respect for John, which by that time I had lost. So, I was kind of impressed that Dougal would have that, because he was an independent spirit. I saw that as odd. Dougal had a way, unlike myself, of probably ignoring John's weaknesses or other side, and maybe he was pretty generous that way.'

Frost, who was also to climb with Haston on Annapurna in 1970, and who is also in the climbing equipment business now, did notice a similarity between the two. 'John Harlin was a little bit like Dougal in some ways, being almost like a Greek god in his strength and in his style, and in his appearance. But, at the same time, they had mortal weaknesses. They are, in my mind, two quite spectacular individuals: very powerful, very strong-minded, both of them.'

Harlin's strength of will, organisation, drive and undoubted ability to make headlines struck a chord with Dougal who, by this time, knew that only a full-time climbing career would satisfy his hunger for greater and greater extremes. Harlin would provide the opportunity. Although some found the American's quest for publicity and self-aggrandisement distasteful, Haston was able to rationalise that media exposure would give him the time, money and freedom necessary. As Chris Bonington, who should know about these matters in his position of Britain's best-known mountaineering professional, says: 'Dougal saw very clearly that publicity was the vehicle he could use to do all the things he wanted to do, and have money to do them. He certainly did not court publicity, but was not averse to using it.'

Like Bonington later, Harlin's climbs were invariably sponsored, and performed to the demands of a contract: he cut an imposing, plausible figure for potential backers. 'John had this incredibly impressive physique, like a Greek statue, and this tremendous enthusiasm,' says Clark. 'He was also a very positive thinker, good at drawing you into his plans. I think there was a mutual respect between him and Dougal, but I don't think they actually became friends. Dougal was not the type to fall for bullshit, for a start.'

Harlin's dream, almost his obsession, was to make a direct route up the North Face of the Eiger, the most famous mountain wall in the world, and a theatre which undoubtedly suited the American's ego. A theoretical direct route up the face had been mooted for some time. One of the first attempts, in 1935 by Germans Max Sedlmayer and Karl Mehringer, had followed a virtual straight line from the foot of the face to the top of the feature at three-quarters height christened the Flatiron, where they perished in a storm, this spot being known forever after as the Death Bivouac. The successful 1938 route involved much traversing, following the line of least resistance, and Dougal and Harlin, among subsequent ascentionists, considered that it was a huge face to harbour just one route, being some three-quarters of a mile wide at its base and 6000 vertical feet high. A similar notion had occurred to others: two Poles made an attempt in 1961, followed by three guides from the Squirrels (the Cortina version, not the Edinburgh one) and two more remarkable Italian climbers, Ignazio Piussi and Roberto Sorgato, but all these forays were beaten back by a combination of bad weather and technical difficulty.

Harlin was sniffing around the face in 1963, camping at the foot, and, as always, trailed by a posse of media. 'This big, blond guy had this uncanny knack of presenting the right profile to the camera all the time,' recalls a young Creagh Dhu climber from Glasgow, Davie Todd, who was also in Alpiglen with John Cunningham, sitting out bad weather before their attempt on the 1938 route. 'Everyone he was with had a title: Stewart Fulton was the Best Rock Climber in the World, Gary Hemming the Finest Aid Climber, and Harlin himself the Greatest Mixed Climber. He was a real impresario.'

By 1964, the Eiger had virtually taken over Harlin's life, though he was finding upward progress difficult. In February, he made an attempt on the second winter ascent – a well-organised German team had climbed the 1938 route in January 1961 – but his climbing partner was sick, and they retreated. Back in the valley, Harlin found that Piussi and Sorgato, with two compatriots, were preparing for another attempt on the direct, and he managed to talk his way into that party. They failed again. The following June, he was back with Piussi and Sorgato, with Rene Demaison and Andre Bertrand of France also in the team, but again they got no further than the Second Icefield. By now, Harlin had clocked up more hours on the face than anyone, and was gradually forming the opinion that only winter, when the frost had muted most objective dangers, such as falling stones and waterfalls, offered a safe option for what would certainly be a prolonged effort. With newspaper coverage assured, all he needed was a winning team, but a team who would operate on his terms, for in contrast to his desire to make the first direct ascent of the Eiger, almost without exception, the climbers with whom Harlin had become involved so far had one thing in common: they were all far more accomplished technically than he. They didn't really need him. Harlin must have recognised this, without actually admitting it, though he did tell Layton Kor, another potential recruit, that his attempts to date had failed 'because of the wrong companions'. Clark notes: 'Harlin was also a bit of a user of people. When he came to select his team for the Eiger Direct, Dougal was undoubtedly there because he was a pretty good ice climber, not because he was a climbing friend. Layton Kor was there because he could get up bits of rock John couldn't.'

In 1966, Kor was 27, and one of America's most accomplished

rock climbers, but with minimal experience of major mixed routes in Europe. Harlin, with his skill as a headhunter, however, had recognised that on the Eiger Direct he would need someone to cope with the extensive amount of artificial climbing involved, and in this department Kor was considered the nonpareil. But Harlin was rapidly running out of other possible allies: Bonington and Whillans had turned him down. Whillans, the pragmatic Northerner, had always been hard to please where climbing partners were concerned, but in the past had managed to forget personal dislikes and, definitely a man for the main chance, to use people for his own needs. Harlin, however, he considered 'full of bullshit, and a right poser', and even if he hadn't, he considered the Eiger Direct unjustifiably dangerous. Bonington, who eventually did contribute to Eiger Direct in a climbing capacity, says: 'John came with us on the Right Hand Pillar of Brouillard in August 1965 [with Rusty Baillie and Brian Robertson of the Edinburgh Squirrels] and I wasn't totally happy with him, and his plans. Also, I had never climbed in the Alps in winter, and I thought that Eiger Direct was a pretty severe introduction.'

Harlin had made a tentative reconnaissance with Dougal in February 1965, but by the summer of the same year they had fallen out and were no longer talking, and Dougal had returned to Scotland, helping Graham Tiso in his thriving Rodney Street shop. After another refusal from Bonington, Harlin finally swallowed his pride and telephoned Edinburgh. A young climber from Fife, Blyth Wright, took the call in the back shop, and 'got various clues as to what was happening, because we had the first Neoprene-proofed cagoules at that time, and Dougal tried one on, and was saying things like: "Well, if we run into any wetness on this route, we could be in trouble", and I thought: "Aha". It was supposed to be top secret.' Dougal also took the precaution of taking out insurance, but probably withheld some of the fine details when filling in the proposal form.

Wright adds: 'Midway through the climb, when it was on TV and in the newspapers, this guy came storming in the shop shouting "It's cancelled, it's cancelled". Tiso used to sell skis at that time, and he used to do ski insurance for holidays, and Dougal had taken this winter sports policy out. But he hadn't told them he was going to climb the Eiger.'

By Christmas, Haston was back in Leysin, but not in the Harlin basement, and the two Americans and the Scot began their preparations, poring over photographs of the face, compiling equipment and food lists, and continually working on how they could reduce weight on the loads they would have to carry up the face. The Harlin masterplan was to await what he postulated would be a ten-day window of fine weather – one of the confident assumptions that had put off Bonington – and then make an all-out push up the wall. But three weeks of waiting around in Leysin produced nothing but unfavourable forecasts, and a dislocated shoulder for Harlin in a skiing fall. But they could afford to wait. The *Daily Telegraph* was underwriting the project with Bonington, and a young journalist, Peter Gillman, was employed to cover the climb with pictures and words, and they had been able to splash out on the best equipment available, some of it made to order for what Harlin judged were the unique demands of the Eiger in winter. There was even a helicopter reconaissance of the face, with Harlin captured by Bonington on film – in profile, and gazing magisterially down on the mountain's weaknesses.

The price of all this was that Harlin and Haston – Kor was a far more ingenuous, less worldly character – had to swallow the traditional climber's distrust of the press. Eiger Direct was to be Gillman's second major assignment in national journalism after leaving Oxford in 1964. After a brief spell working for the magazine *Town* he got a job on the *Weekend Telegraph*, and when he heard the newspaper had been approached by Harlin, he seized his chance.

Gillman, who was later to become a kind of Paul Gallico of mountaineering, cornering the market on the reporting of numerous expeditions and first ascents at home and abroad in the manner of a specialists sports correspondent, says: 'I wanted to be a part of it, because I had done some climbing, but I didn't know what to expect of these people, Bonington, Harlin, Whillans and Dougal. I found Dougal a gentle, unassuming character, and I got on with him very well. He may have been dour and reticent with outsiders, but he seemed OK with me. He was also very determined to succeed, and I was overawed in the presence of him, and Harlin. Both, I think, were wary because I was a journalist and, quite rightly, because journalists had a reputation for getting things wrong about climbing, and the Eiger has always been a cockpit for publicity. There was always plenty going on there, a lot of toing and froing on the wall.'

Too much, as it turned out, for Dougal's group. At the beginning of March, a panicky Bonington, who was working on a preliminary *Telegraph* piece, telephoned Leysin from Kleine Scheidegg and told Harlin the news he must have dreaded, but half-expected: another party was on the wall and heading up his route. They were Germans, an eight-strong group, and instead of climbing the face in the traditional, ethical manner that Harlin had espoused, were fixing ropes Himalaya-siege style. Serious opposition, indeed. Haston, Harlin and Kor drove round to the Bernese Oberland at once, and Bonington filled them in with the details. For Harlin, it was the worst possible scenario.

In 1965, the American had met Peter Haag, a young German climber, at the Trento Film Festival, and as climbers often do, they had discussed future projects, which included for both a possible attempt on Eiger Direct. They had wished each other luck, and gone their separate ways. But while Harlin was making his plans, Haag had been hard at work, too, and had assembled a far stronger team. Haag was the organiser, but the acknowledged climbing leader was Jorg Lehne, whose personality mirrored that of Haston in many ways. 'Few could match his stamina, not least in all-night drinking bouts,' said his friend Dietrich Hasse in a 1970 obituary in the German climbing magazine *Alpinismus* (Lehne had been killed by stonefall on the Walker Spur of the Grandes Jorasses earlier that year). Hasse also noted that Lehne 'had an obstinacy, and an unfailing reliability for seeing through what he had started', traits that Haston was to demonstrate in full in the weeks, and years, ahead.

With Lehne and Haag, the German party comprised Sigi Hupfauer, Rolf Rozenzopf, Karl Golikow, Gunter Ströbel, Roland Votteler and Gunter Schnaidt, all good friends and members of the Deutsche Alpen Ferien, the German Alpine Club. Although almost all were working class and in many ways outside the mainstream of German climbing, they had managed to secure commercial backing from a publishing company that employed Lehne, and even had a public relations manager at the Eiger's usual base camp, the Scheidegg Hotel. When the world's media discovered that two rival teams were competing for a first ascent on the most notorious mountain face in Europe, the German PR found himself working overtime.

Sigi Hupfauer, a toolmaker who was 60 in 2001 and still climbing and skiing from his home in Ulm despite a prostrate tumour – he was on Ama Dablam in 1999 – has almost exclusively fond memories of the Eiger Direct. There were, he says, lots of friendships formed *in extremis* on the ascent, and he has always kept in touch with Bonington, meeting the Englishman eight weeks before the interview for this book. The Germans also hold Eiger reunions, but Lehne, Haag and Karl Golikow are dead.

'Peter Haag was the driving force for Eiger Direct, and we had discussed it for a long time,' says Sigi. 'We had also trained hard for it, with winter ascents, and were gradually getting more and more excited about it. At first, we tried to compete; we were using fixed line, and they were trying to do it in traditional style, but gradually we got closer and closer.' When Bonington had approached the wall, the Germans had thrown snowballs at him, actions that the rival team construed as open hostility, but this, according to Hupfauer, 'was just a bit of fun. The rivalry was manufactured by the press because, in the end, we needed each other.' The Germans recognised the strength of the rival team from the start: 'We knew about Harlin, but it was the other members that interested us. I knew of Haston, and what he had achieved. Friends, who had come across him on an international meet in Munich, had spoken highly of him. I came to appreciate that he was, indeed, a very hard man. He was very good on ice, and I soon respected him both as a climber and a man. He was quiet, but the type who inspires other people. John Harlin was also a hard man, but also very ambitious – that much was clear. He was the driving force behind his team, but gave his life for the Eiger.'

The story of the first ascent of the Eiger Direct is well enough known. Harlin's notion of a single-push ascent employing bivouacs or snow-holes on the face was soon overtaken by the elements, the small size of his team, and German efficiency, and the rival parties eventually joined forces.

'John and Dougal wanted to do it Alpine style,' says Bonington. 'The problem with that is you have to have decent weather, and the weather wasn't there. I think if the Germans hadn't turned up, we wouldn't have even gone on the wall. Conversely, a party of three was not enough for siege tactics. I found myself on the face involved, and I remember being terrified, jumaring on three-quarter weight rope, and on stretched ropes, too. I got into Harlin's bad books when I agreed that Karl Golikow could climb with Layton. Typical Dougal, he just kept out of things, and clear of the controversy.'

It was an unusual first ascent, to say the least, with an element of surreal melodrama about the whole affair, an act of theatre played out in the full, public gaze, with telescopes and cameras at Kleine Scheidegg trained on the climbers' every move. Daily reports from the international press – Gillman now had plenty of competition – filled the main pages of newspapers, and it became akin to a major sporting event, a drama that enthralled readers and viewers worldwide, with its key elements of danger, rivalry, extreme suffering and, ultimately, tragedy.

Joy Heron, in Edinburgh working on a hospital ward as part of her nursing training, listened to most of the action on the radio, while a comatose patient suffering from an infectious disease lay silently in the bed alongside. Robert and Margaret Haston, at 48 Dolphin Road, Currie, were also delighted to hear the first of the daily bulletins on their radio, Dougal, as always, having neglected to tell them where he was bound that winter. Margaret had even walked into Tiso's shop one day early in March to ask if anyone had seen her son recently.

On the route itself, climbers would retreat from the face to rest in the hotel, and Kor, in particular, seemed to come and go on and off the face as he pleased. One climbing friend of his recalls going into the giant American's room at the Scheidegg Hotel one afternoon during one of the recuperative periods, and being almost overwhelmed by passive marijuana fumes. When bad weather came in on March 11, Harlin suggested that he and Haston should sit it out in a snow-cave for six days, rather than go down, and with Haag and Ströbel having made the same decision, the media had a field day with stories of climbers marooned on the face – and at Death

Bivouac, what's more. Harlin, the centre of all the attention, was in his element, and on the second day, when he developed a fever, was able to extend his role to even more heroic proportions. Three Swiss doctors were assembled at Kleine Scheidegg, to make their diagnoses over the radio. One of them offered the simple prognosis that Harlin should set off, at once, down the fixed ropes to the warmth and comfort of the hotel, but the American was having none of that. As it happened, when he and Dougal did descend, laughing and giggling like naughty schoolboys, after an exercise whose logic escaped many – they even lost the 'sit-off', with Haag and Ströbel remaining doggedly on the face – Harlin immediately retired to hospital in Interlaken for examination, returning a day later to carry on with the climb.

Maude Tiso, who had stopped off with Graham in Kleine Scheidegg to catch up with events on the way to a mountaineering equipment trade show in Munich, recalls the unusual nature of Eiger Direct: 'We were coming down in the train, and it stopped at one of those little crossings, and just when it stopped, John Harlin skied down, and we chatted to him through the open window, which quite impressed our three-year-old son. But then the next thing we knew, we had driven into Germany, and there was the newspaper and the headline was "Harlin killed", and we just couldn't believe it because we'd had this big, happy, smiley face just talking into the train. It was hard to take in. But we had a really good time meeting up with them, and you could see in that sort of situation Dougal seemed comfortable; he was in his element, and in those conditions you saw his best side. He was either talking about what the climb would be like, or what they were going to do.'

Unsurprisingly, there were criticisms from other climbers of the siege tactics, and what Whillans famously described as 'the slowest race in the world', but after Harlin fell to his death from high on the face, just after Dougal had vacated the same, worn 7mm fixed line and with a successful conclusion in sight, there is little doubt that it turned into a major epic and a monumentally difficult climb, under the most harrowing circumstances. Nor were there any dissenters to the view that, on the final day, after a sodden night spent with one leg on the face and the other dangling in space in a sling, Haston produced one of the most bravura performances in the history of alpinism to lead Hupfauer and Votteler to the summit.

Hupfauer takes up the story: 'On the morning of the day of the accident [March 23] Jorg Lehne set off first, up the fixed ropes, followed by myself, Roland Votteler, Dougal, and then Harlin. Then we had the radio message that someone had fallen; we didn't know who, and we were looking round to find out. Roland was my best friend, and I was concerned it was him, but then he turned up, and we knew it was Harlin. We were really shocked, but in many ways it made us closer. Golikow and Layton Kor had already had one great day climbing together, and now we wanted to achieve the summit as a true team. Then came the storm, and we were huddled together in the ice-cave. My main worry was losing my fingers. My face and eyebrows were frozen, and I couldn't see twenty metres ahead. It was absolute hell when the five of us set out for the top. Going for the summit, the ropes froze into the ice and snow, and we couldn't use them. We were using short bits of rope, or just climbing solo.

'At last, we met Chris Bonington in a snow-hole on the top, and had time to eat and drink, and toes and fingers started to warm up. Dougal's recommendation for frostbite was Scotch whisky; I didn't drink whisky at the time, but now, when I see it, I think of Dougal and smile. There was no time to celebrate. Roland had been hit by a stone, and Dougal and the others needed medical attention for frostbite.

'Since then, I have lost other friends, Lehne, Golikow and others, and seen a lot of fatalities, but I will never forget Eiger Direct. I met Dougal later in Munich, after the 1975 Everest expedition, and also in Nepal where I was trekking. I feel his death even today. He made an impression, and people like him only come this way the once.'

Eiger Direct was to make an impression on a lot of lives. Of the Germans, Lehne lost a big toe through frostbite, while Votteler and Ströbel had all theirs amputated. Hupfauer was the only one of the German summit party to escape serious frostbite. Haston and Bonington needed extended treatment, too. Kor retired from climbing to become a Jehovah's Witness, though he still retained memories of the Eiger, not all happy.

'It was years before I could even think about climbing, with a smile, after Harlin died,' he told American photo-journalist Ed Webster. 'I used to sob like a baby. Harlin and I had a lot of plans. People criticised John for his publicity-seeking, his way of selling his own climbs. It finally caused he and Royal to part; after their climb on the Dru, they couldn't even speak to one another, which I always thought was really too bad. John was a mover, though, a man who loved to get things done, and head on to the next project. The more I got to know him, the more I found we had things in common. Harlin was a man of action, and when he was killed, life just wasn't the same. For me, and for several others, his spirit was irreplaceable.'

Dougal, Kor believed, was equally motivated and borne along by 'an almost prophetic ability'. At his home in Colorado, Kor still has his copy of *Eiger Direct*, Haston and Gillman's joint account. The dust jacket is worn, and a dedication inside the cover reads: 'To Layton, a small token, Big Daddy of the Great Days. Dougal.'

Harlin's family apart, the climb's most lasting imprint was on the psyche of Haston. *In extremis* on the summit icefield, when Lehne and Ströbel had taken most of the gear ahead, and neglected to fix some of the ropes, he had fought his way up a sixty-degree water-ice slope without an axe or hammer, and had 'gone to the limit'. But he had also embraced the risk like a lover. At times, the privations and suffering had evolved into something close to euphoria. When looking over the edge, he had felt in total command of himself and the savage environment, and when he returned to ground level, it confirmed what he had long suspected: it was the only thing in life that could offer a momentary happiness. Bev Clark believes that 'he had stayed in control in an impossible situation. His partner had just died, and he was getting frostbite. It was a remarkable display of will. It was the same later, surviving a bivouac on the South Summit of Everest. That's real control of the head.'

* * *

After the Eiger, Dougal suddenly found himself projected from an obscure Scottish climber into an international figure, approaching something akin to pop stardom. Though one of five to reach the summit, the climb, named the Harlin Route in honour of his fallen comrade, was to become more closely associated with him than any of the Germans. He was the quiet achiever, the strong, silent type who could be relied upon under any circumstance, the mysterious, brooding stranger riding to the rescue. In the climbing world he was plainly different anyway, his unusual, clean-shaven, almost aesthetic looks setting him apart from the popular image of the bearded climbing hard man. It struck a number of chords, particularly in female breasts, and fan mail from girls he had never met started to arrive at Dolphin Road, one addressed to: 'Dougal Haston, Eiger Climber, Scotland', which was delivered.

He went on a lecture tour, and spoke in public for the first time, his quiet, understated and modest manner making his feats seem even more notable. He swallowed an aversion to medical waiting rooms, and the smell of antiseptic, to have his uneven, tombstone-like teeth capped and straightened. He was a star.

Dougal's performance on the Eiger, however, also altered his perceived image of himself, and not in a way that would find universal approval among his former friends. Joy Heron, who was to be ditched by Dougal later that year, but who stayed with him at Clark's flat in London while he recuperated from Eiger Direct, reflects: 'Some say he changed after the accident [in Glencoe], but I believe he changed after the Eiger in 1966. Even more than usual, he tended to keep his thoughts to himself. In my view, it was a change for the worse. It might have been the fact that he had more money, and more freedom, but he was definitely a different person.'

Andrew Wightman, his university climbing pal, met Dougal after one of the Eiger lectures, and remembers that 'he was polite to me, but distant. We had been good buddies, shared a hell of a lot, but it was as though I was something from a previous history. Normally, we would have gone out for a few drinks, but he wasn't interested.' In his autobiography, Haston tells of finishing the Eiger, and 'coming out of the darkness into the light, and the exploration of that light offered so many possibilities that my mind could scarcely cope with the contemplation of it all'.

In private, things were somewhat darker and, writing to himself just after his return from the face in 1966, an entry headed 'Analysis' noted:

I have achieved my greatest climbing ambition, but as stated previously, I would not make it a stopping point. Others to come seem like achievements of lesser magnitude, but must be treated with the same seriousness as the major. I still feel the urge to fight with the forces of unknown walls. It has almost become a necessary part of life for me. I am searching into self, and I must undertake these tests in order to reach a degree of happiness – temporary though this may be – before the next test. These tests are not stepping stones to one big test. They exist as separate wholes, the tackling of which is one complete function in my term of existence. The results of the continuous on self and general action is being observed carefully – on my chosen path of delving into extremes, I am becoming more complete. A great hardness is setting in, and I am becoming increasingly able to treat the petty and mundane with utter contempt. I have a few friends in the true sense of the word, but no one will complete this path with me. I don't think anyone shall – I don't think I want anyone to. It is too difficult. People do not really understand. Often certain of the attitudes are called selfishness. The latter is a sin in the eyes of the masses. Why? They are too conditioned to mass thinking. One as an individual must think of self – I do not mean that one must hurt others – but the ones who get hurt are usually the purveyors of the petty, or whose minds are not broad enough to realise that some seemingly hard 'selfish' decision is really an altruistic one. I will do many things for people I respect, and for fools nothing. They deserve to be trampled on. One has freedom at birth. Why should one submerge or lose this freedom in attempting to help others who also had this, but lost it? The masses are not free, as they become bound by the morass of cant which rules society. Most accept a life sentence in the imprisonment of general rulings. The freedom we are born with is the freedom to live as freely as possible within certain laws. This is the freedom I pursue.

Thus spake DH.

Little wonder that some new acquaintances, from then on, though ignorant of Dougal's libertarian, Nietzsche-like notions, were often to offer the opinion that Haston's taciturnity could well have been mistaken for arrogance.

After a lengthy spell with Bonington in a London hospital, where they shared a hyperbaric machine in a successful effort to cure their frostbite, and found time to formulate a hypothetical future expedition to the South-West Face of Everest, Dougal threw himself, not totally wholeheartedly, into the new professionalism. He sat down with Gillman in London to produce a book, *Eiger Direct*, which was rushed out for the summer of 1966. Haston provided the dramatic accounts for the climbing, while Gillman successfully provided the link, as he had done via radio throughout the climb from Kleine Scheidegg.

'It was a very obvious thing to do,' says Gillman. 'The money seemed a fortune at the time, although I can't remember how much. The third-person stuff was from me, the dramatic first-person stuff from him. He stayed at my house for a while, and basically just wrote all his stuff down in longhand on paper.'

Dougal was seeking new horizons elsewhere, too, with much of his past ruthlessly discarded. It was as if he had drawn a line in the sand. Towards the end of 1966, Joy Heron had finished university in Edinburgh, and started packing her bags ready for a trip to Leysin, and a reunion with Dougal. Two days before her departure date, a letter with a Swiss postmark landed on the mat of the flat in Valleyfield Street. 'It was from Dougal, telling me that he had found another girl, but it was too late to cancel my ticket, of course. But I did go out to Leysin, where I met Royal and Liz Robbins and Yvon Chouinard, which really motivated me to come over to the States.'

Ironically, Joy, who now lives in Glenwood Springs, Colorado, and works as a midwife, married Dougal's Eiger partner Layton Kor, the couple having since divorced. She says: 'I was very much in love with Dougal right up to the point he said it was over. It was a good relationship. I don't know about marriage, because I don't think I thought about Dougal as a marrying kind, but it was tough on me when he broke it off.'

Dougal, operating on his own terms, as always, did want to stay friends with his ex-girlfriend. 'He did like to keep in touch later.

When he went to Cerro Torre [in 1968] he communicated with me from base camp, and the letter he wrote was kinda like the old Dougal. I was surprised. He said he was coming back through the States, and that he would get in touch, which he did, by phone. But it never happened because he wanted me to go to wherever he was, and I wasn't in a position to do that, and I was also thinking, by then, that this relationship was over: why should I go and chase him?'

Joy married Kor in 1969, the year that Dougal also got married.

'I was living in Boulder with Layton and already had one of our kids, and that was the last time I saw Dougal. He had been giving a lecture some place, and stopped by next morning rather hungover. I had a crying kid by that point, so it wasn't a great reunion. I think he had come by to visit me, rather than Layton.'

* * *

In February 1967, Haston was back on one of his unknown walls, this time in the company of a small, bespectacled extrovert from Wigan called Mick Burke. The partnership had begun without much promise, the climbers having had a drunken argument in a Leysin pub, and staggering outside to settle the matter in time-honoured fashion. Sense had prevailed, and they had gone back inside arm in arm to continue their discussion on future climbing plans. Dougal had wanted to go for the North Face of the Matterhorn – probably the easiest of the Big Three north faces alongside the Eiger and the Walker Spur – which was still awaiting a first British winter ascent at the time. Burke wanted a training climb, so they eventually compromised with a trouble-free ascent of the Gervasutti Couloir on Mont Blanc du Tacul above Chamonix. Six days later, they were in Zermatt. Dougal had failed twice before, in summer, on the north face, and wanted a winter ascent, not for the kudos attached to a first British ascent, but 'to even things up' – not with the mountain, but with himself. In any case, winter offered the peace and quiet he craved far away from 'caves full of sleepy people reluctant to part with the stale, artificial warmth of humanly created heat. In winter, the mountains seem to regain their primitive, virginal pride, and no more do the howling, littering summer masses tramp their more accessible flanks.' Away from the crowd he found so maddening, the North Face of the Matterhorn was climbed in three days, the only notable incident on the ascent being Haston's now regular bivouac nightmare of being pursued down a cul-de-sac 'by a huge, screaming army of armchair critics'. Fortunately, he wakened just in time.

In Currie, Robert and Margaret first knew of Dougal's success when they saw the newspapers, but as his father said: 'He is like that. He never tells us when he is going to make a big climb. I don't think he wants to worry his mother.' The Hastons' younger son did return home in early April, however, not long after Margaret had been diagnosed with breast cancer. Moriarty accompanied him to 48 Dolphin Road, and when they left, remembers catching sight of Margaret waving goodbye from an upstairs window. She died on April 26, at home. Robert survived his wife by five years, until May 1972, when he succumbed to broncho-pneumonia in Edinburgh's City Hospital.

In climbing terms, Dougal in 1967 was in a similar position to that of the struggling supporting actor who suddenly lands the leading role when the star falls ill. He took over from Harlin as director of the International School of Mountaineering in Leysin, having already decided to make his home there, and job offers poured in. He could take his pick. Bev Clark wanted him to help with a ski film he was planning to make in Verbier, there were plans for a trip with a small team to Cerro Torre in Patagonia, scheduled for 1968 and, a sure sign that he had made the big time, an invitation from the BBC to take a leading role in one of the first televised climbing extravaganzas – the Old Man of Hoy in Orkney.

Initially, Haston approached this with some misgivings about the 'commercial despoiling of the sport', but the money was too good to turn down. TV climbing was a new fad, and the Old Man of Hoy followed experiments of varying degrees of success on the Eiffel Tower [starring Chamonix guide Gaston Rebuffat], Kilnsey Overhang in North Yorkshire and Red Wall on South Stack, Anglesey. Surprisingly, because movements in climbing, particularly the artificial climbing that Dougal had been designated to undertake were slow and ponderous, it caught on for a time, possibly with the TV audience who were later to find a novelty in junk sports, such as tractor-pulling and ten-pin bowling. Whatever the reason, for a time the BBC lavished a great deal of licence-payers' money on climbing projects, presumably in the vain hope that one day someone would fall off.

As Dougal put it, even more sardonically: 'Someone, somewhere in the murky depths of the BBC production had thought it a good idea that new routes should be climbed, and proceeded to draw lines on the Old Man of Hoy to [Pete] Crew and I, with the hopeful purpose of an everlasting memorial on a dotted line on the SE arête.'

The other participants on Hoy were the acknowledged cream of the British climbing aristocracy, with only Don Whillans missing. The Hoy party included the legendary 'Human Fly' Joe Brown, Chris Bonington, Tom Patey, Haston's partner-designate Crew, and his companion from the summer Eiger, Rusty Baillie. John Cleare and Hamish MacInnes were among the cameramen, and the commentator was former Olympic steeplechase champion Chris Brasher, who had also dabbled with climbing and was by then a noted sports journalist. Dougal and Crew had been cast in the roles of the thrusting young guns, but most of the scenes were stolen by Brown's veteran straight man and the bumbling clowns, as played by Ian McNaught Davis and Patey. The programme was one of the most successful in the history of BBC outside broadcasts, and no other TV climb would get close. As in a successful Hollywood film, the casting was just right, the location could hardly be bettered. Even the weather, unusually for the far north of Scotland, stayed fine for the programme, which went out live on July 8 and 9.

The Old Man, a monolithic, 450-ft sandstone sea stack just off the island of Hoy, came close to matching Brown as star of the show. It was climbed for the first time in the summer of 1966 by Bonington, Patey and Baillie, when Bonington had taken some extremely evocative black-and-white pictures. It wasn't long before, with a little discreet prodding from Patey and Bonington, someone at the BBC decided that a televised mass climbing assault on the stack was a must for the summer schedules. The British Army helped with ferrying of supplies, which included five-star food and a plentiful supply of the local grog. The Haston and Crew route took the unclimbed south-east arête, and after the first day, with Dougal performing efficiently if a little laconically, there was a 'bivouac' which consisted of blow-up mattress, sleeping bag, hot food hauled across from the mainland, and a bottle of Talisker. A greater contrast with the privations of the Eiger and the Matterhorn it would have been difficult to find, and the whole weekend obviously sat uneasily with Haston. He was a pallid performer on camera, in any case, and the artificial climbing elements – not his favourite mode of climbing – on the south-east arête slowed things even more. He was happy to take the BBC money and indulge their lavish hospitality – the party on the last night is still recalled with awe, by those who can remember it, but in private he harboured a scorn for the whole project, and something close to contempt for some of his fellow climbers, Brown in particular. Writing at the time, probably in his luxury bivouac on the stack, he wrote disparagingly of the climb and some of his colleagues, and even got sniffy about Brown's working-class roots. For a man who constantly referred to himself as 'working class', in many ways it is a masterpiece of rambling paranoia, and should perhaps be looked on as evidence of Dougal's insecurities and self-doubt more than the failings of anyone else:

I find the present company so facile, so boring, so insular. The climbers – aware that they are in the public eye. All except Crew, perhaps playing the envisaged role, smug in the adulation of the British climbing public. These people have lost the essence of the extremist. Some never really have been. Some are buffoons, and content to be that. MD happy when he is holding court with his jolly witticisms. Unhappy when anyone else takes the field. Smug, pompous, full of his role as the stumbling buffoon second. He has never really seen the edge of the void – both physical and mental. Contemptuous of persons who keep quiet and think. Why talk inanities? Speech for me is something to be used for enjoyment and learning, not trumpeting blasts of empty noise. Then there is Brown – so like Whillans perhaps – but not even so entertaining. One discerns the plumber always. The opinions and speech are still those of a working man. They have aged and have many years of climbing experience. The adulation is assured. But why doesn't he realise that it is insular? He is not – never has been – an international name. He has pushed, but never to the limit. The extremities of the mind could not be for him. Now old in adulation has the fixed opinions, the dogma. Why can people like him never consider the opinions of others? Life is for living. How many times have I thought something as being absolutely correct, only to change my mind? No matter what people propound, he always comes back with the smug, canned opinion. Reasonably likeable surface people, yes, but not to be chosen for the tasks of probing – probing, always probing into the realms of what is possible in the world and the mind.

A gathering
Of the shells
Of the climbers
They have been
It is a contradiction of what the strivings of the extremist are all about.

Dougal had been due to take over officially at ISM in June 1967. Hoy had delayed that, and it was his Creagh Dhu pal Davie Agnew who had had officially to open the new era of the school. Now Haston hastened back to Switzerland to begin life as a climbing instructor, but within a far more formulated agenda than his freelance gambollings up and down Glencoe with Eley and the Scottish Mountaineering School. Dougal rationalised that he would have to give up most of his summers to the demands of teaching basic rock and ice climbing, but he also planned 'advanced' courses, which might satisfy his need to continue to perform at a reasonably high level, and as director he could always grab the most proficient students for himself. One of his early instructors, the Canadian Chic Scott, was to take one particularly promising beginner up the extremely serious Brenva Face of Mont Blanc. As he had stated on the Matterhorn, Dougal was also clear in his mind that only alpine winters offered a sufficient test for his mettle now, and 'overcrowding in the Alps was common in high season. Mingling with shouting crowds was not my idea of alpinism.'

For many of his friends, however, it seemed a surprising vocation.

Top-class climbers, with few exceptions, seldom make good teachers, being far more concerned with the demands of their own ambitions. At Haston's level, like many other sports, climbing is often a matter of instinct, and for the same reason that George Best would never have made a football manager, some extremely skilled mountaineers have found it impossible to pass on their skills to lesser lights. Dougal, in any case, was far too concerned with his own mountain experience to bother much about others.

Bev Clark, for one, found justification for this view when they took part in a film which was to document *La Grande Traverse des Alpes*, from Kaprun in Austria to Grenoble in France on ski, a feat first achieved by the legendary Walter Bonatti. Dougal was there nominally to look after the participants, and as a general factotum, but 'he really pissed the BBC producer off,' says Clark. 'There was a film unit, and we were the crew. Dougal was supposed to be the head guide, and Ginger Warburton and myself were the others, far more qualified than the actual "actors", as it turned out. Every time the expedition got into trouble, the film crew would bail them out. Dougal upset the BBC guy because, instead of acting as protector and head guru, he would simply disappear at high speed over the nearest ridge, and out of sight. Dougal, in fact, was an awful instructor. In Leysin with ISM, he would occasionally go on guided expeditons with clients, and again he would just vanish into the distance. He seemed incapable of modifying his level of performance to take into account the weaknesses of others. The client would be staggering around on his own on the glacier, and Dougal would be in the hut drinking a beer. The client would get really pissed off, but when Dougal went into climbing mode, that was it. He had a reputation to live up to.'

When Dougal began his ISM courses in the summer of 1967, however, he was taking over a template which Harlin had established with some success. There were enquiries from many parts of the world, particularly the United States, where the deceased former director had built up a number of contacts among the university climbing clubs and educational establishments. But Dougal now also had something of his own to sell – his name. His first brochure was framed by a cover picture of himself tackling the overhangs of the Old

Man of Hoy, above a logo that said: 'International School of Mountaineering; Director, Dougal Haston'. He had a good selection of itinerant staff to help him, including his friends Whillans, Agnew and Clark, and the ideal location high, but not too high, in the Vaudoise Alps with Geneva and its airport, Chamonix, Grindelwald and Zermatt within a couple of hour's drive.

For Dougal, Leysin had other attractions, too.

VAGABOND KING

They are not long, the days of wine and roses
– Ernest Dowson, *Vita Summa Brevis*

At 1263m above sea level Leysin is one of the highest villages in Switzerland's French-speaking canton of Vaud, yet is still within easy reach of Geneva or Zurich airports. By rail, an enchanting 135k journey from Geneva, skirting Lac Leman and passing through Lausanne and Montreux in the Rhone Valley, lands travellers at Aigle, and the start of the climb to the village on a road with only a few of the hairpins traditionally associated with that country. The village is also served by an electrified, narrow-gauge railway, which terminates above the village, and there is also a regular post bus.

Leysin's records date back to 1446, but it was only at the turn of the previous century that its mountain air and relative accessibility gave it worldwide fame as a healing centre for tuberculosis sufferers. Many buildings, with wide doors and balconies built to accommodate patients in their beds, still offer evidence of its former incarnation. The discovery of antibiotics in the 1940s made it redundant as the Lourdes of the TB world and in the 1950s the village began to develop as a tourist centre. The opening of the Leysin Tours Company and the arrival of Club Med in 1956 made Leysin a useful winter sports alternative to some of the bigger Swiss resorts, and its walks and limestone peaks made it an attractive summer holiday area. In 1956, too, the Grand Hotel – a former TB sanatorium – was reopened for tourists, and other former clinics followed its example. The Tour d'Ai–Berneuse ski-lift was constructed in 1957 to produce a small, intimate skiers' resort, suitable for intermediates and beginners in the main.

These were the golden years for Leysin, and when the American

School (Mission: 'To educate students to be responsible, productive and ethical citizens with the skills to think creatively, reason critically, communicate effectively and respect peoples of other cultures') opened in 1962, offering secondary and university education to students from many lands, the village enjoyed something akin to a boom. By 1967, when Dougal went to live there permanently, the village was able to accommodate some 5000 tourists in its various hotels, pensions, chalets, apartments, schools and camping sites, with shops, restaurants and a range of ancillary attractions to match. Half the 3000 permanent residents were foreigners, mostly American, giving Leysin the cosmopolitan feel it enjoys today. Most residents are fluent in English, and Guy Neithardt, who was born and raised in Leysin and worked for several years at ISM until 1976, wondered at times 'if I was in America or Switzerland. Most of the time, I was thinking more in English than French.'

John Harlin was sports director of the American School when he dropped everything, first to start his own climbing school in 1965, then to attempt Eiger Direct in February of the following year. As far as a location for a potential university of climbing went, he could hardly have found a more suitable place than Leysin. The whole area was rich in rock-climbing possibilities, largely unclimbed at the time, with the Tours above the village within easy reach from the top of the Berneuse *téléphérique*. Early students often found themselves on first ascents, and one of the world's great Severes, Le Miroir, is just down the valley. Although Leysin has no permanent snow, the weather is more reliable than some higher resorts, and Chamonix, Zermatt and the Bernese Oberland are all within two hours' drive. Lesser-known but extensive climbing areas, such as Arolla, the Aiguilles Rouges and Les Diablerets, are even closer, the French border a 45-minute drive away and the St Bernard Pass, the doorway to Italy, 90 minutes distant.

For all its perceived grandiosity, Harlin's idea of a climbing school offering small, mobile courses able to take advantage of favourable conditions anywhere was sound, and at one hundred dollars for a week considerably cheaper than the established alpine schools, or employing the services of a guide. When Dougal took over, he made it a deliberate policy, too, to undercut all the rival alternatives and attract the traditionally impecunious British.

Like the Scottish School of Mountaineering, Harlin's International School of Mountaineering owed a lot to Bev Clark, who in the summer of 1963, the year before he was jocked off by Harlin and Haston on the Grandes Jorasses, had run into the American in the Pen y Gwyrd, the traditional climbers' pub just below Llanberis Pass in North Wales. They did a couple of climbs with Clark in the lead – Spectre on Clogwyn y Grochan and Brant Direct – and then Harlin had explained over a pint that one of his dreams, among many, was to open a school in Leysin, taking over a building there and combining academic study and alpinism.

'I was interested,' says Clark, still looking for a way of making a living from climbing. 'I agreed to invest in it, as I was a supply teacher at the time, and saw it as a way of getting out of that. It started eventually in 1965, and as the director of my climbing school in Scotland was in prison at the time, it wasn't a question of letting Dougal down, and there was always the opportunity for him to become involved later. So we decided to close the climbing school in Scotland, and went out to Leysin.'

Initially, it was to be called the International School of Modern Mountaineering, with Clark finally persuading Harlin to drop the 'Modern'. As it happened, ISM was an evocative and easy name to market – it still is – and Harlin managed to attract some healthy bookings and charm some big names on to the personnel list. In the first year, with Harlin and Clark, the climbing instructors, at one time or another, were Mick Burke, Dougal's partner on the Matterhorn in winter, Stewart Fulton, the Scot who was working in a tool shop in the village, and who was on the South Face of the Fou with Harlin and Tom Frost, and Davie Agnew. Royal Robbins deputised for Harlin when he went off to Eiger Direct in the winter of 1966, and Don Whillans also took courses occasionally. All the original staff were seasoned climbers, but none was a qualified instructor, and it was only when Pete Boardman became director in succession to Dougal in 1978 that ISM employees were encouraged to get a professional qualification, in the form of a guide's carnet. But the lack of badges seemed to matter little to the original clientele, in the main American, lured to Leysin with the promise of climbing alongside Harlin or his first-choice fantasy staff, Rene Demaison and Walter Bonatti, who ultimately had other matters to attend to.

Robbins, who was to have a lasting fall-out with Harlin after their climb on the Dru, says: 'Charismatic, I think, is a fair adjective to use about John; he certainly sold me on his vision of a climbing school that would have the best climbers in the world, and the highest ideals. Bonatti and Demaison, who John had promised in the brochure, never showed, though. Leysin, I thought, was a charming little Swiss village on the south side of a mountain, and slightly less charming when you get close and see all the institutional buildings that were there.'

Agnew who, like Dougal, had long before decided that there must be more to the world than rainy weekends in Glencoe, but was still going through a transitory, not wholly amenable, stage in his life – friends remember him breaking the fingers, one by one, of an Australian sheep farmer, who had hold of him by his privates during an argument in a pub – had been one of the early arrivals, competing in the British Ski Championships above the village in 1964.

One of his first jobs in the winter of 1967 was to teach Dougal, Burke and Whillans some skiing technique, which they managed with varying degrees of success and enthusiasm.

'Don wasn't very good, to be honest,' says Agnew. 'It was just a utility thing for him, to get to the foot of winter routes. Dougal was quite a bit better – he was a little bit more athletic, which was the main difference between those guys, and Mick turned out to be a half-decent skier. I think they started realising the importance of learning to ski just to get into the routes. I had a lot of time for Don. I know he used to get a bad ride because he never carried his load on expeditions, and that kind of stuff, but there was a gentle side to his nature. One of the things about Don being in Leysin is that, when Harlin got killed, it was Don and Audrey, his wife, that told his wife and arranged the funeral when everybody else was in pieces.'

There was mutual liking and respect, too, between the hard-bitten little Lancastrian and Dougal, initially built on their working-class origins, mutual indolence and fondness for drink, but later maturing into a teacher-pupil partnership similar to the one he had enjoyed with Jimmy Marshall. On Annapurna and the South-West Face of

Everest in 1970 and 1971, they were to form a formidable team born, like every good pairing, from a recognition of each other's strengths and weaknesses, until Dougal eventually decided, in 1972, that the Whillans weaknesses were beginning to overwhelm his strengths, and it was time to move on.

It was a classy team of instructors, all of whom managed that perk of the job, some recreational climbing. Many of the classic routes on the Tours bear their names, and Agnew managed to climb with Dougal virtually every day. There were other perks, too, with the odd little gem being unearthed among the students.

'Some of them were very good climbers,' says Chic Scott, the noted Canadian mountaineer. 'My best client was a young American kid, who came over when he was 15, and the year after, he came back and wanted to do the North Face of the Dru. I ended up taking him up several quite serious climbs, and then the last climb we did was the Brenva on Mont Blanc, which is a pretty good climb to guide anyone, never mind a 16-year-old. The mixture was guys like that, and then others who just wanted to hang out with Dougal and well-known climbers.'

Dougal's first year in charge at ISM, 1967, got off to a delayed start when the Old Man of Hoy intruded, and it was then discovered that, when working out the itinerary, Clark and Dougal had been looking at an out-of-date calendar, so that every course commenced on a Sunday, with all that involved for clients in difficulty in travelling. But Harlin had left a sound basis for the future, and when he died on the Eiger there was every indication that ISM could become a success. An average of a dozen students a week booked in throughout the four-month season from the start, and after an initial preponderance of Americans, the courses became more cosmopolitan and international. One of the first students was a young American Larry Ware, who went to Leysin in 1967 and has never left: 'I went there on a whim, and finished up staying the rest of my life. For the fortune of one hundred dollars a week, I was to meet some of the greatest climbers of the day, do some of the most outstanding climbs and become, without too much ado, one of the alpine elect.

'At least that was the impression given by John Harlin and the first brochure. On the first day, "for training", we carried mattresses up to

Solacyre, and next day climbed into a bus and headed for Chamonix. We walked to the foot of the Petits Charmoz, then learned to use our ice axes descending the M Couloir, still packed with snow. In early June. I remember the instructors, Stewart Fulton, Ted Wilson and Bev Clark, being quite a bit more frightened by our insouciance and independence than we clients were.'

The basic introductory course lasted six days, and the one hundred dollars included room and board at Club Vagabond. The first couple of days, the Monday and Tuesday, would be spent up in a quarry, just above the Solacyre ski-lift on the edge of the forest, where clients would learn ropework and the basic principles of rock climbing. Two or three days on the limestone Tours high above Leysin would follow, with competent clients being led up the Chimney Route, and the more proficient ones heading for the Sphinx. Towards the end of the week, there would be an ice-climbing day, with the whole course piling into a six-seater Opel Kadet, the school's transportation, and driving over to Chamonix and the Bossons Glacier, where they would be shown crevasse rescue – Agnew once impressing a group by hauling a 'casualty' bodily out of a crevasse, like a cork out of a champagne bottle – and given an introduction to ice climbing. There would be an hour in Snell Sports, an outdoor equipment shop in the town, where everybody was given an opportunity to buy equipment at a favourable discount, before heading back across the border. What appeared a sophisticated, high-powered operation to wide-eyed beginners from Nebraska or Boston, however, was not quite the case.

'Of course, crossing the borders was always interesting for two reasons,' says Chic Scott. 'First of all, none of us had work permits, and we were all there illegally, and secondly, the car was illegal. It always had bald tyres, and they were always giving us trouble for the car. Every time we crossed the border, we wondered whether we were going to get thrown out of France or thrown out of Switzerland, or end up having to live in no-man's-land in between. It really was, basically, an illegal operation. The guides were not certified, the equipment was not up to par, and courses that we offered were courses in hard climbing and hard drinking, which is not quite what guides are supposed to teach. But nobody complained. That was the 1960s and 1970s, when the whole world wanted that sort of rebellious thing, and so people came from around the world to get a little touch of the freedom and wildness.'

According to Guy Neithardt, the school was granted a lot of leeway, particularly by the Swiss. 'It was so important to the village that they used to turn a blind eye to things like tax, and other formalities. None of the instructors were properly qualified, although there was usually back-up from Leysin guides. There was no programme, as such, just a bunch of guys taking people out, no organisation whatever. There were no serious accidents, thank God.'

It was a narrow boundary between success and disaster at times, though. Bev Clark clearly remembers the first ISM course, with his party leaving the Aiguille du Midi *téléphérique* station bound, unroped, for the classic Plan-Midi traverse, and one of the American students taking a long slide down the Chamonix side, and eventually stopping himself by accidentally digging his heels into the snow. ISM could have ended there and then.

By the 1970s, though, helped enormously by Dougal's reputation, the school's fame had spread, and clients came from all over the world. One particularly multinational course featured customers from Giessen in Germany; Chicago, Illinois; Victoria, Australia; east Jerusalem, Kelso in Scotland and York in England, with all that involved in terms of cultural differences, although all invariably spoke English. But Dougal and his staff were also having to cope with the individual quirks of clients. The school questionnaire sent out to customers included, perhaps unwisely, a space for 'special needs', and the inevitable requests came back: 'I am a lacto-ovo-vegetarian, can you accommodate me?' and: 'Will my hard contact lenses freeze in cold conditions?' The most common question, however, was: 'Will I be instructed by Dougal Haston?'

Usually, the answer was no, though he never told them that. He was prepared patiently to stand in the bar and answer their 'silly questions', according to Blyth Wright. 'One American was just full of himself: I did this, and I did that. Dougie was just standing humming away quietly, and the guy stopped for a while, and Dougal butted in: "No, tell us some more about how great you are." That dry sense of humour could be quite a weapon.'

Chic Scott believes that 'Dougal was a climber primarily, and if he had his way, he wouldn't go guiding at all: he would let people like me take the clients out and do the guiding, and he would just be the big-name star who attracted them. Occasionally, he would maybe spend a little time with them, and he would come down and drink with them in the bar in the evening. But the clients who came to Leysin, for the most part, wanted to hang out with the stars, and they wanted to get instruction from leading-edge climber to guides, and they got both. But I soon learned the first rule of guiding in Leysin: "If you stay up all night drinking, make sure your clients stay up with you." And it was a great rule because, otherwise, you could wake up hungover the next morning with a bunch of chirpy clients who were bright as pennies and wanted to go climbing. You wanted them hungover, too.'

The sore heads and dry mouths were provided by a famous Leysin establishment, whose charms were summed up memorably by Jimmy Marshall when he said: 'I never went to the Club Vagabond, but it always sounded a bit like the SMC club-rooms to me.' ISM's spreading fame, success and occasional notoriety owed as much to the accommodation in which it housed its clientele as the attractions of its big-name instructors, and sublime, alpine surroundings.

* * *

Club Vagabond had been opened in 1962 by a Canadian, Allan Rankin, and a Rhodesian, Ken Tait. After Tait's death in a road accident a Dutch homosexual, Luc van der Kaay, and an Australian, Joan Seeman, joined the consortium. Rankin was a former Pan Am marketing executive entranced with the idea of finding a cheap boarding-house in the Swiss Alps, which would become a meeting place for travellers. He found the place of his dreams in an old sanatorium overlooking the village, close to the Solacyre lift and within staggering distance of the American School. The accommodation was on four floors with bed space for 40, and there was a bar and reception area through swing doors on the ground floor, and below that a night club and disco called the Ice Cave.

Rankin, who still lives close by, says: 'We were lucky because the Vag coincided with an era, and it became a phenomenon of the times. It was the time of travellers, all of whom had a certain amount of disposable income, but not enough to justify going round the world living in three- or four-star hotels. In those days, too, there was a certain guarantee that if you left home for a year there would be a job waiting when you got back. In the Vagabond, we had found the right place in the right time. Leysin was already fairly cosmopolitan, with the American schools, and the locals, having had half a century of people with health problems, now had a whole new clientele.'

The Vagabond clientele included the students at ISM, who were housed there from the start at priority rates arranged by Harlin, plus an astonishing, polyglot mix of travellers, draft-dodgers, leading-edge mountaineers, boozers, drug-takers and a few bewildered locals. It was primarily a place for the young, but the Vagabond transcended every boundary of age, sex and nationality. A night in the bar would mean a meeting with the world. And it was, says Rankin, 'unbelievable party night every night' – with loud music, drink, conversation, sex and occasionally drugs. For Dougal, a participant to a greater or lesser degree in all of these, the Vagabond, like 369 High Street in Edinburgh, became a home from home. It also served one other useful purpose, providing him with the secretariat to promote the school, write letters to potential clients and handle all administration. Before long, all he had to do to run the school was to show his face occasionally and sign and bank a few cheques while he got on with the real business of life.

'Dougal was king of the Vagabond,' says Chic Scott, the Calgary-born climber who became one of the first Canadians to have an impact on the international climbing scene, and was one of the founders of the renowned Banff Mountain Film Festival.

'I can still picture exactly the way he came down the stairs every night, and how he liked to have two sides of support, the bar and wall. He liked to be in a corner, so that he wouldn't fall down, and so that he had his back to the wall like a Nevada gun-fighter, and so nobody could sneak up behind him. You came into the bar, and Dougal was over there in the corner and, of course, if you were someone like me, a 20-year-old impressionable climber from Canada, there was a little pitter patter in your heart, and there he was, the star. Dougal really was, physically and emotionally, and to his admirers, very much like Jim Morrison and Mick Jagger. He was the Mick

Jagger and he was the Jim Morrison of the climbing world. He had that sort of face, the high cheekbones, very drawn like he had been taking drugs and booze for a long time, or hanging out at 27,000 ft too long. He just lived life with that passion that was very much admired in those days, and we said that's the way you gotta live.

'Dougal is the only person I have met in my life who was truly larger than life, like a Shakespearian hero. Heroes are not necessarily good guys, but they are big, really big personalities. Dougal's life was tragic. It was very Shakespearian, but you know he was larger than life and the rest of us. Dougal climbed the great mountains; he eventually hung out with the great stars, he wore the sunglasses and the scarf around his neck like a Hollywood movie star, and he could carry it off. He's the only guy who could make the rest of us look like a bunch of fools. Dougal could carry if off, we couldn't. I remember I did buy a colourful, pink shirt one year. Dougal wore bright colours, a pink shirt and a flashy sort of scarf around his neck, and he was like some goddamn Italian movie star. We just looked ordinary.'

Scott, who was only five years younger, admits that he hero-worshipped Haston, as does Guy Neithardt, who remembers Dougal introducing him to local rock climbs, and offering him the lead 'as a part of the education. I was a young boy, and I looked up to him, and I learned so much from him.'

Scott remains convinced, too, that Dougal became a sort of mentor for them simply because 'I never questioned him, I loved him and admired him in a way, and also I never knew anything about his chequered past, and I never knew anything about his car accident. In fact, I didn't know about that until 1977 in Calgary. We had a wake for Dougal, and Bugs McKeith was there, and he told me about the accident. I never knew about it all those years. So I think Dougal really was happy in my company because, to me, he was still untarnished, and he liked that, and also I didn't talk very much either – and I didn't disturb the silence. He didn't even ask me himself to work for him; he asked my girlfriend to ask me, and I've always wondered about that, why he didn't just come up to me and say: "Would you like a job, would you like to do some guiding?" So anyway, I went and talked to Dougal, and I said: "Well, I'd love to work for you, but I've never guided, and I don't know how to do it," and he said: "You know how to do it: just be careful." For me it was marvellous. I was a young kid from Canada with stars in his eyes, and here I was in the great European Alps, and sort of hanging out on the fringes of these big stars and, basically, I was asked to be a guide and asked to participate, and sort of given a free hand. Dougal never told me what to do after that, he just said: "Be careful." But it's the way Dougal was. He was just very lean on words, and I was very lean on words at the time.

'I owe a great debt to Dougal. He was the guy who gave me my break, and it's had its ups and downs over the years, but it's going pretty good now, and he's the guy who got me started. Oh, he never talked. Occasionally, I used to go down and visit him down at his apartment, and Dougal and I would sit there for hours together, just looking at climbing magazines and climbing journals, and occasionally saying: "Oh, have you seen this one?" Or: "Look at this one." There was just silence. Annie, his wife, had this joke about me sort of leaving the house and Dougal didn't even realise that I had arrived. Martin Boysen used to call me Dougal's batman. I was his gopher, and I trusted and admired him without reservation, and he liked that because everybody else knew him as something else, as a bit of a drunkard, a bit of a scoundrel, and I was totally ignorant of all of that, and I was just this curly-headed kid from across the water, who saw him as what he really wanted to be, just a great mountaineer.'

Dougal's climbing career, unlike those too numerous to mention, thrived alongside his marriage, mainly because he would never allow it to interfere. As he was to write later: 'Her attitude towards my climbing has been magnificent. No attempt at suppression. If there had been, it would have ended long ago.' In his autobiography, his marriage merited one, short sentence. 'One other significant event that year, I finally married my girlfriend Annie' – at the end of a chapter devoted to climbing in Yosemite. Even that was put in at the insistence of his publishers, who must have thought that a full-time woman in his life may have had some relevance.

* * *

Dougal had met Annie Ferris in May 1966, when he had returned to Leysin from London following his hospital treatment for the frostbite suffered on Eiger Direct. He and Mick Burke had been drinking in the Vagabond bar when two attractive English girls, Annie and Beth, walked in. Annie was tiny and pert, with the face of a pixie, but with a confidence beyond her years. She was an excellent conversationalist, was very well read, and adored music. There was mutual attraction all round from the start: Dougal paired with Annie, Beth with Mick. The girls were working at the club as cleaners and, like all the other domestic staff at the Vagabond, were paid a pittance, but given free board and lodging. There were compensations: 'We had a ball,' says Annie, who was born in Chiselhurst, Kent, on October 23, 1942. Her mother died when she was ten, and being an only child, she was immediately dispatched to a boarding school, St Mary's Hall in Brighton where, as she puts it: 'I basically managed to screw up everything I tried.' She and Beth, who was from Sevenoaks, met at Guy's Hospital in London, when both were training as nurses, and in April 1966 reached the fateful decision to take a working holiday in Leysin.

'We had never met a climber in our lives, until then,' says Annie. 'They were a completely new species. I was going to marry a doctor: it was going to be Dr and Mrs Bowen-Simpkins, but that soon ended. Beth had just had a miserable fall-out with her boyfriend, and we were working in casualty when a girl came in with a plaster cast on her leg, and looking very brown. She'd been to Leysin, and proceeded to talk about Leysin and the Club Vagabond, where they took English girls as bar staff, cleaners etc. Peter, my fiance, said: "Why not go with Beth because I have exams to do?" And that summer, Beth met Mick, and I met Dougal, which rather finished my life as a genteel doctor's wife. This was a brand-new species, a rough-and-ready species. It was quite a scene, with some amazing characters. This funny guy called Don Whillans would come over and sit with us, and he would drink pot after pot after pot of tea then, without looking at his watch, out would come the beer. You'd be in acres of laughter, and then analyse what he said, and he hadn't said much. It was just the way he said it.'

Beth, who was to marry Mick Burke, remembers that the first inkling they had about the existence of climbers was when she read about Eiger Direct in a newspaper while they were in London. 'Annie said: "Look at this" and I said: "They must be mad" and she said: "I think you're right." We had just done our training and were on a year's post-grad and I, for one, was looking for change. Everyone around was dying, and I had had enough of nursing. I needed a break. I had been on ski holidays, so I loved the mountains. The Vag was full of Canadians and Americans on motorbikes. We cleaned the rooms, starting at six a.m. and watching the sun come up. Leysin was like living in a film set, too perfect to be true. We first met them in the Vagabond one night; they had done a lot of climbing and drinking together, and were fairly inseparable. Mick would tell stories and make people laugh, Dougal was just there. I remember them coming back from the Matterhorn so pleased with themselves. Dougal always had this aura about him. You would look at him and wonder how on earth could he cope on a steep hill, never mind a mountain, he was so pigeon-toed. He had a fresh sort of complexion, and couldn't even grow a beard, so he was never as scruffy as everyone else. He was certainly attractive to women, and he had wooed quite a few, I believe.'

Annie reflects: 'I think Dougal thought: "She looks a bit of all right" and Mick obviously thought the same about Beth. It was love at first sight for both.'

It was then that Dougal remembered that Joy was on her way over from Edinburgh, and his hastily written letter to tell her that their romance was over arrived too late to stop her catching the flight. Her arrival in Leysin caused minor complications, but Royal Robbins and his wife Liz looked after her, and though Joy was deeply hurt, there were no scenes. The Robbinses, with another visiting American climber Yvon Chouinard, prompted Joy to go to America, where she has lived since.

Annie and Beth, for their parts, were so smitten that they took up jobs in the local hospital, La Beau Site, and the two couples shared an apartment in the Villa Florence for a time. At the end of the summer, all four went to En Vau in the Calanques, where cliffs 400 ft high rose out of the turquoise-blue Mediterranean, and where most visitors slept in the open. Annie recalls the boys' outrage when they insisted on washing their hair – with the water supplies they had carried in from Cassis – and Mick and Dougal singing choruses of the tune of the moment 'Yellow Submarine', before plunging into the sea. There were long, loving days spent snorkelling, picnicking and drinking, with the occasional climb thrown in. Annie dutifully tied on the end of Dougal's rope – she was, after all, in love – before deciding that it was not for her, though she developed a lifetime devotion to the outdoors. While Dougal went on his expeditions – Cerro Torre in Patagonia in 1968 was to be his last major trip as a bachelor – his wife worked extra night shifts at the hospital, so that she could do her own travelling. While he went to South America, she headed for Squaw Valley, California. It was an unusual marriage. 'I believe, to be honest, Dougal was quite relieved that I never got interested in climbing,' says Annie. 'I never interfered with that, but I cherished my independence, too. One of the reasons we decided not to have children was because I would literally have been left at home holding the baby, and neither of us would have wanted that.'

Leysin and ISM were slowly providing Dougal with the lifestyle that he had long craved. In winter, he had some of the last great problems of the Alps on his doorstep, and summer consisted of four months' work with the school with, perhaps, another two or three free for rock climbing. The income from work was just sufficient to meet his basic needs, which had never been excessive. He had never shown any great interest in money, and whether by accident or design, the business did not expand too quickly. That would interfere with his real career and, besides, away from the hills he had already proved himself chronically lazy. And, of course, he now had a woman who loved him on his arm, a non-climber quite willing to endure, and indulge, his anticipated long absences on expeditions. What is more, she could match him drink for drink in the Vagabond. The perfect wife, in his eyes.

* * *

The year 1969 began well, and along the course of the master-plan he had mapped out. In March, he was with Bonington in the Argentiere basin with their eyes on the Cornaux/Davaille Route on the North Face of the Droites, a route long on both men's winter wish-list. It had been tried before, by the German Eiger Direct trio of Jorg Lehne, Gunter Ströbel and Karl Golikow, using similar fixed-line tactics. Dougal wanted the one-push approach, and with Bonington similarly motivated – and with a photographic commission from a magazine – the friends set out for the empty Argentiere Hut on skis. Haston's lessons from Agnew came in useful on the approach over unstable snow; Bonington, far less accomplished, fell over every couple of turns. At two a.m., dozing in their sleeping bags, both were wakened by the sound of boots tramping across the floor above, and then down the stairs. Next morning, there was no sign of another occupant, and no tracks in the fresh snow outside. The same thing happened the next night, and it was only later, when flicking through the hut's climbs book, that Dougal found the entry: 'Guardian killed by avalanche in the couloir on the Aiguille d'Argentiere'.

A similar incident had been experienced by Dougal and Jimmy Marshall a few years earlier, in the CIC Hut on Ben Nevis, when both had heard footsteps in the darkness, and after the Argentiere episode Haston developed a respect for, and an interest in, the supernatural. He was convinced that the guardian was still fulfilling his ghostly duties in the hut.

The Droites were taken out of their plans by bad weather, and Haston and Bonington made do with a first winter ascent of the North Face of the Argentiere, ascended over hard ice plastered with powder snow, and one bivouac near the top. Bonington recalls that, and another winter attempt on a new line in winter on the Grandes Jorasses, as 'some of the best climbing I ever did, not just with Dougal, but with anyone. We were totally in tune with the environment and each other, and Doug Scott was to express similar sentiments about climbing with Dougal later. On the Jorasses, I think we probably exchanged eight sentences in three days in a snowhole. But it was a comfortable, relaxed silence. He was really at home in situations like that.'

It was turning into a year of contrasts. Bev Clark had enlisted Robbins' and Dougal's help for a ski film set in Verbier, and having been admitted to the Club Alpin Suisse and the élite French Groupe Haute Montagne, Dougal felt qualified sufficiently for some independent guiding, and extra cash, from leading clients over the famous skiing Haute Route from Chamonix to Zermatt. It was Bev, too, who suggested the trip to Yosemite (the Californian national park being far more user-friendly for non-climbing wives) and they set off at the end of April, with Jan Clark and Annie in tow. Dougal had never been to Yosemite, but already felt an affinity with America's foremost rock-climbing area through his friendships with Royal Robbins and Kor, who had made their names on the huge, sun-drenched granite walls. The techniques they had evolved, and their proficiency in artificial climbing, had been demonstrated with startling effect in Europe on the Dru and the Fou and on Eiger Direct, by Kor.

Dougal continued his love-hate affair with aid climbing, at which he was far from adept, according to Clark: 'He was pretty hopeless, to be honest. It was far too mechanical and complicated for him.' Dougal proved far more able in handling Yosemite's main, objective danger, the predatory brown bears that roam the park on the lookout for tourists' edibles. Dougal, as was the fashion, had tied his food sack high in the branch of a tree but, unfortunately, had attached his tent guy-line to the same branch, and he was disturbed in the middle of the night by the canvas swaying alarmingly. The bear came out worse in the subsequent encounter, with a naked Dougal springing out into the night brandishing a piton hammer, the beast retreating into the forest. 'It must have been a very young, and very craven, bear,' says Clark. 'But when we looked at the tree later, there were these huge slashes in the wood, so full marks to Dougal. He certainly had guts.'

Clark's climbing holiday came to a premature end when, after sweltering and hammering their way up the East Face of Washington Column, he bruised his elbow in a fall on the approach to the North-West Face of Half Dome, and Dougal was forced to team up with an American climber from Boulder, Jim Logan, while Bev sat it out drinking beer under a polythene sheet 'tent' by the river. The holiday ended with an eye-opening Grade Six, the South Face of Mount Watkins, climbed with Rick Sylvester before duty called – in the shape of an urgent telegram from Agnew – back in Leysin.

Dougal and Annie were married at Leysin Church in October that year, with Luc van der Kaay and Allan Rankin as joint best men. After three years together, she admits that the proposal came by surprise: 'I was amazed when he popped the question. I honestly think Dougal one day decided he wanted to be respectable. He thought it better to introduce clients to his wife rather than girlfriend. After the ceremony, I spent a week trying to get Eley to leave.' For his part, Dougal's old Currie friend was just as taken aback. 'I thought, if he would get wed, it would be Joy,' says Moriarty. 'They were very close in every way, and then just drifted apart. Women were not going to interfere with his climbing, certainly Annie didn't. She didn't climb, though, not like Joy. But he made a decision, and that was it.'

The couple settled down to married life, moving into an apartment in La Coccinelle block, Beth and Mick having returned to England. It was in the Rue du Commerce, a couple of hundred yards downhill from the Vagabond, and Annie received early hints that being married to a climber would have its drawbacks, particularly in a mountain village like Leysin. 'They used to call me La Petite Coccinelle [Ladybird] in the shops, and I got on fine with the locals. I loved Leysin, but in many ways, after London, it was like living in a goldfish bowl. Everyone knew each other's business. At one time, everyone wanted to visit us, and I remember once we even had to knock on our own front door to get in. We were plagued by hangers-on, plagued by them, but I could always escape to Lausanne, Montreux or Vevey. Dougal, for some reason known only to himself, just put up with people lolling about on our furniture, and helping themselves to our food and drink.'

Despite Haston's hatred of conformity, Leysin and the school provided an ordered life with a day job, a meal at home or in one of the village restaurants in the evening, and then drinks in the Vagabond at night. But there were still the occasional flights from normality to keep him occupied. Allan Rankin had been in the club one night in early 1974 when Dougal came in brandishing a book, *The Eiger Sanction*, and insisting that 'this will make a great film'. Within a week, quite coincidentally, he had received a letter from the Swiss/American mountaineer and film-maker Norman Dhyrenfurth, asking Dougal if he would be prepared to help with training Hollywood star Clint Eastwood and his actors in basic climbing techniques, and then act as safety officer on Eiger locations. Dhyrenfurth, leader of the successful 1963 Everest West Ridge expedition, which placed four men on the summit, and the less successful 1971 climb, mentioned a salary of around five hundred dollars a week plus half that again in expenses, and Haston and the school would be acknowledged in the credits. It meant a sixth trip back to the north face for Dougal – he had helped John Cleare with a documentary *The Climb Up to Hell* in 1968 – and was also to have tragic consequences.

* * *

The Eiger Sanction was written by a retired college professor operating under the pseudonym of Trevanian, and concerns a libidinous art teacher and collector Jonathan Hemlock (Eastwood), who finances his hobby by performing the odd sanction (assassination) for an obscure US government bureau. He is forced to take a case where he must find out which member of a climbing team is the Russian killer who is his target, by joining an expedition to the Eiger North Face; why the sanction could not be performed at sea level is never made clear. Dougal was also asked for advice on Eiger locations and for comments on the script, and he pulled no punches: 'I have heard mention of shots of actors leading. This is definitely not on, unless they are on very easy terrain. The description of the methods of descent are also totally fatuous. As for holding a weight with hands – bullshit! Also, bivouac just above Eigerwand Station – there's none.'

The director and star was Eastwood, with support from Jack Cassidy (father of David), George Kennedy – who, despite being cast as the perennial heavy in many movies, turned out to be one of the most amiable men most of the climbers had met – and Vonetta McGee, the love interest. The crew was to include well-known climbing stars, such as Martin Boysen, Guy Neithardt, Bev Clark, Dougal, Ian Nicholson and Dave Knowles from Glencoe, and Chic Scott. Dhyrenfurth was in overall control of climbing matters on the mountain, and John Cleare was the mountain sequence photographer. Much of the filming was done in Monterey County and Yosemite National Park, but Eastwood had, quite rightly, reasoned that it would be hard to find a suitable backdrop to fill in for the Eigerwand, and the wall and its environs were to become the film's European location. The meticulous Eastwood had also intended to do many of his stunts, and booked in for the alpine introductory course at ISM.

'Clint on the Eiger, he was great,' says Scott. 'He did most of his own stunts – he was very courageous, and he was very good with us, an absolute gent with not a trace of ego anywhere in his make-up. I showed up on the set, and I sort of walked into the Scheidegg Hotel, and was immediately invited to sit down to lunch with Norman and Clint Eastwood. Here I am, just a member of the technical crew, no big deal, and I'm sitting having lunch with Clint Eastwood. Clint was very, very low key. He worked hard, and everybody liked him.'

Blyth Wright, who had arrived in Leysin that year, found that one of his first jobs was to spend three weeks with actors who had not climbed before, teaching them to look and move like Eiger aspirants, which they managed with varying degrees of success. Most of the climbers considered Eastwood a natural. However, the production got off to a bad start when Nicholson, a member of the Creagh Dhu and a famed Glencoe hard man, was thrown out of Switzerland after an incident in the Vagabond. Wright and Haston had introduced him to the local hooch, and Wright takes up the story: 'The evening wore on . . . so Ian comes over to me – and you must remember Ian is just newly married, and a great champion of the married state – and he says: "See that guy sitting over there chatting up Annie, I'm going to have to hit him." Well, if you knew Annie, you would realise it wasn't him that was chatting her up, it was the other way about, but Ian said: "No, no, no, that's what you have got to do is to hit him." So smack and immediately, of course, the bloody place is full of police and walkie-talkies.'

Nicholson was escorted to the border and, despite a plea to Haston to allow him back on the set, that was the end of his participation on *The Eiger Sanction*. The dental bill for the Vagabond punter was two hundred Swiss farncs, paid by Dougal, and which, despite several requests from him over the years, was never paid back.

But far worse was to follow on the second day of filming. Scott recalls: 'I was told that Hollywood likes to shoot the hardest scene first, to get it out of the way, rather than go all the way through filming and then find you can't get the last scene, or something. So they started with the hardest scene first, and they actually wanted me to take a fall over a ledge on the West Flank. I refused. I'd spent, by then, 15 years hanging on as tight as I could, and I just couldn't bring myself to throw myself off and, anyway, something definitely did not feel good about it.'

It was Dave Knowles who deputised, but with the light fading and most of the rest of the crew being evacuated in a hurry – 'safety officer' Dougal was back in the hotel taking a shower – a large rock was dislodged from above, crushing Knowles to death. For the superstitious Scott, the whole thing was almost too much: 'A day before he got killed, Dave and I had spent the whole day fixing pitons and ropes on the Shattered Pillar. We had climbed up the Rote Fluhe on ropes that Dougal had fixed earlier, and we had traversed out. I nailed out to the left, and I think Dave and Martin nailed out the right, and it's really weird, but basically it turned out we had made a giant cross with the rope. That night, I bought the bottle of wine at dinner, and I ordered the most expensive wine on the list, and it was called the Tears of Christ and then the next day I had this strange premonition, which saved my life. I ended up being the guy who had to go into Dave's room and pack up all of his stuff to take back. Dave was dead and, yeah, that night we all got really pissed, and the next day Hollywood told us we all had one-hundred-thousand-dollar insurance policies, but I think it was too late for Dave's widow.'

Eastwood was devastated, but the show had to go on. Dougal was moved sideways from his allotted role, and Hamish MacInnes came in to take over the safety aspects. 'Hamish, of course, was far more methodical and switched-on than Dougal,' John Cleare observes. 'He had run the mountain rescue in Glencoe for many years but, more importantly, wouldn't take any bullshit from the Hollywood types concerned about time and money.'

The Eiger Sanction, which included a special dedication to Knowles in its end-credits, opened to mixed reviews in 1975, though most critics agreed that the mountain sequences were fairly special. One wrote: 'An abundance of fairly well-written, tough-guy dialogue make it fun to cheer for Clint Eastwood in this espionage thriller. But the story and the rest of the characters are short on sense and believability. A couple of tense mountain climbing scenes aside, much of this film is downright laughable. For Eastwood fans only.'

* * *

Back in Leysin, the Hastons got on with married life. At around eight p.m., after an evening meal, they would walk up the hill to the Vagabond, where they would stand drinking for most of the night, usually in the same corner, Annie invarably lasting the pace as well as Dougal. He drank pints, she drank wine. Most guests, visitors and clients thought they made a handsome couple, though many friends considered it an unlikely union. 'I think she could hold her own with the booze all right,' says Scott. 'But to be honest, I don't know why they married because they were quite different. Annie was a little bit of a cultural snob, and Dougal was just a drunken, climbing bum like the rest of us, and why she was attracted to him, I don't know. She's the sort of person who would have wanted to marry some man who had some money, who could take her to the Paris opera: she would like the high living. Of course, Dougal could provide some of that, once he was famous. As for Dougal wanting to get married for respectability, I don't buy that. I can't see the clients even giving a damn if he was standing there with a couple of bimbos on each arm, right out of a *Playboy* calendar. They would have loved it.'

It is unclear whether Dougal or Annie was unfaithful first, but in the sexually charged, promiscuous atmosphere of the Vagabond, with copious amounts of drink involved, it is hardly surprising that both were to stray. As with so many high-risk sports, there is much amorality in climbing, a feeling that normal rules of convention simply do not apply. At one time, it was fashionable for climbers to leave restaurants without bothering to pay and to pilfer from foreign supermarkets, and soft drugs, excessive drinking and the occasional fight were part of the scene in the 1960s and 1970s. Infidelity, too, seemed to have been remarkably endemic in Dougal and Annie's group, which contained a fair smattering of the world's top mountaineers. There were affairs with wives of friends, and even friends and widows of friends, and the Hastons played their full part, living in what amounted to an open marriage and disregarding all normal rules of convention until they separated in 1975. But that was the freedom espoused by Kant, and what Dougal felt was his right. At night, he could often be spotted chatting to a girl in one corner of the Vagabond bar, while Annie was engaged with a man in the other; she had an affair with one of Dougal's best friends,

Dougal a fling with the wife of one of his best friends. Virtually anything went.

'I never saw them openly fight, but I was always aware that there was infidelity in their marriage,' says Scott. 'They were sort of hurting the other. I had the impression that one would be unfaithful to hurt the other person, and then vice versa. But it was that time of the century; everybody was sleeping with everybody. Annie and I got along very well. I mean, I was the nice Canadian kid who was sort of inoffensive and not very dangerous, and not a powerful personality to be threatening, and I was friends with everybody. Some of the others, I think, were just to piss Dougal off.'

Bev Clark comments: 'We shouldn't be too hard on Annie, because she did bring a lot of positive things into Dougal's life, like books and music. I certainly think they were in love, but they got married and then decided to grow up afterwards. But being around Leysin was being a spectator to all Annie's infidelities.'

Haston, however, was hardly a shrinking violet. His status and fame were powerful aphrodisiacs in their own right, but combined with his unusual looks and what most females saw as a quasi-tragic, brooding demeanour, they proved a powerful combination. Nor did he have to do much chasing. There was a never-ending carousel of female staff or travellers passing through the Vagabond, many of whom found the silent Scot brooding in the corner irresistible. Beth says: 'I think he made some women feel he needed looking after. He knew that, and probably expected it.'

Occasionally, Dougal did make an effort, without ever feeling comfortable. Uncomfortable not in the sense that he believed a liaison might damage his marriage, but that it might damage his climbing. He wrote to himself to describe one liaison with a Marie in Paris, calling it 'A Moment in Time':

> At our first meeting in London over a year ago, I thought there could be something between us. In the drunken cataclysm that follows an Eley meeting, I had contemplated a flight to Paris. I am not frustrated – seldom am. But in the drunken ramblings on sex which always happen when friends as close as Eley and I get together, and instead of looking in Edinburgh – which is

not too difficult – I suddenly thought of Paris, and Marie. I suppose the urge seemed pointless at the time and, anyway, I was due back in Leysin to see Annie, and there would be suspicion and possible scenes, scenes which have little point to me, but which I suppose must loom large in a woman's mind. Spoke to Marie. Then letter arrived from her. We return Chez Elle, and Scotch sends its bewitching, soothing fumes round our heads. Talk Drink Talk Drink. Dinner for two in warm Paris night, elder children capering like children. I now know why Paris holds a spell on people. Through the confusion, a whirl of talk and food and wine and ignoring others, and 'Let's Spend the Night Together' on the jukebox. The only thing that exists is a potential of supreme happiness on this tormented earth. Go to her room, and for me sudden deflation. I sink down in chair in a torpor. No thoughts, no feelings, just empty. Then it comes, the solution, and my mind and senses begin to operate again. There is now a need, so needful that feeling flows beyond the capabilities of conveying meaning. We close and finish. The next I do not feel like putting down in descriptive form. It is a sin against a night – a night which should perhaps be left in the mind. The impression is there forever. Memory recalls it, but never adequately. The fusion of mind and body is not for you, cannot be for you. My control must be for my mountain way of life. But the pushing of my body gives me the ability to assimilate great experiences. And ours was that.

Thus spake DH.

Blyth Wright, who worked at Leysin in 1974 and 1975, and had a close-up view of the Haston marriage, notes: 'Dougal, I would say, was a relatively enthusiastic participant. But it was an unusual relationship in a lot of ways. He obviously liked a quiet life, and didn't want any hassle. Nor did we. There was one New Year when the club bar didn't really shut, so we were drinking at the bar until eight in the morning, then it closed. The staff finally decided they had to go to their bed. But a lass called Linda, who worked in the ski shop next to the disco, had a bottle of whisky, so we were all sitting around the floor, and when we scoffed that, we were just getting started on

Linda's brandy when the ski-shop door burst open and in walked Annie. I leapt to my feet, loudly declaring: "It wisnae me, it wisnae me." Annie was quite cool about it, she just said: "It's perfectly all right, Blyth. I appreciate that he's perfectly capable of doing it all by himself." Later on, when things died down, Dougal was speaking to Annie, apparently, and Annie said to Dougal: "What on earth was that performance from Blyth?" And Dougal said: "Oh, he's just accustomed to Scottish wives." '

Annie believes 'we had some fun times, some ups and downs like every interesting relationship,' while her friend Beth believes that 'Annie was always very self-contained and independent, but I always felt she needed more looking after than she let on. Some people saw her as quite tough, but in nursing I saw another side to her. She should maybe have met, and married, someone a little older.'

*   *   *

By 1973, a year of little activity for him on the mountains, it was plain that Dougal had seen the beginning of the end of his marriage, writing:

> Present state of mind is not too good. A summer of work and suppression of ambition. Contact with lots of people with character. 'Friends' made. There is also a period of dislike of people around. An analysis of my present emotional attachment shows that it is going through a period of negation. We are still friends in the true sense of the word. Yet there is a numbness of feeling inside me very often. My climbing is not being suppressed. In fact, A's attitude towards my climbing has been magnificent. No attempt at suppression. If there had been, it would have been ended long ago. It is the attempt at suppression in the mixing with other girls and general social mixing that is going to cause a break – if there is going to be a break. The nature of human relationship is such that two people must get tired and bored with each other, if they attempt to spend every available part of the day and night in each other's company. Ours is something I don't want to give up, but will if I feel that conventional norms are creeping in. If my freedom

is not impaired, it will continue. It is the best I have ever had, or am likely to have, but must give up if it impairs the chosen course of my life.

Why do people
Not understand
That a man
Who lives constantly
On the edge of the abyss
Must be difficult
To live with
On the ground?

Those decisions that one makes when climbing are often extremely difficult. There are many choices. They all involve life. Once one is taken, it has to be acted upon with everything one has. Often the same decisiveness is employed to moves on the ground. Sometimes the situation does not demand it. Often one is wrong. It's hard to steer a middle path if one is an extremist. One seldom can if one wants to stay at the extreme level. The mind must be kept at a trained pitch of hard decision.

The marriage to Annie, however, might have lasted a little longer had he not committed the cardinal sin of all libertarian relationships: he fell in love with someone else. And as so often in cases like that, Annie knew it before the other two parties did.

Ariane Giobellina, inevitably, met Dougal in the Vagabond. She came from a third-generation Italian family, and had lived in Leysin all her life. As a very young girl, she had been silent and withdrawn, an aspect of her personality with which Haston empathised, and admits that she was quite often beaten by parents for her lack of responsiveness. Like Guy Neithardt and a number of other local teenagers, she had been to the Club Vagabond while still under-age, a 15-year-old, but it was not until the summer of 1972 that she noticed Dougal in the bar.

Ariane, who was 11 years younger, says: 'I didn't know who he was, although I knew the effect he had on me. I definitely wanted to know him better. We talked, and he told me he was going away, so the first contacts were very superficial. It took a long time really. In 1972, he was going to Everest, and he told me he wouldn't be back until six months later, so I said: "OK." I thought things must take their course. Then, when he came back, I had plans to go to the Far East, and I wasn't going to change that. But, we made plans to meet in Greece, and we did. It was a secret meeting. All the rest went to Mykonos, and we met somewhere else. I knew about his marriage, but at that stage we hadn't talked about a serious relationship. In fact, he had told me it was the opposite. He was simply living for the day and, anyway, he said he wanted to try and make the marriage work. For a few months, I went less to the Vag. I went to a different pub, and he walked in there one night. I think, by then, he had time to think. For me, it was always clear from day one, but I didn't want to push anything. From then on, it was a different type of relationship. I found in Dougal a very warm human being, a caring person prepared to share himself.'

Their similarities proved one of the attractions. She believed in reincarnation, numerology and astrology, and there had always existed a mystical pocket somewhere inside Dougal. Being Scottish, he also believed in ghosts. Both were withdrawn, and in many ways troubled, and they took a great delight in slowly demolishing the barriers. Unused to the sensation of caring absolutely about someone else, Dougal attempted to dissect the relationship, and 'attempt a clinical look through a series of questions, answers or even just random statements. There is a considerable age difference – 11 years to be exact – but it does not seem to matter. Why? A) I relate very easily to younger people, and B) A relates easily to older. She has for her age a mature, if as yet undeveloped, mind – not intellectual in approach, but quick to grasp, and very difficult to fool. Would probably treat a person less mature, younger than or of a similar age, with some contempt. Could be hurt, withdrawn, but handle it inwardly, and in this way bring a remarkable similarity to myself. The year in the east caused a certain maturity to appear in an already precocious person. On return, I did not want to put the relationship together again with its only too obvious difficulties – frankly, it did not seem worth it. Then one day in late March, I woke up feeling desperate for her company. Now we relate in solitude for long periods.'

Annie, believes Ariane, had known they were in love long before they did, and there was the occasional scene. 'I would be talking to Dougal – and this is long before we got really close – in the Vagabond, and Annie would be talking to a man, and I would be thinking that this is OK for both of us when she would come over and there would be raised voices.'

When Annie finally agreed to a separation, and left to find work as a nurse in Lausanne, she believes that she got on better with Dougal than when they were married. She would visit Leysin, and they would go out for dinner. 'We were better friends apart, we still respected each other.' As for Ariane: 'I do recall a letter Dougal wrote to a mutual friend in Canada, who must have moved, and the letter came back. He had said: "Annie and I are living apart, and I am leading a monastic life." And I thought: "Monastic? Ariane?" But it is all water under the bridge between us now. We are totally amicable.'

Beth believes that 'Ariane was totally in love with him, and I think they would have gone on to have a family, and maybe turned him into more of a home animal. Ariane was a much gentler person than Annie, but Dougal loved them both in a way.' Chris Bonington says: 'Annie was longest with Dougal, but I could see why he moved on. Annie was a superb bon viveur.'

After Annie's departure, Ariane moved in with Haston at the flat in Rue du Commerce. 'He asked me to move in. He took me climbing, and I liked it from the start. One reason for the attraction was an unspoken understanding of certain things. Many times we would sit in silence, but still be able to communicate. For me, this was something deeper than happiness – it was a confirmation of what you had felt deep down.'

Dougal committed himself totally to the relationship, after the usual lengthy period of analysis. From Everest in 1975 he wrote her long letters on the official South-West Face headed notepaper, invariably beginning: 'Greetings favourite person', and he also wrote in his Science Exercise Book No. 7: 'Slid into [Camp] Four to find some pleasant letters, many from A consolidating our position. We have something.' A year later, in Squaw Valley on April 19 (his thirty-sixth birthday) and on the way to Alaska for his last major climb, he reasoned that 'there is no doubt I could spend a lot of time with her, in fact as much time as I am prepared to spend with anyone in one place at one time, and away from the mountains. Very, very tempted to teach her to climb, so that we can enjoy that part of life together. I feel she could be good – if not [it] is an experiment gone wrong without any real loss. But it is good to see the psychological barriers slowly crumble, as she realises she has met a genuine person. The slow process of this mutual happening has been pure pleasure, and remains (and shall remain).'

By then, he had stopped signing off his essays in the manner of Nietzsche's Zarathustra. Perhaps he had realised that he was a man, not superman.

IN HIGHER PLACES

The true leader is always led
– C. G. Jung

The period between 1968, when he came back from Cerro Torre in Patagonia, and 1975, when he went to Everest and he and Ariane Giobellina set up home together, was to be an extraordinary era, even by the lavish standards Dougal imposed on himself. He managed, without any discernible difficulty, to juggle the hedonistic lifestyle of Leysin, and its heavy drinking and casual seductions, with the monastic asceticism required for making new routes on high mountains. It was either ambrosia or porridge, but this had always been a life of polarity; everything attempted, and mastered, being taken to almost absurd extremes. If he had retired from climbing and taken up golf, he would have got down to scratch within two or three years. Until the appearance of Ariane, the succession of desultory relationships continued, without much effort in the way of romancing and pursuit required on his part. A close climbing friend recalls a Canadian girl approaching Dougal after an expedition and, in the manner of a male disco predator, informing him: 'You've been highly recommended to me.' Another female fan wrote from Alhambra, California, to tell him that she felt instinctively that he was her soul-mate, though they had not met. She offered to dance an Irish jig for him, and say hello in Welsh, French, Spanish or Russian. 'I am your female counterpart, free, happy and a little crazy. Oh, and I will be in Europe soon.'

His boozing was alarming, even to climbing friends who were no strangers to over-indulgence. At the Club Vagabond, he would drink himself insensible, without the need for any company, and staff became inured to the sight of him hanging on to the bar rail in an effort to stay upright. He was invariably last to leave, ushered out by the last, patient barman, in the early hours. Chic Scott remembers watching Dougal going up stairs from the bar to the main level of the club with all the dogged concentration and effort he had applied to the climb up the Summit Icefield of the Eiger. 'He had a hand on the banister and one on the wall on the other side, and he was taking about 30 seconds to a minute to negotiate one step, he was just so focused in concentration. He could barely stand up, and here he is walking. But he would not fall down.'

Allan Rankin quite often found himself carrying his friend over his shoulder down the hill to his apartment in the Rue du Commerce, and some binges lasted for days. After *The Eiger Sanction*, when everyone who had worked on the film had pockets groaning with Hollywood dollars, one bender went on for seventy-two hours, with twenty hours a day devoted to alcohol. It would begin at nine a.m. in the apartment, with Scott and Guy Neithardt and one or two others seated on the balcony in the morning sun, Cinzano and lemonade in their glasses, and the Rolling Stones or Vivaldi on the record turntable in the background. They would drink and talk until noon, then head to the Vagabond to be served hotdogs in the bar, the food washed down with a few pints of beer. At two p.m., when the bar closed, a short walk up the trails and through the meadows led to l'Horizon, a chalet/restaurant above the village, and they would sit there in the sunshine on the *terasse* and drink wine and talk until around five, when the Vagabond opened again. At seven p.m., it was back up the hill to l'Horizon and a *boeuf fondue* with the house wine and a few cognac *digestifs*, before returning to the Vagabond and a session on the house speciality: depth charges. These were pints of beer in a mug with a short glass of Drambuie dropped in – 'like a depth charge'. At two a.m., when the Vag closed, a short walk led to another nightclub, La Grenier, where the surprisingly rational party would listen to jazz and other music and, in Scott's words, 'shuffle around the dance floor a little bit. We'd drink Scotch whisky until six o'clock in the morning until they shut down, and then we'd come out in the grey morning light, and everybody would wander home, go to bed for a couple of hours, wake up and have a shower – and at nine o'clock we'd be back at Dougal's again. This went on for three days.'

Dougal also took occasionally to smoking the Euro-chic Disque

Bleus, to which Mick Burke had introduced him – holding the cigarette with exaggerated care between thumb and first two fingers, and puffing out the smoke without inhaling. Neithardt, on a bivouac on a first winter ascent on the Monch that he made with Dougal, remembers him scrounging cigarettes 'because we were awake and cold, and it was something to do'. Dougal justified his excesses with the thought that 'one cannot live at the extreme all the time; the tenseness and strain would drive one over the edge. A few weeks of easy living and female company are good training for coming ordeals. The contrast makes the eventual hardship even more appealing.'

It was only his superb fitness and a remarkable constitution that granted him almost immediate recovery from his dissipations and allowed him to get away with abusing his body in this manner (although the memory was a little hazy at times). That, and the knowledge that a bigger fix, his ultimate addiction, was always round the corner. For all the drink, late nights and women, when an expedition or major climb approached there would come a time when he would down his last pint, leave the fags on the Vagabond bar, and head off into the hills to 'walk on some muscle'. He despised running, and training invariably consisted of high-speed, solo rambles and scrambles, often heavily laden, on the hills above the village. When the time came to dig out his passport, pack his rucksack and look out the times of the flights from Geneva, he was ready.

'You could almost call Dougal a partial alcoholic,' Annie suggests. 'It was a very, very heavy drinking scene in the Vagabond. Red wine was, is, our scene, but when an expedition was coming up, then it was serious stuff. He concentrated totally on that next trip.'

After his mastery of the Alps in winter, it was time to consider the next stage of a climber's logical upward progress, and a look ahead at the greater ranges. Cerro Torre, which would be his first major expedition, struck Haston as a worthy arena in which to test himself – he had never looked on mountains as the opposition – being an unclimbed, theoretically at least, granite spire in distant Patagonia, with some formidable defences. Although just over 10,000 ft, Cerro Torre is situated on the edge of the continental ice cap of South America, and because of its most western position in the Fitzroy group, bears the brunt of the winds that sweep across the cap at up to 200mph. Its vertical rock faces become swiftly plastered in snow and ice in bad weather, and the mountain is capped by a permanent, overhanging mushroom of snow. All in all, though dwarfed by its neighbours and offering only 5000 or 6000 feet of actual climbing, it represents one of the most fearsome mountain challenges in the world.

Haston knew the history of climbing in the area – he still possessed the SMC copy of Marc Azema's *The Conquest of Fitzroy* for research – and Cerro Torre had a strange, almost mystical, aura that appealed to him. In 1959, the Italian climber Cesare Maestri had claimed a first ascent via the South-West Ridge with Austrian Toni Egger. But Egger had been killed by an avalanche, probably on the descent, and Maestri had been rescued in a delirious state near the foot of the face, half-buried in the snow of the Torre Glacier. Maestri was to claim that both had reached the summit, but there were no photographs, and he could offer only sketchy details of the technical difficulties. An earlier failure by Walter Bonatti, the greatest alpinist of his generation, and subsequent failures by other strong parties increased the scepticism, and Maestri's return, in 1970, with a compressed-air drill to bolt his way to the top for a 'second ascent' did little for the plausibility of his original story. Most of Dougal's party believed that, if they did get to the top, they would be making the legitimate first ascent.

Dougal, who rarely came up with mountaineering initiatives, had been invited to Cerro Torre by Mick Burke. The other members of the party were Pete Crew and the unknown quantity – on a major route with Dougal – in the towering form of the spectacularly laid-back, Manchester-based schoolteacher Martin Boysen who, after a spectacular entrée into the British rock-climbing scene, was making a name for himself as one of the country's leading alpinists. Jose Fonrouge, an Argentinian climber, joined the party, and the now ubiquitous Peter Gillman was there on an assignment for the *Sunday Times*, his main employers by this time. Annie, ever independent, was going along as far as Buenos Aires, from where she intended to head north to meet friends in California. Dougal was to join her after the expedition.

In Buenos Aires, Fonrouge steered the party and gear through customs in record time, and a few days were spent in the indolent pleasures of Argentina's most European city, before they set off on the journey south, initially by air in a frighteningly unstable DC3, to Comodoro Rivadavia on the coast, followed by a trek on foot to base camp close to the Torre Glacier. Horses carried the heaviest gear, the climbers humping the rest to base camp over flat, arid landscapes haunted by withered witch trees and colourless moraine. And all the while, Cerro Torre towered and mocked overhead, with not a single weakness apparent in its armoury.

Their target was the untried South-East Ridge, and Haston was to produce a performance of almost freakish drive and doggedness on the unsuccessful attempt. He carried loads up to base camp almost in a frenzy, and with Crew suffering from bronchitis, took on the workload of two men.

In his diary, but never to their faces, he railed at what he perceived to be occasional laziness in his colleagues, particularly Crew and Fonrouge, and once on the mountain, he pushed out most of the way in front. At one point, the weather kept them in base camp for thirty-seven frustrating days, and destroyed most of their fixed ropes with an ice-cave dug out on the col beneath the final tower. They were forced to fix the route again, and during one fifteen-hour day – after Dougal knocked a rock down on to Burke's head, and with Crew 'in a bit of a state, and not much use for any front work' – he produced a monumental effort of will-power and technical climbing ability to get back up to the col, with the almost certain knowledge that the attempt was doomed to failure.

As ever, there were lessons. During the enforced stay in base camp, while the others occasionally swore and cursed and huffed and puffed, Dougal concentrated on total relaxation, reasoning that there would be many more phases like this to interrupt expeditions. He managed to surprise even himself with his ability to switch off totally, reading, making notes and producing written theses on topics such as the sociology of knowledge. He was, by then, a master of the art of keeping feelings, whether of happiness or frustration, to himself. Of the expedition, he wrote: 'Sometimes, one finds it difficult to retain a sense of perspective about the ultimate objective. There are days when it seems climbing has never existed, and will never exist again.

One also finds difficulty imagining the world outside – hence, the world is a few square yards. There are no chains, but one seldom goes far from camp. Perhaps a brief look at the sky to confirm that it is really bad, and a return to the present norm. It could be called infinite boredom. It is, in a sense, that one is being forced into a state that one would not normally choose to exist in. But achievements of the end to which this period is a means will make an eventual return to the outside world more enjoyable.'

The moments of quiet introspection also produced a poem, 'Cerro Torre Pre-dawn':

> This is the time
> The time of indecision
> Here night crosses day
> And day struggles with night
> And who knows
> What will happen
> Night is history and
> Morning probable future
> Probable future may not happen
> History may never
> Have been
> Shall we always remain
> Suspended in the present?

The expedition, after one last night without food and drink on the col, and with the wind whipping spindrift over their sodden sleeping bags, decided to retreat 'like beaten soldiers from a lost battle'. Back at base it was time to reflect.

As he had done with previous failures, particularly on two setbacks on the North Face of the Matterhorn, Dougal wrestled with his conscience for a short time. Was further progress really an impossibility? Had he done everything within his power to force the climb on towards success, or had he succumbed to personal frailties? In the end, he decided that there was nothing more he could have done; he had pushed to the limit, and at once began to focus on the next objective. He headed north to meet Annie, who had been charged with the transport arrangements for the return home, and the trip ended in archetypal Haston drunken disarray: 'My job was to get two tickets back from America,' says Annie. 'He was going to make his way north. I did get two air fares, but then Dougal met this Swedish guy whose idea of breakfast was half a bottle of vodka, so it was like two parts of a magnet, and we finished up getting, guess what, the Greyhound bus back across to the east coast.'

* * *

It was while basking in sun by Yosemite's Merced River in May 1969, that Dougal learned that a Bonington application to the Nepalese government for an attempt on the unclimbed South Face of Annapurna had been approved, and he could start looking forward to his first trip to altitude, with all that entailed in hopes, fears and ambition. He had discussed the face with Bonington during one of the bivouacs on the Argentiere in the winter that year, Dougal assuming, quite rightly, that he would be an automatic choice for any major British expedition. He was Bobby Charlton to Bonington's Alf Ramsey, the first name down on any team-sheet. Though he did not, as Bonington admits, 'suffer fools gladly', the leader's careful selection process – not necessarily choosing the best climbers, but the most compatible – made it unlikely that he would run across half-wits at 26,000 feet, and as he had showed on the Eiger Direct, he had a priceless ability to stay out of the limelight and clear of the controversies that marred so many expeditions.

Bonington recognised the essential selfish nature of Haston on the hill, but also knew that he was no shirker. 'Dougal was quite happy to let others do all the organising, until he was in a position where he wanted to be. He was the ultimate prima donna, if you like, but he fitted in easily and well on expeditions, and there was never any aggro about what Dougal was doing, or not doing. He was happy to carry loads and fix rope and support other climbers, but I knew, and he knew, that eventually the time would come when you could slip the leash, and let him go.'

Compatability on climbing trips, for Bonington, usually meant known friends, and Annapurna was to see the opening bow of the Bonington Boys, the British climbing élite of the Himalaya who were always in the newspapers or on television, giving public lectures using their pooled selection of slides, and contributing to the inevitable expedition book. With sponsorship for expeditions at a premium, the Bonington Boys, in many ways, had cornered a very limited market, and they were regarded with less than total affection by the climbing hoi polloi, though this may have had more to do with jealousy than any other factor.

On Annapurna, as well as Haston, Burke and Boysen, Bonington chose Nick Estcourt, an old climbing friend and near-neighbour in Altrincham, and Mike Thompson, another chum from Sandhurst. There was also a base camp manager, a Gurkha signals officer named Kelvin Kent, and a doctor/support climber, Dave Lambert. Bonington's agent, George Greenfield, had also canvassed for a leading American climber to be included, for considerations not far removed from the demands of sponsorship and selling the expedition book's US rights. Tom Frost, a leading Yosemite Big Wall practitioner and known and admired in Europe as the softly-spoken, unsung hero of the South Face of the Fou, was approached, and accepted. According to Frost, Dougal had also played a role in his selection: 'I met Dougal in Yosemite in 1969, and he's the man that talked me into going on that trip when he was over here. I thought I'd give it a go, and he said: "Frost, get up there." And he showed me the picture of the face, and talked me into coming, and I'm really grateful that he did that. The climb was sort of overdue, for me. I had been doing a fair amount of climbing and mountaineering since the early 1960s, and so here I was finally saying: "OK, I gotta get serious about life." '

Frost, a Mormon, eschewed cigarettes, drink and bad language – sins practised, to a greater or lesser degree, by all the other expedition members – but he managed to get on well with everyone. Dougal, in particular, was intrigued by the old Mormon concept of non-monogamy. 'The Brits were a wild bunch,' says Frost. 'But there wasn't too much of that going on really, because we were all pretty impressed by the size of the mountain, and we worked together quite well. Anyway, in my mind, that wasn't a very big issue.'

Some of the other members had been led to believe that it was the American's first trip to the Himalaya, but without publicising the fact, he had climbed with Sir Edmund Hillary (when plain Ed) in

1963 on Tagar. There was also a fabulous rumour still doing the rounds that he had worked for the CIA, erecting listening posts in the Nanda Devi sanctuary to monitor potential Chinese nuclear activity over the border, a tale that Frost does not exactly deny: 'Those are great stories,' he responds enigmatically. The deputy leader was to be Don Whillans, who could also have been considered a friend of Bonington at one time, the men having co-operated in a remarkably productive climbing partnership in the early 1960s. This culminated in the first ascent of the Central Pillar of Freney on Mont Blanc and a successful expedition to the Central Tower of Paine in Patagonia in 1963, but since that time the relationship had gone gradually downhill. Bonington grabbed the plum of the first British ascent of the North Face of the Eiger – the climb that brought him to public prominence – after several attempts with Whillans, and Bonington still believes he was not forgiven for that. There were other problems. From his days in the 1950s as a lithe, gymnastic rock climber, who was one of the finest British exponents, by 1970 Whillans had deteriorated into a caricature of the flat-capped, abrasive, beer-swilling Northerner with a cryptic answer for anything and, if that didn't work, an equally effective pair of fists. In that time, too, he had watched with ill-concealed scorn as Bonington rose from the fresh-faced novice of his early alpine days to his position as the ultimate climbing entrepreneur, in the eyes of Whillans motivated purely by money.

Whillans had also been written off a dozen times as a mountaineering force, but had always managed to confound critics in the end. On Annapurna, stimulated by the drive and ambition of Haston, he was to do so again, he and the Scot forming a partnership similar to that of Hollywood's favourite Western theme: the aged sheriff and his feisty young deputy cleaning up the town. Or, in this case, the mountain. They were happy to use each other, and feed off their individual disparities without coming even remotely close to friendship. The differences in personality, physique and temperament were obvious, but both were driven by the same motive: climbing a mountain and getting back down again in one piece. As so many observers have pointed out, they did make an unlikely pair, but the same is true of virtually every successful climbing partnership: Harlin and Haston, Jimmy Marshall and Robin Smith, Tasker and Renshaw, Messner and Habeler, Bonington and virtually anyone. Probably the only roped pairing who looked, acted and spoke alike were the identical Burgess twins, Alan and Adrian.

Bonington says: 'On Annapurna, I believe Dougal saw Don as an invaluable mentor – for that stage of his climbing career. If you climbed with Don, you resigned yourself to do most of the cooking, and Dougal led every single pitch until the last day. He took all the pressure, all the weight off, as Don got fitter and fitter. And then, of course, on the last day, Don just took off and left Dougal behind.'

Dave Agnew believes that, for a couple of years at least, Dougal – who referred to the older man as 'Dad', Whillans calling the Scot 'Jimmy' – thought of Whillans as the greatest mountaineer in the world. 'Dougal said to me: "Whillans is the man." I think that takes a bit humility to do that, and you don't hear too many mountaineers of that calibre, or who have been in the kind of situations Dougal had been in, admitting that. There was this compassion about Don, which a lot of people don't often attribute to him. On Annapurna, and on Everest later, when they ran short of food, it was Don who would open up the last can or tin of pâté, and say: "Here you go, Jimmy, you eat this." Don survived on tea and cigarettes, and as far as Dougal is concerned, he told me later that Whillans saved his skin. He looked after Dougal.'

Haston was fond of telling the story about Whillans picking up a copy of Tolkien's *Lord of the Rings* during the Everest expedition in 1971 and snorting 'Fucking fairies' when asked his opinion, and he also liked to portray Whillans as a man for whom climbing was a job of work, like clocking in on the factory floor. 'Don didn't have a romantic thought in his head,' said Dougal. 'To him, you get the job, you are sent out to do it, and you do it the best you can.'

But Whillans enjoyed the stimuli of mountain countries and travelling, and was interested in his surroundings and different people. He got on famously, for example, with the Sherpas on every Himalaya expedition he was on, and once returned to his home in Rawtenstall, Lancashire, from Rawalpindi by motorcycle after an expedition to Trivor, simply to broaden his horizons. This was in 1961, and involved a 7000-mile trip through Pakistan, Iran, Turkey and Yugoslavia, and he managed it all without a single punch-up, though it was a close thing at times. No one could picture Dougal, at least in the early 1970s, undertaking a journey like that.

Whillans also had one thing that Dougal lacked: experience of the Himalaya and altitude. Dougal, like Burke, Boysen and Estcourt, had been no higher than Mont Blanc, and the overriding fear in the back of his mind as the expedition approached was that he would not cope with altitude, and find himself unable to acclimatise. 'I feel ready for a move to the bigger challenge, but I can also imagine my despair if I find my years of experience suddenly invalidated by some physio-logical defect. The thought keeps coming back, and there will be no solution until I am actually on the mountain,' he wrote in December 1969. He also dreaded pre-expedition injury, and decided to under-take no winter climbing early in 1970 – departure month for Annapurna was March – for fear of frostbite. Training was skiing in the powder snow above Leysin, but even this was done within circumspect limits. He could not afford a broken leg.

Whillans, in contrast, believed his training began on the walk-in, and undertook no physical exercise whatsoever, apart from the short walk from his house to the pub in Rawtenstall. But it worked for him, and he had proved himself a dozen times over at altitude. He was also one of the most safety-conscious climbers. Dave Bathgate, for one, said he would have trusted Whillans with his life. 'Dougal probably had much more in reserve stamina-wise than most other guys, but Whillans was the one I always thought was in control. I would have followed that guy anywhere. He was always weighing the job up, and what the odds were. Maybe Dougal learned a lot from Don in that respect. They were a good team, both with a dry sense of humour, and both with the same type of drive. I don't know if it was a love of hills, or just like doing a job and going home again, because neither ever let on about their motivations.'

Mike Thompson who, as a social anthropologist, found plenty of casework in the company of the climbers on his two major Himalaya expeditions, Annapurna and Everest '75, and wrote some bitingly witty Tom Patey-esque observations on both, was amazed by the amount of time Whillans spent at Annapurna base camp, simply gazing up at the South Face for hours at a time, working out the fall lines of the avalanches and potential sites for camps free from objective danger.

Annapurna was to prove the metaphorical high point of Whillans' career. He was the first man to the top via the South Face, as it turned out, and one of the few Himalaya climbers operating at the highest standard to die in his bed.

The south face of Annapurna, the tenth-highest mountain in the world and the first 8000m peak to be climbed, was a logical extension of a climb like Eiger Direct, with a small team committed to a large face. There could be little Sherpa support in the way of load-carrying on such a technically difficult route, and lead climbers would have to muck in and ferry supplies up and down the face. The equipment was superb and, helped by sponsorship from the Mount Everest Foundation and the largesse of Thames TV, who were sending a camera crew and reporter, the Annapurna team of 1970 lacked for nothing. There were double boots with Neoprene over-boots and a made-to-measure Mountain Equipment full down suit per person. The revolutionary square-frame tent invented by Whillans, and marketed as the Whillans Box, was one of the main reasons – the others being a Whillans prototype climbing harness, a range of waterproofs bearing his name and the odd rucksack design – that 'working-class' Don was able justifiably to declare that he never did any work.

On the walk-in, with little in the way of organisational logistics to worry about, and able to attune his mind to the task ahead and the business of getting fitter by the day, Dougal began to feel more confident by the minute, despite the prospect of the most technically difficult Himalayan climb ever attempted. The trek to base camp was passed in the routine to which Dougal's companions were to become accustomed over the next three years. He would rise and breakfast with the expedition en masse, then take off alone along the trail winding over easy foothills from Pokhara and up through the breathtaking Modi Khola gorge into the vast mountain-ringed amphitheatre of the Annapurna Sanctuary. In 1970, this was not the densely populated trek it was later to become – Nepal had re-opened its doors to mountaineers in 1968 after a four-year ban – and Dougal, with his colleagues as much as four miles behind daily, enjoyed the solitude of the bamboo and rhododendron forests and the distant views of Machapachure and Hiunchuli, which guard the entrance to the sanctuary, and glimpses of the high, glacial basin that was to be the site of base camp. When the others arrived at a designated spot for lunch or dinner, they would find Dougal already there, in his other accustomed expedition mode: flat on his back reading a book or writing. Bonington thought he had already acquired one of the prerequisites of Himalayan climbing, energy-conservation bordering on total indolence.

Whillans, however, had mastered this art long beforehand, and Dougal was soon to discover on the face that his new mentor applied the same principles of doing as little as possible to the business of climbing. Any partner of Whillans tended to find the workload divided unequally. Doug Scott, Haston's future climbing partner, recalls a day on the international expedition to Everest in 1972 when, having pushed the route ahead and almost exhausted himself, he returned to find Whillans in the tent, trimming his beard. 'Dougal learned a lot from Whillans, particularly about pacing himself,' smiles Scott, not without affection. 'One day in 1972, I went up to Camp Five on my own, solo to 26,000ft, and was coming back down the ropes, and I shouted to him: "Get a brew on." I got back and, of course, he hadn't made any effort whatsoever, so I finished up not only brewing, but making the meal as well. I passed it over, and said as sarcastically as I could: "I'm not your bloody wife, you know", and I'll never forget his reply as long as I live: "You're not one of these people who moan about a bit of cooking are you?" Dougal would certainly have to do the cooking with Don, but at that stage of his climbing development, he'd be happy to play second fiddle.'

In his role of deputy, Whillans had been sent ahead by Bonington to reconnoitre the climbing difficulties and, in between sweeps of the face with his binoculars, had managed to spot, first some giant footprints at around 14,000ft, and then a shadowy, pedestrian figure which he took to be the Yeti. This discovery produced some pleasing early excitement for the Thames TV crew, and a few headlines for the newspapers back home, as well as adding a few more pages to that thick volume entitled 'Don Whillans' Book of Tall Stories.' But he had done his work astutely on the reconnaissance, and his customary, detailed analysis broke it down into five segments: a lower icefall, an upper icefall, a forbidding ice ridge, and the rock band and summit cliffs. He believed that six or seven camps would be needed on the face.

Whillans and Dougal were paired from the start, and despite a lot of spring snow, they soon established Camp Two at around 17,600ft, where what looked reasonably easy ground led to the big couloir. Evidence of the Whillans mountain nous was demonstrated almost immediately, when huge powder-snow avalanches rushed past all night without touching the chosen site. Dougal was also happy to note that, having pushed up to close to 20,000ft next day, he had not suffered problems with the altitude. Frost and Burke also made a strong team initially, and the climb was pushed out swiftly to Camp Five. But, as Dougal had predicted before the start, personal ambitions then started to intrude. Boysen and Estcourt exhausted themselves cracking the ice ridge, as did Burke and Frost on the rock band. The load-carrying took its toll, too, and the party suddenly began to seem very small. When Bonington decided to send Haston and Whillans to the front, out of order, to speed things up, there was a long and acrimonious radio conversation between camps, with Bonington finally pulling rank – and pushing his big guns out ahead.

The incident, and the resulting acrimony, left a large imprint on the memory of Frost, one of the few who could honestly claim to be a recreational climber. A man noted for his conciliatory, easy-going nature, he was surprised by the dichotomy of individual goals mixed uneasily with the overall concept of close teamwork, and he says: 'I wasn't over there as a professional climber, like many of the others. I recognised that, with a number of the climbers, it was really important to them how they came out in the public eye. On the mountain it was an important issue for them, whereas I was just there as a member of a team to climb a mountain. There was a television crew there, and Mick was the cameraman for up high, but every time we came down to base camp, we'd be interviewed. It was a matter of who climbed well and did well, and who reached the summit, and this and that. Just like climbers today, they need to have the media coverage to get sponsorship. I was just a recreational climber. I recognised the difference as we went through the expedition; by this time, I saw that I was there really for different reasons than a lot of the others. It just sort of came up, when we had that controversy about who was going to go out front. The ice ridge was below the rock band, and at that point I was climbing with Mick, and we all just took on a regular rotation. It was a privilege to be leading rather than carrying. That was the main activity that had to go on, and we all spent most of our time doing that. It was a controversy. I mean it was about the only controversy that we had, and it was a matter of experience. I favoured the idea that everybody got treated equally, and you went out in front when your rotation came up. That's just the way I was looking at it. Others obviously disagreed.'

As was to be the case so often in the future, Whillans was seen as the culprit, the lead-hogger, with Haston cast in the role of the unwitting accomplice. But Dougal didn't care a jot for the opinion of others: 'We are simply going better than any other pair, and they should all realise that. Mick and Nick are both suffering with altitude, and Martin has an infection, probably caused by cut hands failing to heal. People should realise we are a long way from the top and, in the end, it will prove to be the right decision.' Right decision or not, there was still a major confrontation, which almost led to blows, between the pugnacious little Lancastrians, Whillans and Burke, on the walk-out, and he, Estcourt and Boysen never totally forgave Whillans. They were, however, to have a form of redress within two years.

Haston's drive and ability on his first Himalaya trip also made a big impression on Frost, and no one could ever have accused the Scot of not doing his fair share of work. The ultimate accolade came from the Sherpas, according to the American. Frost, who has a strange habit of speaking of everyone, dead or alive, in the present tense, says: 'I really was impressed that the Sherpas had the greatest respect for Dougal. They saw that he was a man that was stronger than they were, and that was really unusual. He received a tremendous respect from the Sherpas, who understand stuff like that. He was willing to do all that kind of work that they specialised in and, of course, that's what it was essentially about on the majority of the trips. When I am with him, he is very quiet, very introspective, and he doesn't make with small talk: the strong, silent type. It doesn't bother me because I don't talk myself. I don't make small talk. We could go for days without talking, and be quite happy. He makes a very strong focus, on what he's doing, and he is very strong physically. He'll put up with anything or anybody. He's just a businessman when it comes to climbing, and he's very good at it. I'd say that he and Don are an excellent combination.'

Even with the Big Two in front, the successful ascent of the South Face of Annapurna was still a marginal thing, and turned into a desperate race with the approaching monsoon. Most mornings were as cold as either man could recall anywhere, and it snowed most afternoons, making climbing an impossibility. Any upward progress became a test of dogged perseverance, with Dougal doing all the trail-breaking through fresh, soft snow – and the cooking every night.

Dougal wondered if his willpower, despite all the training, would last, writing: 'It's a case of one leg after the other, what a senseless existence. W behind me, but unable or unwilling to go to the front. It's too much to hope, I suppose, that he will ever actually get his fucking finger out, and make a brew. Too late to change now. Funny, but in a way I relish being out in front all the time. If my will lasts, my body can. At times, I question my sanity. This is what I have worked for all my life, but where is the pleasure? The happiness, I know, will come later, but how long will it last?'

Once, setting out from Camp Five, he dropped his rucksack containing all his personal gear for Camp Six, but he knew better than to waste valuable energy in swearing or feeling sorry for himself, and simply swung back down the ropes to find a spare sleeping bag and food. He and Whillans survived for four days above the rock band on raisins and porridge in the case of Dougal, Whillans managing on cigar smoke. But on May 27, the mountain cracked just before they did, the weather brightening sufficiently to allow an early start, and one last attempt to establish Camp Seven. As it turned out, they sensed they were near enough to the summit to make it in one push. A short snow ridge led to the final 800ft of mixed ground, and with Dougal carting the redundant tentage and also having problems with a crampon strap, Whillans forged on ahead for the first time towards the summit ridge, visible through swirling cloud a short distance ahead. When Dougal got there a few minutes later, his partner, the ultimate climbing pragmatist, was already preparing the abseil. There were no words, not even congratulations.

On the way down, they met Frost and Burke on their way up for their summit attempt. Words, wrote Dougal, seemed superfluous. 'I did not envy them, and they undoubtedly envied us.' Dougal found it hard to even wish them luck, and contented himself with describing the route. With yet another storm imminent and both men almost wiped out by the labours of carrying loads and lead-climbing, he didn't give much for their chances, and he was right; Burke sat down in the snow just above Camp Six, and Frost didn't get much further.

Bonington ordered the evacuation of the mountain, but with the expedition over, Ian Clough was killed by a serac fall just below Camp Two. He and Thompson had been on their way down, and though the latter ran clear, his companion had no chance. As the film crew filmed what they thought would be the routine arrivals back at base, Thompson staggered weeping into the camp, producing some horribly memorable footage. The expedition left for the trek back to civilisation on the same day as the funeral, just below Base Camp.

* * *

Haston was fond of Ian Clough. He had done some of his best climbing in the Dolomites with him, and the Englishman was one of those rarities: a cutting-edge climber who managed to get on with everyone. In Scotland, it had once been fashionable to sneer at Clough for his over-indulgences in aid – his ascent of Point Five Gully on Ben Nevis in 1959 had taken five days – and the standing joke in Glencoe was that, if you wanted some free gear, you just went out and de-pegged a Clough route. Dougal had found in Clough and his wife Nikki invaluable support in the wake of the Glencoe accident – the couple had a cottage in the village – but Dougal also knew that along the course he had set for himself, there would be casualties. The lesson of Clough's death was not lost on him: after two months spent on the face and with Annapurna eventually 'conquered', the mountain had had the last word. It was a scenario that was to become horribly familiar in many subsequent Himalayan expeditions, and Dougal determined never to let his guard down. As for his success on the peak, it seemingly took him no closer to solving the great mysteries: where he was going? Why was he going there? Where would it all end? But he resolved to continue the search, writing on arrival back in Kathmandu a week later: 'Annapurna is already in the past, and it seems as though there has been a metamorphosis. I now aim to write and analyse much more. I have gone casually through life too long. I often have unique experiences. I must attempt to analyse. Too simply have I analysed my motives for climbing. I must now set down my states of mind on important occasions, to see if I can come closer to solving the puzzle.'

*   *   *

There were other, less metaphysical matters to concern him, in particular the damaging physiological effects of performing at altitude. He returned to Leysin over a stone lighter than he had set out, and was to discover within the next few years that climbing above 25,000ft was, for him at least, a tightrope walk between maintaining sufficient body weight and strength with what little food was available and total enervation. His willingness to take himself over the limit did not help, and twice on Everest, in particular, film cameras were to capture him in a state of almost total collapse, while his colleagues, the bulkier Whillans and former rugby forward Scott, appeared untouched. Whillans, who could justify his valley excesses and aversion to any sort of training with his own unique qualification for Himalaya climbing – 'Try and start off twenty pounds overweight' – looked positively sylph-like after long spells at altitude. Scott, who weighed more than thirteen stones, also had more in reserve. Dougal, with far less superfluous flesh to spare and a high metabolic rate, would come back looking emaciated and sickly. This, and the fact that not everyone on his large-scale expeditions always pulled their weight, was something he came almost to resent. It does not require much detective work to work out the villain of this piece in his autobiography, written after Annapurna: 'Usually thin and very fit, I need food like a racing car needs petrol. If I don't get it, I lose a lot of weight, which I can ill afford. It's fine to starve for a week or two, but it is damaging over the long type of haul we were on. There are various theories on the kind of condition one should be in when going to the Himalaya.

Some favour going completely unfit, and slowly getting fit towards the end of the expedition; the only trouble with this kind of thinking is that those who pursue it rely for long periods on the ones who are fit initially. It's almost a parasitic feeling to have someone dogging your footsteps, knowing you are going to get weaker, while the person behind is getting stronger, and is probably going to come through better in the end. Someone has to do it to ensure progress, otherwise everyone would be sitting at base trying to outmanoeuvre each other in not breaking trail. I have always gone in good shape and lasted right through, doing a lot of leading, which is the most exhausting, on the mountain, but in the end have been right on the limit. Others play more cautious games.'

*   *   *

Back in Leysin after Annapurna, the pounds came back on swiftly with a few desultory months with ISM and in the Vagabond before preparation began for his next test, the ultimate one. If he thought self-interest had blighted Annapurna, he was soon to discover that the bigger the mountain, the larger the ego. The combination of the highest peak and some of the loftiest conceits in the world was to prove disastrous in 1971.

The South-West Face of Everest had been attempted twice by Japanese expeditions, in 1969 and 1970, and the projected 1971 international expedition had had a chequered history, even before the climbers set off for base camp in March of that year. Bonington and Haston had first discussed an attempt as far back as 1966, when both were in a London hospital recovering from frostbite suffered on Eiger Direct. By chance, their doctor there was Michael Ward, the medic on the successful 1953 expedition, and though they asked Ward to consider leading an attempt, the idea was overtaken by more attainable projects.

Others also had ambitions for the face, however, most notably a group of Norwegian and British climbers who had met on the Troll Wall in Romsdal, Norway, in 1965. In the first flush of friendship, they had conceived plans for a lightweight trip to the Antarctic, and from there ambitions grew and grew until they were discussing first an attempt on Nanga Parbat's Rupal Flank, and then Everest's South-

West Face. Colonel Jimmy Roberts, a retired Gurkha officer who ran a trekking business in Nepal, became involved at the Kathmandu end. Roberts, who had played a major role in Norman Dhyrenfurth's successful American West Ridge expedition in 1963, took on the role of leader, but gradually the project became more and more engorged, and when Roberts independently received a letter from Dhyrenfurth inviting him to join another South-West Face expedition, a merger was inevitable. A small trip to climb in the Antarctic had, in five years, metamorphosed into an attempt on the highest, unclimbed wall in the world, but these things do happen in a sport fed by aspiration, and not always by logic. The intimacy inherent in the original ideal had gone, too, and when Dhyrenfurth and Roberts began to assemble a team, they found they were bringing together a small army of strangers, many of whom had not climbed together before, and who couldn't even find a common language.

None of this bothered Dougal, who was happy to be wafted along in the trail of the organisers and fund-raisers, with the certain knowledge that, within a couple of months, he would once again be out in front where he belonged. Confronted by the fallibilities of others, he could afford tolerance because they were never going to get in the way of his personal objectives. And anyway, as Bonington has noted after Annapurna, 'he seemed more relaxed with others. He had reached a sort of establishment position, and he was far easier company. Personally, I always found him easy to get on with, but there were areas that were closed before Annapurna. After that, for someone to go out on a big mountain and climb with, you couldn't really ask for anyone better.'

Bonington and Haston had been sounded out as early recruits for the 1971 expedition, which was billed as 'international' less for the desire to foster global goodwill than the need to raise finanace from any source for such a massive project. Bonington, who was to be Dhyrenfurth's climbing leader, accepted twice and withdrew twice, the second time finally. Dougal accepted without conditions.

Dhyrenfurth's plans for the mountain, however, turned out to be even more grandiose and idealistic. Leader of the ground-breaking American expedition of 1963, which saw four Americans on the summit and an astonishing traverse of the mountain up the West

Ridge and the down the South Col route – by Thomas Hornbein and Willy Unsoeld – he wanted to split the party, with half attempting the South-West Face and the other a new, direct line up the West Ridge. Dhyrenfurth's reasoning was based on the fact that, as both had a similar starting point, they could share initial work through the Khumbu Icefall before diverting to their individual objectives. If he succeeded on both, it would be hailed as the most outstanding feat in Himalayan climbing history.

To Dougal, the attraction was in the Face route. The mountain still awaited a first British (and Scottish) ascent, but the West Ridge had been climbed before, and the South Col route, pioneered by John Hunt's expedition 18 years earlier, was an unworthy challenge. Even the face, judging by the photographs he was shown by Roberts in the Shanker Hotel in Kathmandu en route home after Annapurna, appeared to be a line without aesthetic appeal. It was essentially a long snow/ice slope set at about 45 degrees, with a vertical rock band above that, and some mixed ground to the summit. If Dougal was disappointed with the potential technical challenge on offer, however, he rationalised that the logistical problems, with the altitude, capricious post-monsoon weather conditions and the juicy-looking Rock Band at three-quarters height, would be sufficient test for his mettle. He would also have to learn a new discipline, that of climbing with oxygen, with the Rock Band starting at around the height of the Annapurna summit. It was, after all, Everest.

Dougal again skied hard all winter in the Alps to prepare himself, but again without risking frostbite on an alpine winter route, and if he needed any help with his motivation, it was provided by regular chatty newsletters sent out by Dhyrenfurth in the months preceding the start date. In February, the final missive arrived with a space at the bottom for each one to nominate his chosen route on Everest, for all the world like choosing direct debit or cheque for paying the gas bill. This was not binding, however, in the democratic and relaxed background that Dhyrenfurth was attempting to create, and the final composition of the various parties was to be decided on the way to the mountain. The demarcation lines were drawn on the long walk-in. Many of the egos – in particular, French government deputy Pierre Mazeaud, veteran Italian explorer and climber Carlo Mauri, and the Swiss husband and wife team Michel and Yvette Vaucher – opted for the West Ridge. Haston and Whillans, with Americans John Evans, Gary Colliver and Dr Dave Peterson, Austrian Leo Schlommer and Toni Hiebeler of Germany, put their ticks in the Face box, as did the Japanese, Naomi Uemura and Reiso Ito, who had replaced his countryman Konishi, a veteran of the two previous South-West Face attempts who had failed to heed Dougal's example and was undergoing mass amputations of fingers and toes in the wake of a 12-day ascent of the Walker Spur that winter.

There was also the obligatory media crew, in the shape of veteran war correspondent Murray Sayle of the *Sunday Times* and the BBC, who had supplied a large chunk of the funds. Driven by this media interest, great ambitions were in the air. Dougal had met most of the expedition at the Shanker Hotel in mid-February, and though hardly a Himalaya veteran, he professed himself astonished by the naïvety of some of the assumptions about the climb. There was talk of BBC cameras on the summit, even from the non-climbing sound man. The Vauchers would be the first man/wife team to climb the mountain, and since there were 33 climbers from 13 different countries, there were opportunities for several more 'firsts'. 'The climb already seems a fait accompli,' wrote Dougal. 'Too few of the people here simply do not realise what they are up against.'

In Kathmandu, Dougal managed to make himself scarce for the two weeks required to pack and unpack the several tons of boxes and stores, hand out and fit most of the gear and sort out the food. Finally, the expedition got into its ponderous gear, the whole massive column of porters, climbers and media leaving Kathmandu on February 28. On the approach, Dougal went straight out to point, as usual, but this time he had some competition dogging his heels: the American doctor Dave Peterson, who also fancied himself as a speed merchant and fitness feak. Dougal had failed to heed one lesson of Annapurna, and refused to pace himself, and the other members would often arrive to find the pair at the day's campsite, sweating but still determinedly bending and stretching and indulging in callisthenics. John Cleare, the BBC climbing cameraman, says: 'Walking into Everest, they would be way ahead, and you would come across one or both down by the river at the next camp doing exercises. Most of us were quite happy to get fit gradually on the walk-in, but it seemed like a trial of strength with them.' Dougal wrote on March 20: 'I seem to spend a lot of the time walking alone, or lying thinking and dreaming. The climb still seems very distant. One good thing is that I seem to be in as a good a state, mentally and physically, as last year [Annapurna]. The two weeks in Kathmandu seemed to help me slow down from the European way of life. Himalayan face climbing is totally new to most of the team, and Whillans and I and Uemura are the only people who have a real conception of what things are going to be like. The thing cannot be managed from the ground, nor can the face be led by anyone who is not completely in tune with the problems. I envisage some difficulty in these regions. The equipment is old-fashioned – I think most of the climbers are, too. I am so glad to have the experience of Annapurna behind me. If my body can stand it again, I know that my mind can take it. The little man has arrived, and it looks as though we should be able to make a good team again, despite his reactionary opinions. I seem to have gone so far away to the other side, tolerance for me now is a very easy thing, as long as there is no direct-contact stupidity. One simply does not want to go too deeply into the problems of the group. The famous South Face of Lhotse is rather disappointing: it doesn't appeal much as a future objective, very nondescript, although undoubtedly difficult.'

Three days short of Base Camp, Whillans arrived with Mazeaud, and with them came the first reminder that the expedition could have problems. Relations between the former Salford plumber and the member of the French Assembly were cool, to say the least. In August 1961, Whillans had snatched the plum route in the Alps, the Central Pillar of Freney on Mont Blanc, a few weeks after a major epic on the mountain involving Walter Bonatti, Mazeaud and a mixed Franco/ Italian group. Four men had died on the descent in a storm and, for some unaccountable reason, Mazeaud believed this gave him or Bonatti a prior claim to the first ascent. When Whillans 'defiled the graves of our colleagues', he was never forgiven by Mazeaud, and the old Whillans syndrome re-surfaced. Bonington, Clough and a Polish climber, Jan Dlugoz, were also on the first ascent with a strong French party hard on their heels but, as always, it was Whillans who bore the brunt of the approbation. A decade later, the mutual animosity and distrust between the Frenchmen and the Englishman was still apparent, and was to play a significant role in the expedition's eventual disintegration.

The Face and Ridge routes were the same as far as Camp Two in the Western Cwm and, theoretically, both teams would work together, particularly through the initial obstacle, the Khumbu Icefall. But at Base Camp on April 4, there were more indications that Dhyrenfurth, an urbane, worldy man, and 'joint leader' with Jimmy Roberts, was possibly too diplomatic to make the harsh decisions needed on an expedition like this, and was already losing what little grip he had on proceedings. Instead of climbing leaders, he appointed 'co-ordinators', with Evans in charge of the Face route, and the Austrian Wolfgand Axt in nominal charge of the Ridge. But Axt was hardly the convivial, easy-going climber prototype. He was into yoga, would do handstands before breakfast, and was also a vegetarian. Bizarrely, he had been put in charge of food by Dhyrenfurth. Evans was a gentle, kindly soul who found it hard to make enemies, but the likelihood of, say, Whillans bowing to the wishes of a man with minimal experience of hard climbing at altitude was remote. The Indian climber Harsh Bahaguna, too, earned sneering approbation, from Mazeaud and the Vauchers, in particular, for his obvious lack of technique on ice. Vaucher wondered what he was doing there, but he was there, of course, for the same reason as the other 13 nationalities – the need to raise finance from as many sources as possible. In fact, Bahaguna, who had been to 28,000ft on the South Col route, put in a strong performance early on.

Whillans, Uemura, Mauri and Haston were first into the tottering wasteland of creaking seracs, and soon ran into problems. Dougal told his diary: 'The second day of exploration [in the icefall] with Naomi was a wild trip lottery in tottering, heat-filled seracs: one or twice, ominous cracks sent a quick shiver floating round the spine. It's a strange objective danger situation – there's no use getting panicky because even a little one can do the trick. I hope there will be a push through to Camp One tomorrow, and that I will be in the van. The party as a whole seems to be working well together, but the main trouble seems to be lack of experience and wild ideas from certain parties. On the days that the inexperienced go ahead, there is always indecision, and people are wanting to try new ideas because they are frightened, and it's obvious they are frightened. Whillans is pessimistic, but mainly because he is suffering from vertigo. But I still have high hopes for the international aspect. I find myself more and more in a lead position because of ability and know-how. Last year taught me a hell of a lot, and a combination of this and the professionalism I have attained in the last few years seems to be making a fair to middling Himalayan mountaineer out of the kiddy. A fair degree of ruthless thinking is needed – something you know me capable of. So many people here seem incapable of making positive decisions by themselves, they are always looking to others for guidance – this I find strange in such high-class mountaineers. Even though one of the youngest, I find myself being turned to for opinion and advice – which is fine by me. Some of the older ones are humble enough to ask for advice. I don't know if I have this ability!'

On April 5, after two weeks in an icefall even more hazardous than normal, Camp Two was established, and the two teams split up. Dougal examined the face for the first time at close quarters. It looked promising, with a good covering of snow over the lower rocks and, as usual, Dougal broke it down mentally into climbable sections. From around the 6500m mark, the initial wide, steep flank of ice and rock from the Western Cwm narrowed at 7000m into an increasingly steepening couloir, the Central Gully, which ended in the 400m of the Rock Band. Above the Rock Band, the difficulties looked as though they might ease, with snow slopes alternating with short rock sections. The Rock Band would obviously provide the crux, though Japanese attempts in 1969 and 1970 had postulated that one or more gullies would cut through the band with relatively moderate climbing. Much would depend on the build-up of snow in the gully.

By April 18, Dougal's early confidence was fading somewhat. There was a backlog of supplies at Camp One, at the head of the icefall, and radio contact with the various leaders was proving problematic. There were mutterings about rotating leads, but no one turned up at Camp Two to take over. The Haston-Whillans Japanese quartet were forcing the pace without tangible support from below. Some of his companions' performances were also falling far short of Dougal's high ideals. The Austrian Schlommer, in particular, aroused the wrath of both Britons, with his complaining nature and prima-donna attitude; at times he expected a Sherpa to be employed to carry his personal gear.

Dougal wrote in a barely suppressed fury: 'The day before my thirty-first birthday, and I have just finished a two-week spell above Base, where Whillans and I reached a height of 25,000ft on the face. When it's cloudy, it's like Siberia, but when the sun is out, it's like Blackpool or a Himalayan Calanques. Food is pretty crap – I force myself to eat. Whillans eats fuck all, which isn't making him any faster but, as usual, you can't tell him. The others, except the Japs, don't seem to have the sense of urgency that this bloody problem needs. Already our team seems very small. Hiebeler, I think, is fucked. He is just not acclimatising at all. Schlommer is lazy, and seems to be wanting to be carried to the top – as I've said before, a typical, dull, plodding Teuton. Of the Americans, John Evans is a really good guy, but may fuck himself by doing too many trivial things. Also doesn't have the experience for the job. The other two OK, but I don't think determined to shine climbing-wise. Whillans seems to be taking more time to acclimatise this year, but the old will is still there. Both Japs – good climbers and competent. I came down to Base because you really can't rest at Advance – too high at 21,500ft. Whillans opted to stay up because he's too lazy to come down. It should be interesting to see the comparison in performances.'

In Camp Two one night, having seen at close hand the capabilities of the other members of the expedition and the state of the mountain, Haston and Whillans had conducted a hypothetical sweep, half-jokingly working out who was favourite for the 'chop'. On Dougal's birthday, April 19, he learned that their ghoulish jesting had become horrible reality. He wrote: 'My birthday but a sad one. There has been a weather sock in, and last night Harsh Bahaguna, Indian member, died from exhaustion and exposure while descending from Camp Three to Camp Two. Don't know the full details, but he had been up for two weeks pushing himself hard. Awaiting details in still atrocious weather of what to do with body. Sincerely hope they opt for burial in the Western Cwm, as it will save a full-scale rescue in very bad conditions. Hope to hell this snow doesn't keep up, otherwise we're in trouble.'

Dougal, who had pushed the Face route almost up to Camp Four, near the top of the couloir, had gone back down to the relative luxury of Base Camp, with its foam mattresses, tea brewed by Sherpas and lavish meals when the bad weather arrived, and he heard the full story only later, although sketchy details came in over the radio from time to time. Bahaguna and Axt had been at Camp Three when the storm – so severe it was to last for ten days – blew in. Without waiting for the weather to clear, they decided to head back to Camp Two, and compounded the error by not staying together. But there were other circumstances which contributed to the tragedy. The West Ridge team had had trouble establishing a route from Camp Two in the Western Cwm to their Camp Three just below the ridge proper, mainly because of the snow conditions, but also because of the indecision that Haston had noticed earlier. Initially, the Norwegians Odd Eliassen and John Teigland with Bahaguna had tried to climb directly out of the Western Cwm to the ridge, but the technical difficulties defeated them. When Vaucher and Axt took a turn in front, they found an icefall blocking the line up to the ridge and, unable to climb this, they made a detour by a descent, a traverse below the obstacle, then an ascent to the line the Americans had taken in 1963.

On April 18, Axt and Bahaguna were still hard at work, and had decided that Camp Three should be moved higher on to the ridge proper. It was while they were doing this that Vaucher and Eliassen decided to straighten out the route round the icefall, circumventing the downhill section by creating an even longer – around 400ft – horizontal traverse. It was here that Bahaguna had come to grief on the way down, Axt arriving alone just before dark. He told the others that he had heard the Indian shouting, but strangely had failed to go back to discover why. A search party that included Whillans, Vaucher, Eliassen and Mazeaud set off at once, and as they approached, the Indian's screams could soon be heard echoing round the storm-tossed Western Cwm. They found the unfortunate climber near death, and still eighty feet away from safety at the end of the traverse. His gloves and a crampon had gone, and his hands and face were coated with ice. When Whillans arrived, he attempted to lower the stricken Indian to the shelter of a crevasse below, but the rope was too short, and with the storm worsening and the rescue party themselves in danger, Whillans took the only option available and turned back.

Bahaguna's death, and the manner of it, occasioned an inquiry at Base Camp next day, with Axt quizzed in the manner of a court-martial. One or two blamed him, without reservation, for not staying with the Indian and for not being roped, though with fixed ropes there was seldom a need for such formalised climbing. The Vauchers and Mazeaud snubbed Axt openly later, and the whole episode and its aftermath heightened the tension in an expedition already close to breaking point.

The storm was to maroon everyone in their various camps, and it was ten days before Bahaguna's body could be brought down, though climbers at the Advance base had occasional views through the cloud of a black shape lying on the ice slope. During one temporary break in the weather Dougal tried to get out of base and up to Camp One with five Sherpas and supplies, but after six hours of struggling through waist-deep snow, he gave up the unequal fight. Two days later the link was made, and the expedition could get moving again with Dougal, this time, determined to stay up until the issue was decided, one way or the other. At Camp Two, he was re-united with Whillans, but with Dougal straining at the leash everything came to a halt again, a state of affairs that he found hard to take: 'Harsh burial to be cremation at Gorak Shep, last grass beneath base camp. It's a pity people's fucked-up sentiments give them leeway to play with others' lives.'

For many, the expedition ended when the flames of Bahaguna's funeral pyre died. Hiebeler left for Munich and home, and Peterson, too, showed little interest in going any further. With supplies and manpower dwindling, it was apparent to Dhyrenfurth that to attempt two routes on the same mountain was unjustifiable. Mauri, Mazeaud and the Vauchers wanted the Ridge route scrapped, too, but their alternative was the 'normal' route up the South Col.

Dhyrenfurth dithered. He agreed, then changed his mind and, like Bonington, he was to find that indecision does not go down well with climbers bowed under the weight of their own egos. Mazeaud, the

Dougal at the high point on
the south-west face of Everest
November 14, 1972

Courtesy of Doug Scott

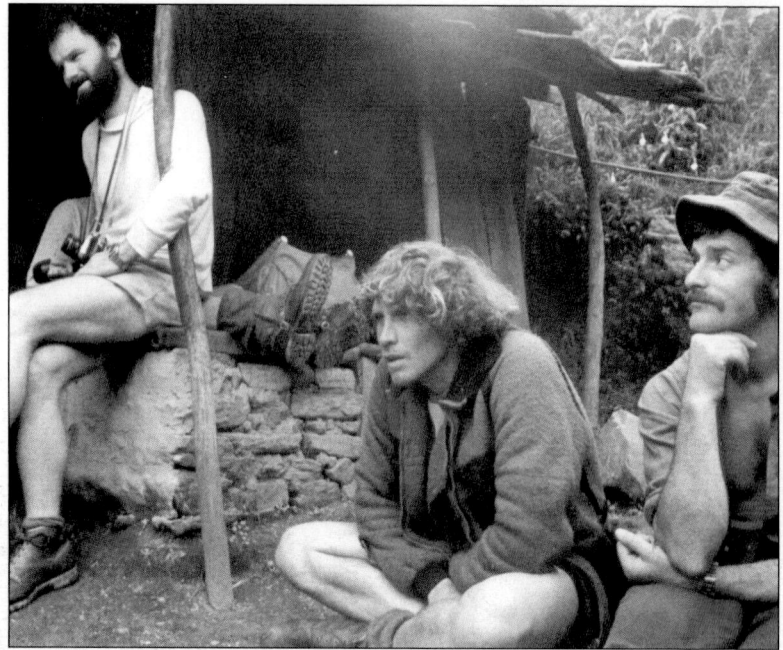

Nick Estcourt, Dougal and Dave Bathgate take a break during the Everest walk-in, 1972

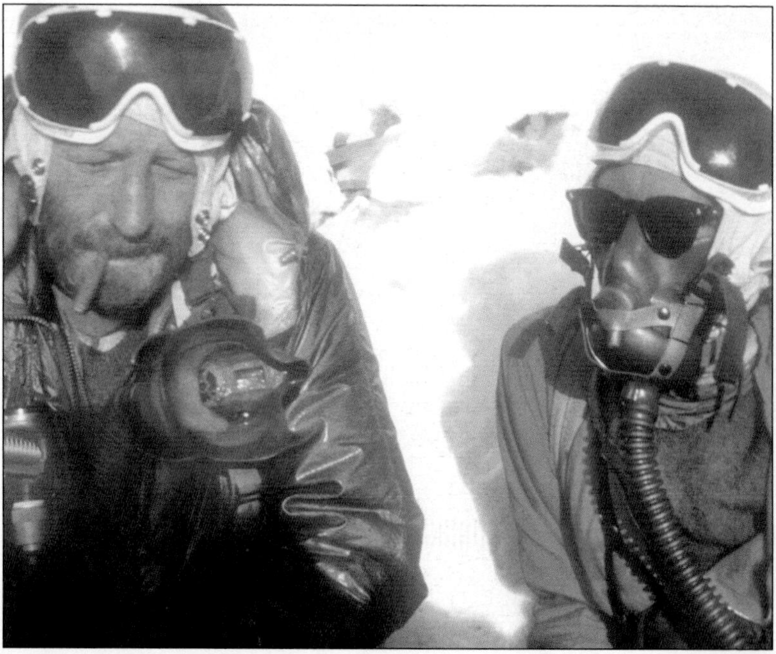

Courtesy of John Cleare

Don Whillans breathes cigar smoke, Dougal makes do with oxygen at Camp 4, Everest, 1971

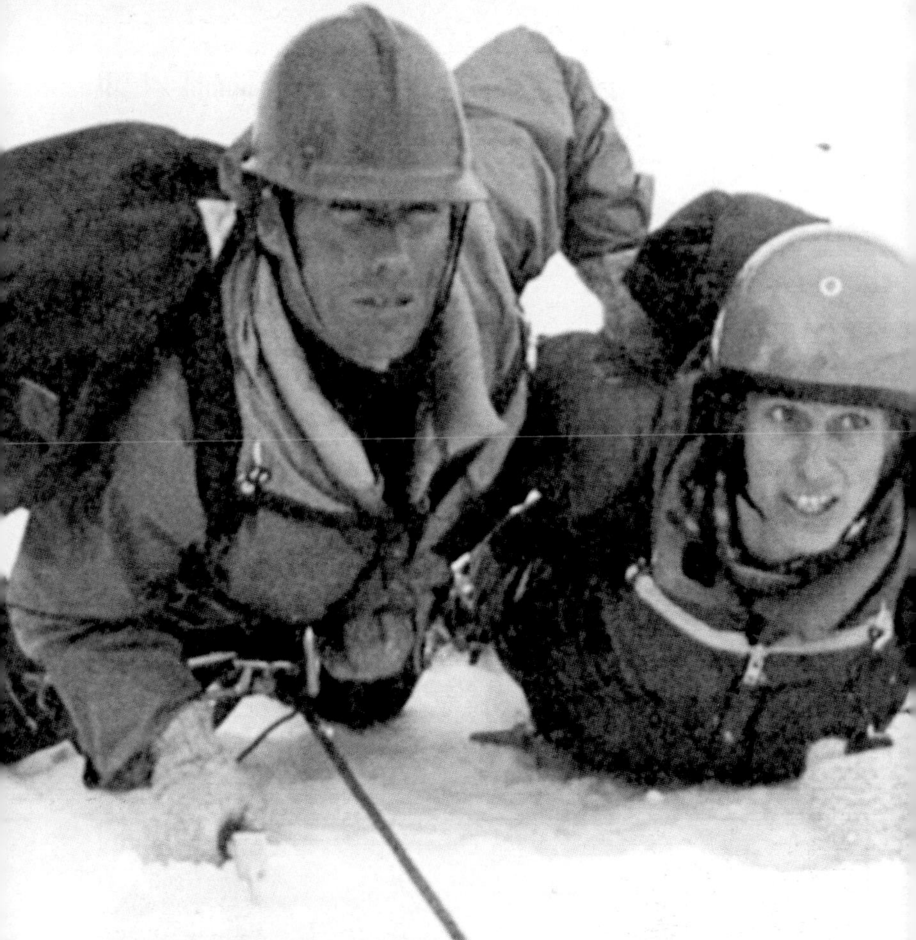

Both pictures courtesy of John Cleare

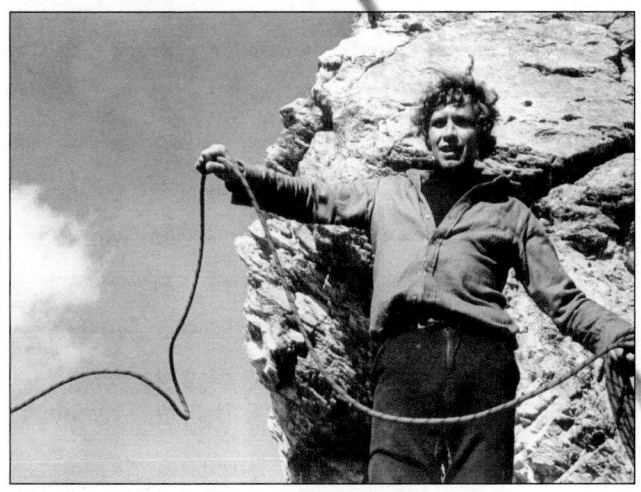

Dougal coils rope on the Eiger West Flank and shows Clint Eastwood the ropes during the 1974 filming of *The Eiger Sanction*

Dougal prepares to move away from the third bivouac site, Mount McKinley, 1976. His last major climb.

Dougal felt uneasy with the official side of fame: here with a presentation at the Royal Geographic Society and piped into Edinburgh's Usher Hall with Chris Bonington and Annie

Dougal shows the enervating effects of altitude at Heathrow Airport on arriving back from Everest in the autumn of 1975; Doug Scott is hardly touched.

All quiet in the Western Cwm ... Dougal nears the top of Everest's
Khumbu Icefall, 1975

Main picture: Ariane Giobellina ski-touring near La Riondaz above the village. The slope that avalanched and buried Dougal is behind and above her left shoulder

Inset: Eley Moriarty and Doug Scott carry Dougal's coffin through the Leysin snows. Ariane is on the right in the dark glasses

Dougal Haston

Vauchers and Mauri (who should, perhaps, have been more compatible and reasonable after his experiences on Thor Heyerdahl's Ra expeditions) had a furious scene with the leader at Base Camp. Madame Vaucher called him a *saleaud*, and pelted him with snowballs. Wounded, they set off to Europe to give their versions, the common theme being that that Whillans was off up the mountain hogging the lead, again.

Half true. Dougal and Whillans, with the two Japanese and an enthusiastic young Sherpa called Pertemba in support, spent three weeks on the face trying to find a way up through the Rock Band but, in truth, with illness sweeping the expedition – Dhyrenfurth was a victim with Teigland, Colliver, Eliassen and Evans – there was no one left to take over. Schlommer expressed a desire to join them up front, but blew his chances when he demanded a Sherpa to carry his rucksack. Axt, shattered by the death of Bahaguna, declined an offer to take a share of the lead, explaining that he had promised his wife that he would not go on the face.

The two Britons went through the motions, and after twenty-one days continuously above 7450m, Camp Six was finally established at around 27,500ft. But with the Rock Band still looming ahead and the cold some minus 35F, and down to their last scrapings of food, Whillans turned to his climbing partner and said: 'We've 'ad it, Jimmy.' Haston agreed. Back at an almost empty Base Camp, Dougal discovered that Annie, his wife, was there, suffering from a mild case of cerebral oedema after coming up from sea level too swiftly. After evacuation, she recovered, but international climbing relations took a lot longer to heal, and the fall-out from the 1971 Everest expedition was to last for several years. The media had a field day, feasting on the international differences, the storm, death, controversy and confrontation, and all on the biggest stage of all. Schlommer, Mazeaud and the Vauchers lambasted Dhyrenfurth and Whillans in print; Roberts, the former career army officer and joint leader with Dhyrenfurth, was accused of drunkenness and incompetence; Mazeaud came out with his famous, possibly apocryphal, statement: 'They expect me, Pierre Mazeaud, Member of the French Assembly, aged 42, to work as a Sherpa for Anglo-Saxons and Japanese. Never! This is not me, but France they have insulted!'

One suspects that some of that may have been lost in translation at the time – Mazeaud claimed subsequently that he said nothing like that – but it poured more fuel on the smouldering ashes of the Everest expedition.

*   *   *

The chief arsonist in many eyes, of course, was Whillans, cast in the role he was destined to fulfil throughout his life. Dougal missed all the ire heaped on his climbing partner, though when the disaffected went into print he was sufficiently stirred to write a long letter to Dhyrenfurth putting his side of the story, and pointing out some of the frailties of other expedition members, Axt and Schlommer in particular. Initially, he had been supportive of the international concept – he ran a business called the International School of Mountaineering – but now he recognised the pitfalls inherent in multi-national expeditions. Many were based on political and monetary expedience. Fonrouge had helped in getting into Cerro Torre, Frost helped with the Annapurna expenses, and the international ideal had certainly got Everest off the ground. (A trip to Changabang in India in 1974 was made possible only by similar liaison with Indian climbers.)

Back in the relative peace and quiet of Leysin, Dougal spent much of the rest of 1971 putting the finishing touches to his autobiography *In High Places*, which he had started just after Annapurna. The book proved to be a fine chronicle of Dougal's climbing career, but told his curious fans little about the man himself. His mother and father were not mentioned, nor his brother. Annie merited three entries in the index, and many other cogent events were left out, including the Glencoe accident. It contained most of what he had written in his school exercise books over the years, but he kept virtually all his contentious views to himself. It was really the face that Dougal had presented to the world most of his life, a subjective view of himself. It was also brief, under 60,000 words, and there is evidence throughout that he had become bored with the project, some fine writing being interspersed with straight lifts from his diary without even changing the present tense. The book, first published by Cassell and Company, eventually came out in the summer of 1972, and the events in it terminated at the high point on Everest in 1971. One of the obvious reactions was that it might have been premature and, in fact, a paperback reprint by Canongate in 1997 did far better business, a foreword from Doug Scott bringing readers up to date with events from 1971 to 1977. As Scott hinted, some of the most interesting, and successful, years lay ahead.

* * *

Undeterred by the controversy of Everest in 1971, Whillans, Hamish MacInnes and Doug Scott – on his first major expedition at altitude – were back on Everest within 12 months as members of another 'international' expedition under the overall leadership of a Munich doctor, Karl Maria Herligkoffer. He was the Don King of mountaineering, a high-profile non-participant who liked to tie climbers to contracts, and whose expeditions invariably had ended in acrimony and lawsuits. He had been organising expeditions to the Himalaya since 1953, when Hermann Buhl made his incredible, solo ascent of Nanga Parbat, and his 1970 attempt on the same mountain had ended in a celebrated climbing incident when Reinhold Messner and his brother Gunther reached the summit via the Diamir Face, only for Gunther to die on the descent. Legal battles ended in a virtual gagging order on Messner. The doctor was no climber, and never went above base camp, but he was a master of litigation. Haston and Bonington had been invited on the 1972 Everest trip – Haston for his abilities as a world-class mountaineer, Bonington for a similar reason plus his organisation and commercial contacts – but both had turned it down. Dougal had learned from 1971, and he had also noticed – which Whillans had not, or had simply ignored – that the other 'international' participants consisted of several of Schlommer's Austrian friends and countrymen. Predictably, the 1972 attempt ended in disarray and acrimony, though it avoided a fatality. The British trio were not allowed into the lead, Sherpas went on strike over the leader's cavalier attitude towards their needs, and eventually the Brits withdrew. The expedition failed at the Whillans/Haston high point of 1971, and the South-West Face of Everest remained unclimbed.

In April 1972, Bonington was granted permission unexpectedly for a post-monsoon expedition. It was short notice, with departure due in August that year, and initially he wanted to go for a lightweight ascent of the South Col route, but when Herligkoffer's attempt failed attention returned to the primary target and Bonington cranked the big machine back into forward motion. To his inner-core team of Haston, Estcourt, Boysen and Burke he added MacInnes, Scott, Dave Bathgate from the Edinburgh Squirrels, and Graham Tiso, who was the obvious choice to organise equipment. For Scott and Bathgate, it was their first invitation into the Bonington inner circle. Kelvin Kent, the young Gurkha officer who had performed his duties of running Base Camp so well on Annapurna in 1970, was invited back, and Jimmy Roberts was deputy leader. The one big name omitted, to the astonishment of the climbing world, was Whillans. Various reasons were put forward for the snubbing: the obvious one was that he was older, fatter, bolshier and even lazier, but people had lived with that on Annapurna and Everest previously. Others felt that, in some ways, he was now over-qualified for any expedition led by Bonington, that his knowledge and experience could destabilise the leadership. The deciding factor, however, was that Dougal didn't want him along. When Bonington started to put his team together, he did the democratic thing and asked his lead climbers to vote for or against the inclusion of Whillans. Most were predictable: Estcourt, Burke and Boysen still held reservations after Annapurna, and gave Whillans the thumbs down; Scott and MacInnes liked and got on well with him, and wanted him in. It was Haston, the man who had once rated Whillans the best mountainer in the world, who had told Agnew that he had saved his skin on Everest, and made no secret of his debt to Whillans for passing on his experience at altitude, who shut the door on the little Lancastrian.

Bonington reveals: 'If Dougal had said he wanted Don along, it would have been very, very difficult for me not to take him. I consulted the core members of the team, and I was given a strong consensus against. He caused too much bloody hassle, to be honest. Dougal had certainly learned what he needed from Don, and he was certainly tired of acting as Don's support. I think he saw as clearly as I did that Don would be a destabilising influence on the team.'

Scott, who admired Whillans and owed him a debt for getting him aboard the Herligkoffer trip, considered his experience on the South-West Face would be priceless, and asked Dougal to reconsider: 'I said to Dougal: "Come on, we owe it to Don to get him on the trip." Dougal said to me quite forcibly: "I don't owe that man anything!" '

After rejection, Whillans – to his eternal credit, he did not utter a word of complaint or condemnation – continued on his own unique way, on the peripheries of the climbing mainstream. He and wife Audrey opened a guest house in North Wales, and Don continued his long-time habit of touring the country in his camper-van, and arriving unannounced at the homes of friends for his socialising sessions. He did go to the Garhwal Himalaya with Scott in 1981, but Alpine-style Himalayan attempts were not his scene, and a later trip to Broad Peak was curtailed by the death of Pete Thexton through pulmonary oedema, Whillans taking on the responsibility of bearing the news to the climber's family. It was Whillans' last big mountain, and one of the world's great climbers died of a heart attack in his sleep in 1985 . . . after a satisfying night in the pub.

Bonington's expedition left on August 21, with Haston and MacInnes going out ahead of the main group, reaching Base Camp in mid-September. At first, progress was good, and by mid-October Camp Four was established at halfway. It was there that the first winds of the monsoon swept in, and upward progress became impossible. The storm arrived in time to trap Ken Wilson, editor of *Mountain* magazine, who had arrived to write one of his highly entertaining and often acerbic background pieces, in Camp One for a week. Wilson had been invited there by Bonington, but his appearance did not please some of the lead climbers. 'Haston and Scott regarded me as a total intrusion on their mountain experience, and just ignored me most of the time,' Wilson confirms.

On November 1, Bonington began his first tinkerings with his climbing order, upsetting Scott and Burke, in particular, by pushing Haston and MacInnes up to the front to tackle the Rock Band out of turn. By now, they should have become immune to Bonington's occasional indecision in the field, but Scott, unlike many others, was not prepared to accept a subsidiary role to Dougal, and the denial of something 'I had had my mind set on for months'. He handed Bonington the ultimate insult: 'You're no better than Herligkoffer.'

Voices were raised, and threats to leave, or be expelled from, the expedition arose, Dougal waiting patiently in the background for the dust to settle. When tempers had cooled, and the expedition got back into gear, he finally reached the foot of the Rock Band for the first time on November 14. He discovered that the gully, seen as a possible route through to the summit snowfields, had been blown clear of snow and now offered an impossibly difficult rock climb at altitude. Everest was over for another year.

All that was left was retreat, and the expedition fatality this time was Tony Tighe, an Australian Dougal had met in the Vagabond. He had been helping out at Base Camp and wanted to have a look in the icefall, but was crushed by a falling serac, near the top, on his first trip in.

* * *

After the phenomenally overblown and controversy-laden extravangazas on Everest, Dougal was relieved to turn his attention to a low-key trip to Changabang in the Garhwal Himalaya, a charismatic, 6864m granite spire that had inspired many mountaineers down the years, but which was still unclimbed in 1974. Haston again had initial misgivings about the make-up of the party. Political considerations made it a joint expedition with the Indian Army, without whom it is highly doubtful if permission would have been obtained, but he was happy with the Brits in the group – Boysen, Bonington, joint leader with Lieutenant-Colonel Balwant Sandhu, and Scott. Haston, who pointed out sardonically that the only successful 'international' projects he had been on were the Old Man of Hoy (with a Rhodesian Baillie) and Eiger Direct (with Americans and Germans), had feared a Bahaguna scenario, reasoning that Changabang would offer technical difficulties beyond the capabilities of the Indians. He was proved correct.

The original intention had been to go for the West Ridge, but closer examination from the Base Camp site near the foot of the Rhamani Glacier, promised too many technical difficulties, and they turned their attention to the opposite flank of the mountain. As they were in the wrong valley, their first objective was to force a route to Shipton's Col, avoiding a long trek to the mountain's south side, and

Boysen and Scott managed to climb a long, dangerous ice slope, which led to a ridge above the col. Even with fixed ropes, the Indians were totally out of their depth, and only Sandhu, with a Sherpa Tashi, managed it. From the camp, a long, narrow ice ridge soared up towards the summit, and it took a very long day to see the ascent through to a successful conclusion.

Dougal wrote: 'Two Indian members became incapacitated through foolishness, or psychological problems. This made the party more unwieldy for any political difficulties, and we could climb as two ropes of three, with an Indian in the middle. Morale was slightly on the slide during the day, and there was some talk of going back to base for a few days' rest, and getting more supplies.

'This, I felt to be a retrogressive step, as we had put too much effort in getting across. Also dangerous, with fixed ropes and avalanche-prone slopes. As we were reflecting and discussing, the clouds slipped to lower-valley level, and we were left sipping tea in a surrealistic, moonlit mountain scene with Changabang sticking up like one of Ludwig of Bavaria's castles. Instead of the Wagnerian overtures we had only the sounds of our sceptical voices. Would it last? Should we go? We gave it an hour to consolidate, but within half were outside packing hurriedly. It was yet another new concept in Himalayan climbing. Not only were we carrying everything with us in preparation for a bivouac, but were climbing at night. It was a long, amazing impression-forming night. Devious route-finding. One pitch involved seven aid pegs, and front-pointing up hard ice with rustling powder sliding in the night. I did most of the leading. The moon dipped and curved behind clouds, and eventually dipped for the night in the middle of a front-pointing pitch. [It] had me groping for a little before a pre-dawn glow assembled itself. Sandhu behaving calmly and confidently, Tashi [Sherpa] frightened and out of his depth, and having to be ushered along in robot fashion. We were only glad that the other two Indians were not in evidence. Otherwise success would have been even more problematical. Problem of deciding on the true summit on flat ridge. Doug and I raced off to make sure, running uphill with the rope trailing in between. Soon caught the others up on way down; everyone tired but no mistakes.'

The first ascent of a major Himalaya peak apart, there were other satisfactions for Dougal. He had felt at ease in the company of a small group of friends, and Bonington and Scott, in particular, remarked that the wall of reserve he had so carefully built up over the years seemed close to dismantlement. There was also strong evidence on the ascent that in Scott, the rugby-playing former Nottingham schoolteacher, he had found a peer in terms of strength, determination and ambition, an opinion confirmed by their performance on the South-West Face of Everest next year, and even more remarkably on Mount McKinley in 1976. In climbing terms, Dougal was approaching his longed-for *Übermensch* state of grace, but most of the arrogance had vanished on the slopes of Annapurna and Everest. He had found satisfaction in his own level of performance. At the end of the Changabang expedition, he wrote: 'By Himalaya standards, it had been a long day – 20 hours – but I didn't feel any more tired than as if I had spent a 20-hour day in the Alps. I wonder if continuous exposure to altitude over the years makes for better acclimatisation. Certainly, I was having no problems on this trip, and mentally all our (Brit) atitudes were good. We were hauling the middle-range Himalaya peaks down to Alpine size in concept, and treating them accordingly, despite the great increase in difficulty. Therefore, creating an advance in Himalayan climbing standards.'

In April 1974, on the way out to Changabang, with the expedition quartered in the Indian Officers' Club in Delhi, the telegram arrived to confirm that Bonington had been granted permission for another attempt on Everest in the autumn of the following year. Again unwilling to tie himself to the back-breaking tasks of organisation and raising funds, Bonington favoured a lightweight attempt, in the manner of Changabang, on the South Col route. Haston and Scott, who basically had only to turn up and climb, wanted another shot at the South-West Face.

If history and experience had taught Dougal anything, it was that no climber went through a career with a 100% success rate. Failure was the progeny of attainment, as the Bat, the Eiger, the Matterhorn and several other of his ascents had proved. To walk up the Western Cwm past the South-West Face towards the South Col would be tantamount to sacrilege, and a betrayal of his entire climbing philosophy, and he and Scott set about trying to persuade Bonington to change his mind.

Bonington, by now too well aware of the amount of work involved as an expedition leader, resisted for a time, but finally agreed, on the understanding that a single sponsor would be found. In the end, via a friend on the board, Barclay's Bank agreed to underwrite the cost of the attempt at a minimum of £100,000. This was a massive amount for that time, and caused a huge stir among Barclay's customers and climbers alike, but it did mean that Bonington could happily concentrate on assembling his grandest Everest expedition yet.

In terms of manpower alone, it was possibly the most powerful climbing team ever assembled anywhere. There was his old guard of Estcourt, Boysen, Haston, Burke, Scott and MacInnes, and in deference to the increasing clamour from climbing commentators – in particular, Ken Wilson – for some more contemporary representation, he included 28-year-old Paul Braithwaite, a brilliant alpinist who had his own painting and decorating business in Oldham, and Peter Boardman, the 24-year-old recently appointed national officer of the British Mountaineering Council. Allen Fyffe, also 28, and an instructor at Glenmore Lodge, was included with Ronnie Richards from the Lake District. Barclays also nominated their own representative, a member of the company climbing club, Mike Rhodes, who was thus asked to make probably the biggest quantum leap in the history of climbing; native Yorkshire gritstone one weekend, Khumbu Icefall the next. Mike Thompson was again invited to do the food, another Bonington pal Charles Clarke was expedition doctor, and Dave Clarke, who ran the Centresport climbing retailing complex in Leeds, took over the Tiso role of quartermaster. Behind them was a Sherpa corps of 33, plus 26 icefall porters, and even more hired hands at Base Camp, for cooking and general chores. The small army – Bonington had cast himself in the role of a mountaineering Montgomery of Alamein – was completed by a four-man TV crew from the BBC. Burke, as on Annapurna, was employed as their cameraman on the face, carting a heavy Bell and Howell 16mm camera around throughout the expedition.

When Bonington's expedition book came out later, the appendices detailing logistics, transport details, communications and medicine comprised almost a quarter, and it was the total antithesis to Dougal's, and Scott's, idea of mountain climbing. But again, they rationalised that it was the only way to get another crack at the South-West Face. There were also a number of climbers unfamiliar to Haston, and some of the defensiveness returned. Boardman, for one, found it hard to get past the reserve on several occasions, and noted what he took to be Haston's 'self-congratulatory air' on 'his' route, when climbing in the company of the new boy. Unfamiliar with the protocol of Bonington expeditions, Boardman, an extremely power-ful climber who hid a dynamic ambition behind a happy-go-lucky exterior, was also prepared privately to challenge the unchallengeable: that Haston and Scott were prima facie summit material, and everyone else was there to help them to the top as best they could. Boardman died on the North-East Ridge of Everest in 1982, but Braithwaite is convinced that the expedition's youngest member had Dougal worked out.

'It's a pity that Pete's not alive, because he would have been able to put his finger on it,' says Braithwaite. 'He was only 24, but he had been to university, and he knew what was going on; he was far more perceptive than the rest of us. We were just working lads, we didn't understand anything. Pete was widely read, too, and knew about all these philosophers – he knew what Dougal was up to. One day, we came into the camp late – we had been held up by something, probably smoking some dope somewhere – and there was Dougal sat on this mattress in this sort of philosopher's pose, with his head rested on his hands and just looking at us as we sweated up the hill. None of us realised at the time, but it was the big thing with him to get to camp first, and be all showered off and looking cool when we all arrived. Of course, he had this polka-dot, red-and-white scarf round his neck – we all went out and got one later – to complete the image. To us, it was just a bloody walk. I can see him now. I am convinced he had deliberately placed this mat pointing in the right direction, so he was the first thing we saw. It was like a removedness, he was sort of telling us that he was different from the rest of us. There were maybe six guys who were the hard core of that trip, and could have gone to the top, but Dougal had this thing that was above this. It was, like, what the hell is he on? He had this edge on us, and he also had this aura that he had built up of this mystical guy in Switzerland with his own climbing school. Dougal's successes were very punchy, and almost as if he had had specific targets, very focused, and in that way he was ahead of his time.

'When we used to go out in the Alps in the late 1960s, Dougal used to appear in Chamonix, and everyone would be gasping and pointing at him, like a bloody rock star – a glam rock star. On Everest, I was just a young lad, and never gave much thought to anything else, and wasn't given to analysis. Dougal was just this God-like creature, who was in front all the time. He was definitely different. It's 25 years since he died, and it's almost as if he hasn't been away.'

Braithwaite is also convinced that the constitution of the first summit party was a fait accompli long before arrival at Base Camp. 'It was certainly no surprise when Dougal and Doug got to the top of Everest before anyone else. Half-way through walk-in, it was established that they would team up together, but it didn't mean much at the time. Five or six others could have got to the top but, to be fair, they worked out those slopes above the Rock Band, and they did a great job there. But there was an awful lot of energy on that trip, and they knew their arses were tailed. They couldn't afford to mess up.'

Bonington had no doubts about his top strike force: 'By the 1975 trip, Dougal was quite clear in his mind about Doug's extraordinary power. In 1972, they hadn't been flung together often, but on Changabang I believe they recognised the strength of the other, and brought out the best in each other. On Everest, in a talented bunch, they were head and shoulders above the rest. I asked Dougal early on, while I was balancing out whether I put my two strongest climbers together, who he wanted to go to the summit with, and he said Doug. Looking back on Dougal's career, and at the three personalities who played major roles in it, I think you could say that John Harlin was a person who gave rise to an opportunity, Don Whillans was a mentor and invaluable for Dougal at that stage in his career, but Doug and Dougal were peers, although Dougal had more experience. They made an extraordinary pair, as they demonstrated on Mount McKinley later, and I am quite sure they would have gone on to do a great many other things.'

There were, however, other notable performances on Everest '75, notably those of Braithwaite and Estcourt who cracked the major problem of the Rock Band, and unsung support climbers such as Mike Thompson. Braithwaite, for one, considered Thompson in the Sherpa class for unselfish, sustained load-carrying. Bonington's planning, aided by computer progamming, worked like clockwork, and Boardman and the Sherpa Sirdar Pertemba – the same Pertemba who had supported Whillans and Haston so valiantly in 1971 on the face – also did very well to reach the top. Burke, who was considered past his peak by Dougal, according to Annie Haston, did disappear on the summit ridge during a solo attempt, but there was consolation of sorts in the view that he must have got to the summit. According to Braithwaite, however: 'The second summit bid was a bodge. It was political, and that's why it messed up.'

The familiar trek to Base Camp went in leisurely fashion for most of the team, with a start at six a.m., a couple of hours' walk to the breakfast site, then an afternoon stroll to the campsite for the evening – usually to find Dougal there, flat on his back, reading and resting and waiting. He wrote: 'Life is good, easy, relaxed with much thinking time and, oddly enough, not much sign of the monsoon. The mornings have been sunny, usually lasting through to mid-afternoon when it rains. But then I am usually inside a tent, so who cares? I walk alone either way, out in front or way behind, after sleeping for two hours in the sun after breakfast. Food is excellent, as good as Annapurna, and I may even gain some weight this time. I even managed to find a tea shop that sold bottled beer.'

Base Camp was reached by the bulk of the party on August 22, with Estcourt and Haston sent ahead to work in the Khumbu Icefall. This time, they were through into the Western Cwm within a week, and there were subtle alterations in the placements of the camps on the way up to the Rock Band, which helped progress. All was going incredibly smoothly, helped by a spell of unusually good weather, and from the end of August to the middle of September, the party built up their chain of camps on the face to Camp Five, in the upper part of the Central Gully at 7800m. On September 9 starting from this base, Braithwaite and Estcourt found a way through the Rock Band, heading up through the narrow, left-hand gully. Braithwaite found it similar to a Scottish gully in winter in difficulty, complete with a small chockstone pitch, and some unstable powder lying on slabs of rock. But then straightforward snow slopes led to an amphitheatre at the top, with a ramp leading out to the right. The ramp produced a fine lead by Estcourt, without oxygen, and it eventually ran out into the upper snowfields. The way to the top was open.

Braithwaite and Estcourt realised immediately that this bravura effort had, almost certainly, taken them down the summit pecking order. Bonington favoured a democratic process – as we have seen, it didn't always work like that – where all lead climbers got a share of the goodies on offer. When the leader began thinking about his summit team, it was more a question of who would get a second shot, after Haston and Scott. These two, already operating in a level of awareness a gear above everyone else, had been tacitly accepted by almost everyone else, but there were still the runners-up spots.

Bonington's biggest problem, as always, was as much about catering for the individual egos of high-standard climbers as the logistics of getting the right numbers of personnel and equipment in place, and his choice of two four-man teams: Burke, Boysen, Boardman and Pertemba, followed by Estcourt, Braithwaite, Sherpa Ang Phurba and Bonington himself, was as much a compromise as anything else, and was hypothetical and wildly optimistic in many ways. And still he couldn't please everyone. His announcement of the summit teams, delivered over the radio, met with mixed reactions. Clarke, the doctor, came on the air almost immediately from Camp Two advising Bonington to step down on health grounds. He had been at Camp Five, over 25,000ft, for two weeks and, according to Clarke, his speech was often slurred – the leader eventually promoted Richards instead. MacInnes, his second in command, announced that he was leaving the expedition at once, officially on the grounds that he had not recovered from being caught in a powder-snow avalanche at Camp Four on September 11. Fyffe was also bitterly disappointed, but he swallowed the news bravely, knowing that he had failed to acclimatise properly, and had not been above Camp Four.

Meanwhile, Dougal ('like Lenin in his sealed train,' as Mike Thompson so appositely put it later) was on his way to the highest camp, immune to the dashed hopes and aspirations of others. On September 16, he wrote: 'The physical person seems to be working well, but no matter how well, there is still an element of blatant hard work in this form of climbing. The mind occasionally flickers on to a distant memory but, in general, hardly working. It is really on the outer edge of existence, and must be taken as a thing in itself, and not held up positively or negatively in comparison with normal existence. Others: Hamish seems to have general troubles. Martin and Pete going well, Martin, of course, being a known, but unreliable, quantity. Pete, despite his youth, seems steady and reliable, with his head in the right place.'

And again on the seventeenth. 'The others decided to go down that day. I stayed up in Camp Four, to think out the mountain and gain some solitude, and also avoid the inevitable Q and A session down below. It's about time everyone got up here and saw the problem, then there wouldn't be so many fatuous questions. This will slowly happen, of course, over the next few days. I settle into my bag, and while the stove melts snow I read some letters from Ariane, drifting and dreaming about the tasks ahead. At two a.m. there was a loud whistling and rushing noise and a great bang on the side of the box. I had had a visitation from an avalanche, which wipes out the box next to me and pushes my one slightly out of shape. Looking outside, I realised at once I had been fortunate in the choice of box – the other one was a total write-off, and anyone inside would not have survived. Not a good, but an interesting experience.'

On September 23, Scott and Haston with Sherpa Ang Phurba moved up past the Estcourt/Braithwaite high point, and found a small notch in a ridge of snow that would serve as a site for Camp Six. Thompson, Bonington and Burke, with the vital loads which would get Haston and Scott to the summit, arrived not long after before departing to Camp Five. Thompson knew his Everest adventure was over, Burke still harboured his own dreams. The next day, they mobilised for their summit bid, moving out of Camp Six above the Rock Band, and running out 1500ft of fixed rope, returning to Camp Six to spend the night sleeping on oxygen. The familiar feeling of controlled optimism returned to Dougal as he waited for the night to pass, the feeling he had first welcomed on the night on Su Alto sixteen years earlier: total commitment, excitement and controlled calm. There was also the realisation that the long road from Black

Hill in the Pentlands was about to reach its apogee. Despite a long day, he felt neither tiredness not discomfort. The stove helped to pass the night with tea, lemon drinks, meat and mashed potatoes. There were bouts of gentle dozing, the occasional dream and a rude awakening to change the oxygen cylinder when it ran out. At midnight, they gave up sleep and began the long process of preparing for the summit, boots, crampons, harness, rucksack and oxygen system all carefully assembled and checked. Scott decided against taking a down suit, to save weight, but took a stove and billycan. Haston carried down boots and a bivvy sheet. They had two cylinders of oxygen apiece.

The route led across a snowfield to the gully leading to the South Summit, but Dougal had trouble with his apparatus, and his attempt could have ended there and then. In a state of controlled sangfroid, the two men patiently dismantled the apparatus, and an hour later discovered that an errant lump of ice was stuck in the tube. Scott led a difficult rock step, which required a number of pitons, and the gully itself proved extremely time-consuming, as it was filled with deep, soft snow. It was three-thirty in the afternoon when the face finally ran out into a snow slope leading to the South Summit. The face was climbed, but what about the summit? They were already past any fail-safe point for turning back, and both knew that they were facing a night out in the open, and what would certainly be the highest bivouac in history. This possibility had been tacitly accepted at the South Summit, when they had started to excavate a space for their bivouac before making a brew, and carrying on towards the narrow arête that led to the Hillary Step and the final summit ridge. Haston led the Step, one of the most famous climbing pitches, and named after the first ascentionist 22 years earlier. Instead of the rock that Edmund Hillary had found, however, it was plastered with snow, and it took Dougal only thirty minutes to lead. By six p.m. they were on the summit . . . trudging up the last few yards together.

Haston's reserve cracked in the moment of triumph and, as well as smiling for Scott's camera, he surprised his colleague by hugging him effusively. He also broke the habit of a lifetime, by taking a photograph. Amid the euphoria, however, the thought of the retreat was already in the back of Dougal's mind. There could be no relaxing yet. At the South Summit, a fleeting ambition of climbing down in the dark quickly gave way to reality and, without another word, both started to work on enlarging the bivouac hole that they had started. All the oxygen had gone, but their stove yielded a few sips of warm water. There was no food and no sleeping bags, and though Dougal wore his down duvet, Scott had just a silk vest, woollen jumper, fleece suit and outer wind suit. But both were physically and mentally equipped to cope; and their minds were brought to bear on the little matters that would add up to survival: warming each other's outer extremities, keeping snow off their boots, making sure they wouldn't go to sleep. They kept warm by enlarging their snow hole, but gradually their minds started to wander; Scott remembers Dougal having a long, convoluted conversation with Dave Clarke, while Scott addressed his feet. The hours passed slowly until a dull, grey light outside the hole finally signalled dawn. They had not slept or eaten for thirty hours, and had spent a night without oxygen in the open at 28,700ft, about the height of the average aircraft flight. But they survived, and after this there was every reason to believe that anything was possible on any future mountain.

The second summit party were on their way up as the triumphant summiteers made their way down, but Burke, laden with cine equipment and personal gear, was already making intolerably slow progress. Nevertheless he, Boysen, Boardman and Pertemba set out for the top in the early hours of September 26. There was an early setback for Boysen: his oxygen set packed in shortly after leaving Camp Six, and he retired to his tent 'howling with frustration'. The others continued in gradually worsening visibility, Burke drifting further and further behind. But the second summit party had the fixed ropes left by Haston and Scott, and their tracks from the South Summit to the top, and they were there by 1.10 p.m. After the truncated summit rituals, Boardman and Pertemba set off down in wind-driven mist, and were astonished to meet Burke a few hundred yards from the top, determined to carry on. Dougal believed that he would almost certainly have turned back, but for the prospect of returning with film from the summit, and his colleagues agreed to wait at the South Summit to descend together. Conditions were swiftly degenerating into a storm, however, and when Burke failed to re-appear, Boardman and Pertemba decided to concentrate on their survival, fighting their way down to Camp Six, where Boysen was waiting.

Burke was never seen again, and the probability is that he walked over a cornice on the summit ridge, his spectacles behind an oxygen mask and poor visibility probably contributing to his misjudgment. No one will ever know.

On September 27, all hope of his survival was abandoned, and evacuation of the mountain began. It had taken 33 days, and one death, to conquer the South-West Face of Everest, and Thompson, for one, wondered if it had been worth it. For the third time, a Bonington expedition had ended in tragedy (Estcourt, Boardman and Joe Tasker were to perish on subsequent trips). 'It was getting like war, premature ageing,' according to Thompson. Estcourt and Boysen, too, had become disenchanted with the 'anticlimax' of the success, Boysen returning to his first love, rock-climbing, and abstaining from expeditions. For Dougal, Everest wasn't even a metaphorical high point. He had been to the highest point on earth, but had been dissatisifed with the challenge offered. There had to be other tests. Everest had been almost an incidental. From Base Camp, he sent Jimmy Marshall a postcard which, instead of bearing something on the lines of 'Reached the top', said: 'Still outsmarting the old fox [MacInnes].' He had posted another one to Chic Scott, who recalls: 'It said: "You should have had more faith" – a reference to the summer of '75, before Dougal went to Everest, when my world was falling apart, and I ended up in hospital with a complete nervous breakdown. In the spring before that, I had been corresponding with Dougal, and I was saying something to the effect that he probably wouldn't make it, and he should be with me. I remember he sent me a letter and he quoted Bob Dylan, and he said: "Those bad dreams are only in your mind." God, I should have saved these letters, but there I was in the psychiatric ward up the Foothills Hospital in Calgary before I recovered, and Dougal sent me this postcard and it just says: "Haston and Scott South-West Face" or something like that, and then underneath: "You should have had more faith." That may be the only postcard he sent, and some day I'm going to get a thousand dollers for that. It's gonna buy me my drink for a whole year when I'm about eighty years old – thank you, Dougal.'

* * *

The aftermath of Everest produced an orgy of congratulation and celebration, almost matching the 'Land Of Hope and Glory' jingoisms of 1953. In Scotland, Dougal was fêted as a national hero. A two-page spread appearer in the newspaper that covered Currie, the *Broxburn and Uphall Post*, which revealed that 'pupils at West Calder High School are walking with a new spring in their stride, shoulders are held back strong and firm, and pupils' eyes seem to shout at you: "Dougal Haston was at the same school as me."' Overnight, the Everest expeditioners became like film stars, pointed out in pubs or on crags, and that included the members who had played peripheral roles. Even the three drivers who took the expedition gear out to Nepal could see their pictures in Bonington's book. There came a CBE insignia for the leader, at long last. But not for Dougal.

After a brief reunion with Ariane in Leysin, he and the others set off on a nationwide lecture tour and, according to Bonington, Dougal proved a subdued, but accomplished, chronicler of the Everest drama. 'Most of the time he was happy just to float through these things, but he certainly wanted to have his share of lectures. No way was he going for fame, it was almost a studied understatement, but there is no doubt that his reticence and the mystery of his persona created more interest. He wasn't a bad lecturer, and by then had developed an extraordinary presence. He was the strongest cult figure British climbing has had, and earned a level of respect for his climbing that was almost beyond what he achieved.'

Many of the lives of the lead climbers were to change irrevocably, particularly the younger ones. 'All I had done before Everest was work and climb, work and climb, with nothing else involved,' says Braithwaite. 'I was on a lecture tour with Dougal just after, and we were in Sheffield and I went into this hotel room, and I was absolutely knackered because I had probably been out socialising, and Dougal was looking round at me and I said: "When are we on?"

"Seven o'clock."

"Jeeesus, we haven't much time."

'And then he turned to me, and said: "Life was simple once, wasn't it?" And, of course, he was right. I think he could see what I was going through. One day you're a climber, and next you're into all the bullshit. But he was five years on, and he had been through it, so he knew what it was all about. Everyone changed after that climb – and someone should maybe analyse it – much more so than the 1953 Everest people. It was quite a demanding time for everybody. We went out as raw climbers with a couple of pros, but the rest were rookies. But in the year after, everything changed; we had to turn up at receptions, give lectures and things like this.'

Dougal returned to Edinburgh, visited old friends, stayed with the Tisos, walked the Pentlands, and was piped into the Usher Hall for his lecture. There were presentations from local dignitaries and plans for a civic reception. But there was also a reminder that he was still an outsider, and the reason he had turned his back on this world, when the Lothian Region convener Peter Wilson opposed the idea of a civic reception 'because Haston is still living in Switzerland'.

* * *

By the time of his return from Nepal, Dougal was a few months short of his thirty-sixth birthday, and though he felt as strong and as motivated as ever, he had been given some food for thought on all his Everest trips. He had gone past the limit with Whillans in 1971, and had been right on the edge in 1975. John Cleare, the cameraman on the earlier trip, remembers clearly the sight of Haston and Whillans arriving back in the Western Cwm, after abandoning their attempt on the face. 'Dougal was on his knees, totally out of it, and literally unable to walk or talk. A Sherpa had to help him into his tent. Don arrived a couple of minutes later, swigging out of a bottle of whisky, smoking a cigar and playing football with a lump of snow.' Their differing states may have had something to do with the share of the workload, but Doug Scott recalls that, in 1975, he was already in the Western Cwm when Dougal was still coming down the fixed ropes on the lower face: 'I think he had slowed a bit by 1975.' Chic Scott, too, saw film of the 1975 ascent, and noticed Dougal's total enervation. 'When he and Doug were back down being interviewed for television, Dougal is absolutely knackered, while Doug Scott, who is a big, strong, hefty guy, looked untouched by it all. Dougal really had little in the way of reserve: he pushed it right to the limit and hit the wall. He had the perfect build, in a way, for certain types of athletic activities, long legs and huge lungs, and very narrow hips, but he had that lean physique which makes you fast the first day, but then you run out of energy – and eventually you are just exhausted.'

The performance of 24-year-old Boardman on Everest had also given Dougal an implicit warning that he may soon have to defend his title as British climbing's undisputed heavyweight champion; ambitious young challengers were around with scant respect for reputations. Nor did he need a reminder that he had eventually overtaken, and left behind, two of his great mentors, Jimmy Marshall and Whillans. Among the instructors who had helped out at his school in Leysin in the mid-1970s were two who could have been younger versions of himself, and who had opened his eyes to modern climbing and its possibilities. Joe Tasker had risen from obscurity to a position of one of Britain's best young alpinists, with a series of first British ascents, including the Cecchinel/Nomine route on Mont Blanc's extremely serious Eckpfeiler Buttress, and the East Face of the Grandes Jorasses. In 1976, with Boardman, he made a fabulous 40-day ascent of the West Ridge of Changabang, the West Ridge that Dougal and his team had considered too difficult two years previously. Gordon Smith, a young Scot, had also set the climbing world alight with a series of innovative ascents, mainly on ice, in Scotland and in the Alps. Dougal may have felt his perch rocking, and said as much in a rare, remarkably candid newspaper interview: 'There are obviously going to be younger, stronger climbers coming along eventually, and one will feel obliged to step aside and make way for them. I know I can't go on forever with the hard, Everest-type challenge. I'll have the urge, but probably not the ability, as the years catch up.'

To Doug Scott, this younger generation was the 'Wolf Pack'. On a trip to K2 in 1980, he noticed that Boardman and Tasker were almost in competition with each other and he, as the older, more experienced climber, was almost peripheral. 'Tasker, Boardman and Dick Renshaw, they were the pack stamping at his and Dougal's heels,' says Chic Scott. 'Dougal was the alpha dog, and he wanted to stay the alpha dog, but he was having to fight, and a lot of the routes he was doing then, particularly in the Alps, were using outdated styles. There was one he spent a lot of time on with Bonington on the Grandes Jorasses [12 days in 1972]. They didn't get it, and I think it was eventually climbed by Alex MacIntyre in a couple of days. I think Dougal's day was coming to an end, at least his day as the leader of the pack. In the climbing world, most climbers are lucky if they get ten years at the leading edge. If you're great, you might get fifteen or twenty. Dougal had had the mid-1960s to the mid-1970s. He had already had ten years, and he could feel the younger guys at his heels by then.'

Blyth Wright, who was also working at ISM in 1974–75 when Smith and Tasker arrived, says: 'He might already have cottoned on to this in a way, when young Gordon Smith appeared on the scene in '75. Joe had a great season with Renshaw in the Alps in '74, and they had some new techniques for the big ice climbs, but then Gordon Smith arrived the next year, and he was using the new ice tools, and they were racing up things like the Shroud in just a few hours. Bev Clark said to me: "It looks to me as though Gordon is doing the Shroud in about half the time it would take Dougal to do it", so that might have been a problem for Dougal. It might not: he might have been big enough to take it and still done his own thing, but it would certainly cross his mind. He was very, very fit, and he always kept himself in shape, although technically in the mid-1970s a new technique was announcing itself over ice and rock. The last routes I did with Dougal, we were still using pegs, which was a bit passé by then. I guess his climbing standard was probably about E2 for most of his life, which is about average, of course. He was a good, solid performer on rock, but on the bigger hills, he still took a lot of catching.'

Doug Scott, who turned sixty in 2001, a year younger than Haston, is convinced that his Everest partner would be climbing today, though he might have had to set his sights lower. Despite problems with knees from rugby wear and tear, not climbing, Scott is still Britain's most prolific expeditioner, with a series of low-key trips to all corners of the world. Post-Everest, he began to favour a rapid, lightweight approach without supplementary oxygen, the ascent of 1975 almost offending him with its heavy-handedness. Haston, who shared that view – the Everest bivouac having shown that survival was possible in almost any conditions with the right disciplines – would certainly have been along on some Scott expeditions, notably the successful ascent of the North Ridge of Kanchenjunga in 1979, which was eventually undertaken by Scott, Chamonix guide Georges Bettembourg and Boardman and Tasker. Bonington, too, insists: 'Dougal had a lot of mileage in him. He would certainly have been on K2 with me [in 1978]. Doug would have wanted him on Kanchenjunga. In many ways, Himalaya climbers peak around their forties, and the only thing that would have stopped him was his interest going in another direction. The intriguing thing with Dougal was this extraordinarly focus, and yet indolence . . . he was quite happy to do nothing. He had a first-class brain and was very widely read beyond climbing, so he may have gone in another direction. That could have happened because of the quality of his intellect.'

It is doubtful whether Dougal would have taken up golf or tennis, but Allan Rankin, in conversation, remembers his fascination with another sport of an epic nature and, in particular, the story of Donald Crowhurst, the sailor who vanished in the Atlantic after falsifying the details of his participation in the 1968 round-the-world race. 'The mystical aspects of that appealed to Dougal,' says Rankin. 'But I also think the idea of setting off alone in a small boat against the seas struck a chord, too. It was not dissimilar from climbing, in a way, and I could have seen him taking up sailing and sailing round the world, or something like that.'

In 1976, however, Dougal's feet were on dry land, and he still had great plans for distant mountains. In the spring of that year, he was due to go to Alaska with Doug Scott, their eyes on a new route on the South Face of Mount McKinley. Proposals to try Dhaulagiri 2 and Everest's very difficult neighbour Nuptse were also in the pipeline (though both were to fall through eventually). It was on McKinley that the partnership with Scott was to reach a remarkable apogee, with a bold, elegant route in ferocious surroundings succumbing to two mountaineers at the top of their form.

At 20,320ft, McKinley is the highest mountain on the North

American continent, and in many ways a fiercer challenge than some of the Himalaya giants: McKinley is close to the Arctic Circle, and the difference in the barometric pressure at northern latitudes affects acclimatisation there. McKinley's latitude is 63 degrees while the latitude of Everest is 27 degrees and on a typical summit day in May, a climber on McKinley will be at the equivalent of 22,000ft when compared to climbing in the Himalaya in May. This phenomenon of lower barometric pressure at higher elevations is caused by the troposphere being thinner at the poles and Scott and Haston also knew that the mountain is buffeted regularly by storms from the Gulf of Alaska and from the Bering Sea. The area almost matches Patagonia in its ability to undergo drastic weather changes, balmy days of glacier travel deteriorating rapidly into a day of survival-snow-cave digging. The intense cold, routinely between 20 and 40 degrees below at night, makes Everest almost tropical by comparison. All in all, a worthy arena for Haston. The two Britons, who were in North America after independent lecture tours, flew in by air taxi from Talkeetna, landing on the South-East Fork of the Kahiltna Glacier, then spent four days on skis and snowshoes humping loads to an old igloo, fortuitously left at the foot of the face. Their projected route led up through a series of couloirs to above a hanging icefield, from where the upper snow basin would give access to the summit.

The first day was a taste of what was to come, with difficult and dangerous climbing over unconsolidated snow lying on ice, the mountain welcoming them with a powder-snow avalanche that almost swept them off the face. The storm blew in after 2000ft of climbing, with 5000ft of mountain still ahead. They were pinned at their first bivouac site for two nights, and Scott admits he began to have second thoughts. 'I said to Dougal: "What do you reckon about our chances?" And he just looked at me and said: "Have you got frostbite yet?" I got the message.'

The weather finally relented sufficiently to allow upward progress, but it took four more bivouacs to reach the top, the pair discarding food and spare clothing for the sake of speed. Dougal described the route in a few words in his pocket diary, but later became more effusive: 'We had climbed rope but, simultaneously, front-pointing forever into a revived storm and relentless wind. Everything was cold,

189

even our souls. Frostbite was waiting to jump at the slightest sign of weakness, but both of us played our own winning game with it. McKinley's climate is tough. We were drawing heavily on all our Himalayan experience just to survive, and it was a respectful pair that finally stood on the summit ridge. It took a few hours to dig a miserable little hole, but free from wind and spindrift, and there we spent an equally miserable night. We had climbed the mountain too quickly to acclimatise, and now we were suffering!'

On the summit, Scott felt that the mountain's 20,320ft felt more like 24,000ft, and on the way down the normal ascent route, the West Ridge, there was a reminder that even a mountain as dangerous and hostile as McKinley attracted the foolish. They were surprised to see figures ahead, who turned out to be two climbers of around twenty sitting in the snow, with equipment strewn all around them. One had yellowing fingers, frozen solid; the other was just sitting stupefied in the snow, his head bowed over his own useless, frozen hands. 'Yellow Fingers was quite chirpy; joking at the coincidence of our meeting at the summit like this. Dougal asked why his hands were exposed, and received a confident, flip reply. We told him that he had frostbite, and that he would probably lose his fingers, and maybe his entire hand. "What do you mean, frostbite?" asked Yellow Fingers. We patiently explained, got his gloves and other clothes out of his sack, and did what we could to make them warmer . . . we heard later that the two lads had to face extensive amputation of fingers, toes, hands and feet, despite the finest treatment available at Anchorage Hospital.'

* * *

McKinley was proof, if any were needed, of the unique physical and mental fitness of Haston and Scott, a graphic demonstration of two men on top of their game. By now rated in the top three in the unofficial table for great mountaineers, alongside Rheinhold Messner and the Frenchman Yannick Seigneur, Haston had finally found the niche he had craved and tried to attain for so long, and this new satisfaction with life and Ariane showed. Most nights, instead of visiting the Vagabond, they were happy to stay in the aparment in the Rue du Commerce, content in each other's company. He made another trip to Edinburgh, with Ariane, and most people remarked on a new contentment in him. He had nothing left to prove, to himself or others. Russell Sharp, his old drinking friend from the Squirrels, saw this new side to Dougal when he came to visit: 'He doted on my son, who I had christened Dougal. He was fascinated by this kid, and dangled him on his knee. I had never seen this Haston before. I was building a house at the time, and he looked over what I had done so far, and then turned to me and said: "I suppose that is your Everest." But there was no sarcasm or criticism in it, and he was right in a way. We all had our own Everests.' To Eley Moriarty, he mentioned his idea of writing a novel, and 'he seemed settled, very settled. I don't know if it was Ariane, the climbing successes or the school, but there suddenly seemed no pressure on him.'

On a trip to the Tisos, Maude was startled by the change in Dougal, but felt sadness that it had come so late in his life.

'Graham had always kept in touch with him, and because he mattered so much to Graham, he was always welcome at our home. I was able to put my personal feelings aside, but then latterly, when he brought Ariane over, to me he was a changed person. We went out for a meal and a drink, and that sort of thing, and he also suggested that maybe we would go out for a walk on the Pentlands with our three boys. You know, women and children, they weren't in Dougal's life. It was as if he just sort of ignored them. But here he was, with Ariane. And the kids and us walked from one end of the Pentlands, and they came from the other end, so we would meet up and picnic, and this was just charming, delightful stuff that Dougal would never have suggested before. To me, he was just a changed person, and I usually dislike when people say that because it rarely is true, but I really found a complete change. Ariane was an absolutely delightful, lovely-natured person, and I think he found a gentleness there that he'd never found before. We spent the whole of that day and the next day together, and I would have to say that, at that point, I felt very, very comfortable with Dougal. I found his attitude was just so different. I don't know what the formula was, but he was just so different; he was delightful company, and suddenly he's an intelligent, interesting man, and for the first time I felt able to share that. We had always had a kind of sort of guarded relationship, where I think he knew that he wasn't my favourite person, but he knew that I respected him as Graham's friend: there was a mutual tolerance. If I had to pick out one aspect of Dougal's life, I would say it was that incredibly significant change. He stopped seeming to be such a driven, troubled person, and you were able to actually enjoy his company. Personally, I think he'd found peace. I felt very sad when I heard about his death because I felt that he had just been on the threshold of something really good, and that seemed such a pity.'

In Leysin, too, Dougal 'opened up a lot', according to Guy Neithardt. 'He usually didn't talk to many people, but suddenly he was stopping in the street to say hello and ask after their families.'

His and Ariane's needs were simple, and he cared little for money. His two bank accounts were in the red. At the end of 1976, the Royal Bank of Scotland account at the Princes Street, Edinburgh, branch showed a debit of £214.20, and a current account with La Banque Cantonale Vaudoise Lausanne had a balance of minus 82 Swiss francs. On trips to London, he happily overspent with his American Express card, usually on trendy clothing at Richard Shops or Freeman Hardy Willis. He turned down a lucrative offer from the travel company Thomas Cook, in September 1976, to guide treks in the Garhwal Himalaya, and his plan for an ISM 'branch' in Canada was less about the commercial opportunities, and more about gaining access to that country's unclimbed areas. The plan was for three or four Alpine climbing weeks with students at Lake Chara, close to Mount Victoria, an advance Alpine course in the Bugaboos, ice-climbing weeks in the Columbia ice fields via the Athabasca Tongue, and one or two advanced rock-climbing weeks amid the excellent limestone of the Bow Valley, near Banff, perhaps staying at the Calgary Mountain Club Hut near Yamnuska.

His Canadian partner in the enterprise was to have been Chic Scott: 'He liked Canada. I remember Dougal and me coming out of the Grenier at six o'clock in the morning, and the sun was just rising; it was just getting light on a grey day. Dougal and I were both quite drunk, and we parted company on the cobble stones, and he wandered up towards his apartment, and I wandered back up to the Club Vagabond to pack my stuff because I was on my way back to Canada. We did correspond. Well, he wrote very short letters – just two or three paragraphs would be a long letter for him. God, I wish I had saved some of his letters. He and I were talking about setting up a climbing school in Canada between 1976 and '77. He was talking about coming to Canada. He had been here in 1974, at my behest. I set up a lecture tour for him through the Alpine Club of Canada, and it was a great success, and he made money and, of course, the Americans picked up on it, and before long he was down in San Francisco and Colorado, and all these places. But, as it turned out, that September morning in Leysin was the last time I saw him.'

In the summer of 1976, Dougal found a spare page in his old science exercise book, and planned out the year ahead. He titled it, in transatlantic corporate-speak, 'Initiative Rough Out'. It read:

June to Corsica, School to end of July, possibly August in Karakoram, September (Jorasses) Switzerland.

October – could be Darjeeling, November – European lecture tour to possibly mid-December, to Goa till end of January.

February–March Alpine climbing.

End March–April back to States.

Novel in Goa. Alternate Feb–March: States or Canada, for winter climbing in April.

May: Nepal, Chris.

He ended with a short postscript: 'Seems as if it could be quite a year, if all works well. Is there any reason why not?'

LOST HORIZONS

That is the land of lost content
I see it shining plain
The happy highways where I went
And cannot come again.
– A. E. Housman, *The Welsh Marches*

Haston had been an enthusiastic, but technically average skier, by European standards at least, since his arrival in Leysin ten years earlier. At first, putting on skis had been a necessary facet of the mountaineering process – an ability at least to snow plough is essential for approaches to Alpine faces through deep powder in winter – but it took some goading from Guy Neithardt to turn him into an expert.

'Yes, I took care of that,' says Neithardt, like the majority of Swiss an expert since his pre-teens. 'Dougal turned into a good skier, in the end, but only after I said to him: "Dougal, until you ski properly, you are not a complete mountaineer." He didn't like that one bit, the thought of not being thought of as the complete mountaineer. So he went out and started to work on his technique, and got quite good.'

'He turned into a bit of a powder hound,' says Allan Rankin. So much so that, with Rankin and Bev Clark, Haston had bought one of the first sets of the specialised Miller Deep Powder skis from a sports shop in Verbier.

By nature, Haston scorned Leysin's regulated, crowded runs, and preferred lonely forays off-piste or ski touring above Leysin. Pierre Starobinski, later to be director of tourism in the village, recalls that, as a teenager, he would often go out in the pre-dawn, climbing to some point by the light of a headlamp, and glance across to another route and see another headlamp. 'I knew it would be Haston or Andre Hefti, and that they would be doing the same.'

194

At the beginning of January 1977, Haston had taken a break from writing his novel and made one of what were becoming his increasingly rare visits to the Vagabond. He failed to return until the early hours, and Ariane remembers waking up in the middle of the night in a panic, to find empty space next to her in bed. Dougal eventually arrived home drunk, and with a deep cut over his eye. 'I gave him first aid,' she says. 'He told me he had just fallen, but I remember this awful feeling of unease, and the feeling went on for two weeks after that. There was no foundation for it. Just something inside was telling me something was wrong. But nothing I could discover was wrong.'

In the last two weeks, Haston dutifully wrote to his target on his novel of 2000 words a day. He would work in the morning, have lunch with Ariane at home and ski in the afternoon, if conditions were right. He finally finished the manuscript, handwritten, on the Sunday and, with a favourable weather forecast, had determined to find some off-piste skiing the next day, January 17.

In the summer of 1976, Haston had decided that a suitable future test would be to ski down the North-east Face of La Riondaz to the Col Luisset between La Riondaz and La Berneuse. His friend Davie Agnew, and others, had done it in the past, but afforested as it was, the slope needed a heavy covering of snow to make it viable. The face looking out to the valley was also known to avalanche, one fall having wrecked a chalet almost at the top of the village. But it was also one of the few challenges available to an expert in the resort, most of the runs being meagre tests even for an intermediate skier.

Ariane recalls: 'In the book, he had described that kind of day, that kind of snow, that kind of weather. He was not unaware of what could happen. He wanted to go alone, at first, but then called me at work at ten a.m. and said that "as it is so beautiful, I wanted to wait for you". I was touched by that, and was looking forward to it. But then my boss wanted me to do some urgent work, and I could not go. Then again came that same feeling, of feeling so low, with no real reason. When we passed my workplace, I kissed him goodbye, and said I would see him later. And then I went racing up the steps, and rushed out of the balcony, but by this time, of course, he had gone – out of sight.

'The summer before, when he had stopped and was looking at the face of La Riondaz, I looked at it, then looked at him, and then he told me he was going to ski that face. I looked at it again, and said: "I will follow you anywhere but this one you do on your own." But then I felt guilty, and added: "I will be down here looking at you."

'And, of course, I am still down here.'

* * *

When she arrived back home from work on that Monday evening, there were no dripping skis standing by the front door and, at five o'clock, it was already dark. Of course, he may have called somewhere on the way home, maybe the Vag, but that vague feeling of apprehension was moving swiftly towards fear. Dave and Joanne Smith, the couple who had taken over the Vagabond from Rankin, hadn't seen Dougal either, nor had Rankin, but all rationalised with her that he would almost certainly have stopped for a drink, and would reappear at any minute reddened by the sun and snow and beers, laughing outrageously at the fuss. Somehow she knew better. Rankin, somewhat apologetically, telephoned Eric Chamorel, head of the Leysin *bureau des guides*. Chamorel, veteran of a thousand mountain rescues, reassured him at once: 'No, no, you are quite right to contact me.' Together with the Smiths and Ariane, they rang round Dougal's favourite drinking haunts, even as far as Corbeyrier and Aigle down in the valley, and when all drew a blank Chamorel set off the chain of telephone calls that would mobilise his rescue team. He contacted Air Glaciers, who ran the search helicopters at Sion across the Rhone Valley and, finally, whistled up the two avalanche sniffer dogs he kept at his home. When the rescue parties met at the foot of La Berneuse *téléphérique*, Rene Borloz, one of the employees, had the idea of taking up, on a Sno-Cat, a large light of the type that illuminate fires, which had been used in a village festival a week previously. They could station it at the top of the lift, and sweep the surrounding peaks. They knew what they were looking for by then.

The rescue team that assembled at the *téléphérique* station included friends of Haston, *téléphérique* employees, and guides and instructors from the Ecole du Ski, and Chamorel organised them into two groups. One party was to take the cabins up to La Berneuse and search from there; the others were to go up the Solacyre lift, in the missing man's tracks. At nine p.m., the powerful beam from the light at the top of La Berneuse settled on what were obvious, fresh avalanche traces on the innocuous hill opposite, and the veteran Air Glaciers helicopter pilot Fernand Martignoni, with Rankin and others on board, immediately took off from the village. Martignoni did not know the terrain, and had to ask Chamorel to pick a landing spot that would not set off another slide. The rescuers noticed later that, for whatever number of landings, the pilot always set down precisely in those first tracks.

Rankin remembers the terrible beauty of the night as the helicopter first flew out a little way south-east, then turned back north. 'I admired the clarity and stillness of a sky lit by a million stars and the awesome view down the valley, and then we turned round to see the awful light illuminating the spot where my buddy was probably buried. It was an incredible contrast of beauty and horror. Myself and Christian Mo, a local ski-school instructor who was strong as an ox, but none too bright, were the two guys delegated to look in the trees. Mo said he had always been afraid of that place since a child. There were obvious traces of a skier, then this break in the snowline. I remember thinking, looking at the turns, that Dougal had probably never skied as well as that, and he was getting pretty good by then. They were absolute perfection. In my time as a 400m runner, maybe once in a lifetime you enter this sublime state where everything is just right, and I honestly believe something like that happened to Dougal that day.'

The avalanche, however, covered a large area stretching down to the stream at the foot of the hill, and the search was not helped when one of Chamorel's dogs caught a scent which turned out to be the carcass of a cow buried by a farmer the previous summer. At daybreak, reinforcements arrived, including 21 aspirant guides who had been climbing in the Les Diablerets range, and more sniffer dogs, but it wasn't until three minutes to two on the Tuesday afternoon, 24 hours after Haston had set out, that one of the men in the line of searchers signalled that his long, glass-fibre probe had hit something soft and yielding.

Rankin remembers: 'The two best athletes in Leysin were Andre

Hefti [owner of an eponymous sports shop and ski-hire business in the village] and Gilbert Felli, then director of the ski school and the sports centre, and probably our best local athlete at the time. These guys were studs, and just shooed everyone else out of the way, and moved in like mechanical diggers. When they found him, I forced myself to look in the hole. It was obvious he had broken a leg in the avalanche, and had got rid of the sticks and one of the skis, although this may have happened in the fall, of course. Dr Klein, who ran a local practice, was waiting in the quarry car park at the foot of La Riondaz with the ambulance, and it was him who told me: "Tell your friends not to wear a *foulard* [scarf]." Apparently, the snow had built up behind his neck, and the scarf had choked him to death. There was no powder in the lungs, as it turned out.'

Haston's death, and the manner of it, attracted headlines and comment round the world, ranging from Robin Campbell's now-classic 'bright blue bivouaced eyes' eulogy in the *Scottish Mountaineering Club Journal* of 1976, to a 'Sun Says' leader in Britain's best-selling tabloid. Some of the newspaper comment, a bane for much of his life, was to haunt him beyond the grave.

The inevitable theorising was advanced on why Haston would ignore avalanche warnings, and head for La Riondaz that particular day. The most extreme considered he may have had a death wish, even been suicidal, but the obvious contentment that Maude Tiso and others had noticed in the past 12 months of his life make that an unlikely concept. Others conjectured that he was an adrenalin junkie, who could get his kicks only in the most extreme and perilous conditions but, of course, he had been in control of most of those situations throughout his climbing career. There was also general astonishment among hastily rented experts that he would choose to ski off-piste when snow conditions were blatantly unsuitable. Locals such as Starobinski and Pierre Barroud, director of the Leysin Chairlift Company, hardly helped. Starobinski said: 'I watched him climb on extreme routes by himself, taking maximum risk, to harden his mind and body for the big face climbs which he would tackle in the Himalaya. He was not a stupid man. He was perfectly aware of the conditions, yet he did not take the safe route. Perhaps he could not see himself as a fifty-year-old climbing and mountain-skiing instructor. That is his secret.'

Barroud expressed his amazement that Haston should go up and ski when La Berneuse was closed off, though, of course, the lower lift at Solacyre was still running. Friends like the Scotts, Doug and Chic, Bonington, Blyth Wright, Guy Neithardt and Agnew were more sanguine, rationalising that if Haston had died, say, in a car accident, there would have been shock, but hardly surprise, because accidents happen. All climbers and skiers above a certain level had taken similar risks, and risks had been a fact of Haston's life for more than 20 years.

Another skier vanished in an avalanche the same day on the Rochers-de-Naye, a few kilometres away, without managing to attract the same theorising on his motives. But Haston was Haston, and the unfathomable enigma managed to keep the world guessing to the end. None of his friends, for example, could find a consensus about the accident . . .

Chic Scott insists: 'If Dougal had a death wish, there were lots of places he could have let go and killed himself in the past. Nobody had more of a desire to live than him. He wanted to go through dangerous situations and come out the other end. But I do think he did have a pain wish. There was something there in the pain and the suffering and the concentration of climbs that gave him solace.'

Guy Neithardt muses: 'I have thought about it a lot since. There was less knowledge about avalanches in those days and, anyway, avalanches are a bit crazy. I remember one of the top avalanche experts in the world was killed in one. And you know, if you took twenty-four profile sections on a slope a hundred metres wide, two will not be the same. It was an accident he had no control over.'

Royal Robbins, who remembers the La Riondaz slope, considered it 'really an inappropriate' place for a man like Haston to die.

Bev Clark said that Mick Burke's death upset him far more than Dougal, 'because I always regarded Dougal's death as inevitable. I always thought that he would push it too far and die on a mountain. When we did the North Face of Mont Blanc de Cheilon, he had really wanted that one. But the clouds came down and snow started falling, and I said: "Well, that's that." And he looked at me, and said: "Not a chance", and started front-pointing up the gully. He had just decided he wanted to do it, and did it. It turned into a real epic, with a rock fall chopping the rope in two, and we finished up soloing it basically. He was certainly capable of overriding caution when he needed to.'

Davie Agnew, who heard the news on Idaho radio – which 'tells you quite a bit about Dougal's place in the scheme of things' – remains convinced that La Riondaz was simply an error of judgement. 'I had skied that face many times, possibly I was even the first. I remember it as a non-retentive, slabby slope, maybe 1000 to 1500ft high. It was really bad judgement, and it made a lot of people quite angry, but these things happen. Maybe he just wasn't thinking, because it was just a good day for ski-ing, and he had just finished the book, so his head may have still been full of writing. Dougal loved to ski, but I don't think he gave much thought to snow. Now there's a thousand books about it, but I recall that even in 1970 nobody recognised the dangers until Eric Langmuir [principal of the National Outdoor Training Centre in the Cairngorms, and later an acknowledged expert] got avalanched over the back of Coire Cas.'

The puzzlement and diversity of opinions expressed in the public post-mortems would surely have delighted Haston who, diary apart, offered only a couple of public hints during his life about what kept him in the business of high risk. Not known for his willingness to talk to newspapers, he did offer one remarkably prescient interview to the *Edinburgh Evening News* writer John Gibson, just after the international Everest expedition in 1971, when he was back home. In answer to the obvious first question, Haston replied: 'If I want to risk death climbing a mountain – and I don't want this to sound melodramatic – it's my privilege. Don't make it sound like you have been talking to some self-styled superman. I like to think I know what fear is all about. I derive a certain comfort from having experienced fear, and knowing that I am going to experience it again. Everyone has fear. It's a healthy emotion – especially halfway up a mountain like Everest. It keeps one's sense of perspective, and it should maintain a climber's respect for his environment. Fear is a good emotion to have, always provided it doesn't turn into panic. That is something else.'

Asked by Gibson if he would ever stop climbing, Haston admitted:

There are obviously going to be younger, stronger climbers coming along eventually, and one will feel obliged to step aside and make way for them. I know I can't go on forever with the hard, Everest-type challenge. I'll have the urge, but probably not the ability, as the years catch up. People – and nearly always people who don't know what they are talking about – say that individuals like myself are pushing their luck, that we'll meet the Grim Reaper sooner or later on the side of a mountain. I never really think about dying on a mountain, although I concede the risks are always there. That's part of the game. But never forget this is a pretty disciplined sport. You know you are going to get into awkward situations, and that they will call for self-control and concentration, and I count myself fortunate because self-discipline kind of goes with the phlegmatic Scottish character. In a tight spot I think about living – not dying.

I have absolutely no religious convictions. When I climb, I find that I have to believe totally in myself, rather than turn to an outside deity. I'm aware that some people in the climbing world regard me as a loner. I never give them any argument. How do I see myself ten or twenty years from now? If I am still here, probably on some expedition, though maybe not in my current role. Maybe not as a lead climber. You make way, as I say, for the new blokes coming up. There comes a time when you move back to the administrative side of expeditions, and that will keep me happy. As long as I am where it's happening.

Haston gave another clue in his novel *Calculated Risk*, the fictional work that perhaps told us more about him than his autobiography. On page 36, the anti-social Scottish hero John Dunlop, tired of the madding crowd on the valley's ordinary routes, escapes to attempt a solo first ascent on Aonach Dubh in Glencoe. The line chosen is the white wall right of Ossian's Cave, the deep slit prominent from the road on the mountain's North Face, and a route that approximates to the line of Kuf, first climbed by Haston with Robin Campbell in October 1963. Dunlop/Haston, however, is unaware that he is being watched through powerful binoculars by his friend Charlie Wilson (a thinly disguised Hamish MacInnes) and as Dunlop advances up the face, Wilson agonises to himself: 'John would come through today's test all right, but that would lead to another and another. Would he ever be satisfied? Could it ever end peacefully for him?'

* * *

There was never any debate about where Dougal would be buried. 'Taking him back to Britain was not an option,' says Annie, who had been collected from Lausanne and driven up to Leysin by the Smiths immediately after the accident. 'And there are a lot of friends in that cemetery – Luc, Luc's mother, John [Harlin].'

The burial was on the twentieth, three days after the accident. Bonington arrived from Chamonix, Doug Scott from England, and Dougal's brother Alec came from Scotland in a black, Celtic mood that alarmed Allan Rankin and, later, some of the Leysin residents.

'Being the biggest, Eley and I got the job of carrying the coffin,' says Scott. It was a dank, misty day, and Moriarty took the front, ploughing head down through a narrow channel cleared of snow up from the roadside, with Scott hanging on at the other end. It was a steep climb to the second-highest level, where the cemetery labourers had managed to dig a hole in the frozen ground and, once, the bearers almost slipped and dropped the casket. Annie, Bonington, Alec and Ariane followed close behind. Ariane disconnected from the formalities, and was there simply as lover alongside Annie's grieving widow. The climbers' traditional garb of duvet and fleece contrasted oddly with the formal attire of the undertaker's assistants and other casually dressed mourners waiting on the hillside, including most of the Vagabond crowd and a smattering of locals. Beth Burke, who had flown from London, was there, and the widow of the man who had vanished close to the summit of Everest two years previously found her own release in the simple ceremony. The two nurses who had gone to Leysin to experience the world, and had eventually married the two climbing friends, were reunited by their deaths.

'I remember meeting Annie at the cemetery,' says Beth (now Bevan), who is still working as a nurse at Greenwich University Hospital. 'We had not seen each other for a few years, and there we were back together, linked again. It was very, very strange. I can remember giving her a hug, and saying: "Look where we ended up now." I used that as my service for Mick because, of course, his body had never been found, and I found it really helpful. For me, it was very moving, and a conclusion in a way. I was sad it was Dougal, but for me it had a different meaning. I felt I was laying Mick to rest, too.'

All that remained were a few formalities. Haston had died intestate, and Annie needed the help of a lawyer, Claude Petitpierre, to sort out the estate under Swiss law. He didn't leave much. Both bank accounts were in debit, as was his American Express account. The climbing gear was dispersed, and the book royalties went to Annie. Ariane kept some personal effects. Petitpierre, a keen out-doorsman, at his own insistence was given a Haston model Karrimor rucksack by Annie, in lieu of a fee. Peter Boardman, later to die with Joe Tasker on the North-East Ridge of Everest in 1982, took over ISM.

Calculated Risk was published by Ken Wilson and Diadem Books in 1979. Wilson had originally shown Martin Boysen and others Ariane's typed copy of the manuscript, and though Boysen had dismissed it as 'rubbish' Wilson decided to go ahead. It was, as he rightly claimed, 'a page-turner', and Doug Scott, in his foreword, believed 'it contained such a wealth of information about this mountaineer that did not appear in his autobiography'. For climbers of a certain vintage, there is also an undeniable fascination in putting real-life names to the fictional characters. Haston, Harlin, Eley, Clark, Whillans, MacInnes and others are certainly recognisable. The hero, John Dunlop, is 'one of Scotland's best mountaineers at the early age of 24'. His Scottish friend George is tall, dark and powerfully built. There are parties in Edinburgh, abortions, punch-ups at the Clachaig, seedy press characters dogging the footsteps of Dunlop throughout his climbing career, a major Alpine winter ascent with a tall, blond American, and other characters familiar to anyone with even a fleeting knowledge of the British climbing scene of the 1960s – or with the life of Dougal Haston. Dunlop's attitude to women is ambivalent, to say the least, and George incurs Dunlop's wrath by putting his pregnant girlfriend ahead of their climbing partnership, a decision that sends Dunlop racing off to Glencoe on his Honda 750 to let off steam (picking up a disposable female tent-sharer on the way). There is also a widely debated passage midway through the book when a skier, looking for off-piste powder on La Riondaz, outruns an avalanche that he has triggered on the face – 'one of the great runs of Leysin'. Blyth Wright, who read an early copy of the manuscript, was convinced that he was reading a letter from Haston describing his own death, and others saw it at eerily prescient, too. But it is the Harlin character that Haston places on La Riondaz to foil the avalanche and, in retrospect, the fact that the author should use a hill overlooking his home as dramatic background is surely no more remarkable than using Edinburgh, Glencoe and the Grandes Jorasses for the same purpose. And Dunlop does find peace, maturing from arrogant, chauvinistic *Übermensch* into a man content with himself and friends, and the book ends, happily, with the hint of a sustainable relationship. Haston, the author, helps his alter ego to win an almost Faustian battle for his own soul.

The novel is no masterpiece, and there are woeful weaknesses in the characterisation – 'Haston was not going to be another Hemingway,' observes Russell Sharp – but as Wilson insists: 'It wasn't a bad first effort.' Haston, had he lived, would certainly have done more work on his raw manuscript; according to Ariane, he was unhappy with the ending, and had still to settle on a title. *Calculated Risk* was Wilson's choice.

'A few days before the accident, Dougal mentioned he had forgotten to put a title to the novel,' says Ariane. 'So I asked him how will he start thinking about it. And he replied that he never thinks about it – it would suddenly come to his head. And then added that, anyway, the publisher had the last say about the title, that the Eiger book should really have been called *The Spider and the Fly*. After the accident, when I was driving through Germany on my way to Britain, suddenly this phrase came in my head, "*Ironie de la Vie*", and I asked myself: what the hell was this supposed to mean? Then, as a flash, the novel came in. So, as far as I am concerned, *Calculated Risk* should have been *Irony of Life*. But I never told it to anyone, as I knew the publisher had the last word.'

* * *

Currie did its bit for its most famous ex-citizen in September 1983 when, outside the village post office at the junction of Riccarton Mains Road and Lanark Road West, and as rain swept down off the Pentlands, a member of the Community Council unveiled a commemorative stone. An anonymous donor had put up the money, and the plaque on the granite plinth said: 'This stone commemorates the historic achievements of international climber Dougal Haston, a Currie boy, who went on to become the first climber to conquer Everest by the South-West Face and the first Briton to scale the North Face of the Eiger. He later died in an avalanche in Switzerland in 1977 aged 36.' Some time after the ceremony, when it was far too late to do anything about it, someone pointed out that the first Britons to scale the North Face of the Eiger were Chris Bonington and Ian Clough.

'Dougal would have had a good laugh at that one,' Ariane notes, with some certainty.

Of all the later homilies and epitaphs devoted to Dougal, perhaps the most moving and credible comes from Tom Frost, the American who went to Annapurna with him in 1970, and who lost his chance of the summit as Whillans and Haston went for the top; the descendant of Brigham Young, sociologically and idealistically worlds apart from the hard-drinking, occasionally foul-mouthed Scot. Frost, who had been at the cutting edge of climbing for many years, and has his own place in American alpine history, still sees the sport through the eyes of a child, perhaps the eyes of Dougal Haston when he ventured from Currie towards those purple shapes in the distance. Frost recognised, above all, what climbing was about when he told the author in 2001: 'I really enjoyed that part of my life. It was one of the highlights of my life, being there on that mountain with those guys. Spectacular. You can't buy experiences like that. Dougal was as big a part of it as any of the others, and it was a privilege to be with him there. He was bigger than life – he was cool as a cucumber all the way through, totally unique. I can't think of anybody else that I can compare him to and say, well, they are similar. A lot of the finest times I have ever had was on that trip. I met my wife in Italy, and we went to England later, and I met some of the Annapurna guys, and we climbed all over England and Wales, and I had a great fortnight's holiday. After the expedition, there wasn't anybody that was enemies with anybody else. As I have thought back, if people ask me: "How was the trip?" I say: "Oh, you know, it was an unparalleled opportunity, a unique opportunity to me with an interesting group of guys. I had a ball." All the British members of the expedition – spectacular, unique individuals, great folks to hang out with, great people to be on an expedition with. Plus being on an interesting mountain and a really interesting route, and breaking new ground, the first big-wall kind of activity in the Himalayas . . . what more could I want?

'As for Dougal today, he will definitely be climbing, there's no question about that. Climbing is him, it's part of him, and I can't imagine him not climbing. The death, and the manner of it, shows me that he's human – he's not a Greek god. That's a delightful, humanising aspect of the Dougal Haston story.'

POSTSCRIPT

I remember skies mirrored in your eyes;
I wonder where you are, I wonder if you think about me
Once upon a time, in your wildest dream.
– Moody Blues, *Wildest Dream*

T he Rue Anna Jacquin lies a few hundred metres from the River Seine in the Paris suburb of Boulogne-Billancourt. Lined by three- or four-storey buildings painted a uniform white or cream, it is a mainly residential area of small houses or apartments, with a Metro station four hundred metres to the west and, on international football days, the occasional swelling roar from the Parc des Princes a kilometre away. The name on the buzzer of the top-floor flat at No. 4 says Haston, and it's a long climb up a succession of polished, wooden stairways and past cool, hushed French landings to the final flight, where she waits. Inside, there is a kitchen containing a picture of Dougal, flashing a rare smile and posing self-consciously with a film camera during work on *The Eiger Sanction*, facing two photographs of Luc van der Kaay on the wall opposite; an even tinier bathroom and a mattress and bedding spread in the alcove of a living room dominated by a bookshelf crammed with classic mountaineering works. There is Buhl's *Nanga Parbat Pilgrimage*, Terray's *Conquistadors of the Useless*, Rebuffat's *Starlight and Storm*, and all the Hastons. No sign, however, of the Scottish Mountaineering Club's long-missing *Fitzroy*. There are unanswered messages on the *respondre* close by, and an old-fashioned gramophone capable of playing 33 rpm records. She likes the Stones. As Annie Haston is fond of pointing out: 'We are still all children of the 1960s.'

She has lived in Paris since 1981. She moved south to Boulogne-Billancourt from Levallois Perret, close to l'Hôpital Franco Britannique, where she worked part-time, in 1999, after suffering a broken leg in a collision with one of those scooters so beloved of young Parisians. Though outwardly frail – she probably weighs little more than six stones – there is a latent toughness and independence. She reminds many, irresistibly, of Edith Piaf. At one time, she entertained plans for a *salon du thé* and bookshop combined, but 'as a middle-aged, female foreigner' found it too difficult to find the necessary finance and help. She smokes dangerously, still loves to drink, red wine mainly, and her reminiscences come framed in a strange mixture of 1960s hip and Franglais. Apart from the occasional royalty cheque from Dougal's three books, she subsists by babysitting one of the children in the apartment below. She gets on a treat with him.

The Hastons made the decision not to have children early in their marriage, and took the necessary steps. Or rather, she took the necessary steps. As he was chronically afraid of doctors, hospitals and operations, a vasectomy was not an option, and she had her Fallopian tubes cauterised; in the early 1970s, virtually a pioneer. 'Dougal hated hospitals. Before Annapurna in 1970, he was suffering from a rumbling appendix, and I persuaded him to go for routine appendectomy because, while it was all right at sea level, it would be more serious at altitude. So off we went to London, checked in at the front desk and, as the porter took us up in the lift, Dougal's face was going greener and greener because of the all-pervading hospital smell. I took his stitches out myself, seven days later, in Edinburgh.'

She has, she insists, no regrets about children and, anyway, she is happy enough to allow *le petit garçon* downstairs to twist her round his little finger.

'We were not children people: we had too many other things to do with our lives.' She still wears Dougal's wedding ring and, like Piaf, regrets nothing. Life as Mrs Haston, she says with an enigmatic smile, was interesting. 'I met incredible people through the climbing set, a life I wouldn't have led if I had been a doctor's wife. I have been away from Leysin for 22 years, and still have fond memories of it, although eventually it changed forever for me.'

There have been men since, including a lengthy liaison with a Dutchman. 'Since Dougal, I haven't exactly been a nun, but in the last few years, no interest. I'm not sure I could live with anyone else any more. Dougal was a pretty hard act to follow.'

*   *   *

By mid-April in Leysin the last of the snows are fighting a losing battle with the fecundity of an Alpine spring. The village is cloaked in an end-of-season torpor, a depression exacerbated by the melting snows pouring on to streets through leaky downspouts. The spooky old TB clinics, equipped with their wide doors and balconies to accommodate beds, may have found new lives as hotels and schools, but still conspire to give the village an eerie feel. On the way up to the Vagabond, the evidence that Leysin is out of fashion leaps out of every boarded shop. Most tourists started to head for the larger, more fashionable resorts such as Gstaad and Verbier long ago. Just up the hill, towards the American School and the redundant Solacyre lift, the Vagabond windows are shuttered and rotting, and the property should probably be condemned. Inside, a fading piece of paper pinned to the noticeboard announces a day's activities from long ago, but there are only ghosts left to read it.

After Rankin gave up there were efforts, notably by the Smiths, to keep it going, and even after it closed a couple of reopenings which foundered. That era passed with the death of Haston. The travellers grew up, found jobs, married, got divorced, and grew old. The survivors may still play their Baez and Peter, Paul and Mary tracks, probably on CD these days, but it's a gesture to something long gone. As Rankin points out: 'You can't turn back the clock.' The Vagabond is owned by a Swiss bank now, and the American college is said to be struggling, but the village has kept its cosmopolitan feel. There are American accents in the supermarket, and Rankin is still there, of course, in a chalet high above the town; he has a terminal case of what Ariane calls Leysin Flu, the affliction that kept Dougal there. Larry Ware teaches at the college, and Guy Neithardt keeps a house in his birthplace, though his permanent home is down in the valley at Ollon, some fifteen kilometres away. Steve Jones, the most durable of the ISM instructors, is into his third decade as a village resident: he even has a Swiss passport.

The cemetery is a couple of kilometres below and west of Leysin, down a twisting road that ends in a couple of parking places at a clearing in the forest. There is a view across the Rhone Valley, and a smell of pine and woodsmoke drifting up from Veyges, the tiny village where Ariane's grandparents once lived. On one side of the road is a cemetery for soldiers from World War Two, sent to Leysin to be treated for TB, and a separate area with a small gathering of tiny graves for children. One is carved with the date 1954–8. Ariane, a cousin of the dead girl, says the father accidentally ran over his daughter with a truck.

The adult plots are on the uphill side of the road, in serried lines facing the valley and divided into rows by lines of privet two feet high. It would be hard to find Dougal without a guide, or if you didn't know his whereabouts. There is a simple, faded wooden cross lying on the ground, and a sign the size of an envelope which says 2242. There has never been a headstone, but this only adds to the simple dignity of the place and, in any case, as with most Swiss mountain villages, bodies are dug up every 50 years to make room for more. Dougal has until 2027.

Ariane stops by occasionally. It is on the route of one of her training runs, and she will pause from time to time to remove the weeds and tidy up the plot. By April, the crocuses at the foot of the grave are already reaching out through the earth towards a warming sky. She lives on the opposite side of the village, running a successful bed-and-breakfast business from the Chalet Ermina. It is the archetypal Swiss wooden chalet with balconies and views, and she has proved an astute businesswoman. She runs her own website from an office dominated by a poster proclaiming 'Determination today leads to success tomorrow', enjoys much repeat business from all round the world, and has plans for another building behind Ermina, on land left by her grandfather. She borrowed, with great courage and aplomb, one million Swiss francs for this.

It seems an ordered life, though the serene normality of Leysin and Ermina are in stark contrast to events after the winter of 1977. Following Dougal's death, she knew she couldn't stay in the village, and set out on what amounted to an extended pilgrimage, to follow in his footsteps. She returned to Scotland and met all his friends – Eley, Blyth Wright, brother Alec and Graham Tiso. Maude Tiso recalls

Ariane's thirst for knowledge about Dougal: 'She obviously had been very, very much in love with him, and she really craved being with people who knew him. She talked for hours with Graham about Dougal.' Tiso was not the only one. She stayed for months with Doug and Jan Scott in Nottingham, and even went some way on some of his expeditions, including Makalu in 1980, where she also met Reinhold Messner.

She travelled around the world and visited most of the world's major climbing areas. She slept rough, forgot to eat and smoked dope; she became a vagabond. An ascent of McKinley in 1979 ended with a spell in an Anchorage psychiatric hospital. 'I didn't know whether I wanted to live or die,' she says. In 1984 she contracted hepatitis and a year later fell pregnant to a Swiss who left her shortly after. Jerome, her son, was born in 1985 and her life now revolves around him, the happy social life of Chalet Ermina and a lazy cat with bright blue eyes called Figaro.

When Dougal died, she had known him for five years, and only in the last two did they become really close. Their relationship was definably complete, however, and there is no bitterness when she speaks of him, and the manner in which he was snatched away.

'Good old Dougal,' she says with a smile. 'So warm and, for me, so perfect. I am thankful now for what we had. But the clock just went round too fast for us.'

GLOSSARY

ABSEIL:	Controlled method of descent, via a friction device, down a doubled rope which can then be retrieved from below.
ARTIFICIAL CLIMBING?:	In free climbing only natural hand and footholds are used; artificial climbing (hardly practised now) involved hammering in pitons or wedges, hanging etriers from them and making upward progress from one to the next.
BELAY:	An anchor point on a climb, used to safeguard a leader or second. In theory if one falls, the other will not be pulled off.
BOLT:	Artificial climbing taken to extremes. When there are no cracks for pitons a hole can be drilled in the rock, a bolt placed in it and the etrier hung from this.
CARABINER:	Used for belays, or runners, this is a lightweight snap-link with a spring-loaded gate which the rope can be clipped through.
CRAMPONS:	Usually with ten downward points and two pointing forwards, they consist of a steel (in Dougal's day) framework attached to the soles of climbing boots.
DIRECT AID:	Artificial climbing.

DUVET: Feather or down-filled lightweight jacket used in cold climes.

ETRIER: Tape stirrup, a short ladder used in artifical climbing.

FIXED ROPE: Semi-permanent rope left in place on a pitch to facilitate ascent and descent.

FRONT-POINT: To climb ice on the projecting point of crampons.

ICE-SCREW: A piton used in ice climbing, but screwed into the ice and with a hollow interior through which the displaced ice passes.

JUMAR: A clamp used for ascending a rope or for protection on fixed ropes on Himalayan climbs.

NAIL: Piton.

PAs: Lightweight, tight-fitting, climbing shoe with very tough rubber sole and rand. Named after the inventor, Pierre Allain.

PARKA: An anorak.

PEG: Piton.

PITCH: Section of a climb, usually limited by the availability of stances or length of rope.

PITON: Once iron or steel, now alloy, 'nail' of various sizes and thickness hammered into the rock with a specialist hammer for direct aid or protection.

POWDER: Unconsolidated, fresh snow, very prone to avalanche.

PRUSIK: The method of climbing a fixed rope using jumar clamps. After the original method which employed a prusik knot.

RUNNNER or RUNNING BELAY:	Sling or piton employed at intervals on a pitch through which the rope is passed to give the leader protection.
SLING:	Rope or tape loop.
SPINDRIFT:	Powder snow, usually wafted downwards by the wind.
STANCE:	A place to set up a belay.
TENSION TRAVERSE:	A traverse by a climber using the pull of a rope to keep himself in balance.
TRAVERSE:	Horizontal pitch.

INDEX